# LOST AND FOUND
# DEPARTMENT

## LIFE STORIES AND SPIRITUAL ESSAYS

## RANDALL HECKMAN

LOST AND FOUND DEPARTMENT
Copyright © 2020 by Randall Heckman

ISBN: 978-1-7363097-0-4

Printed in the United States of America.

*Dedicated to Jaquelyn"Jackie"Keck*
*February 3, 1944 – March 5, 2019*

*"New blades of grass grow from charred soil.
The sun rises."*

*Anne Lamott*

# ACKNOWLEDGMENTS

Thanks to all my fellow writer friends and those on-line doomed like me to push forward, your encouragement is priceless.

My friend and mentor, Doreen Chaky, thank you for wading through hundreds of printed pages and many cups of coffee, editing the rough draft. You're my Northern Star guiding the way.

Clare Eide, thanks for the countless visits when I questioned what and why I was doing this and you always dealt me an ace from up your sleeve.

Thank you, Chuck Wilder at Books on Broadway and all the interesting people I met in the café who encouraged me to keep writing.

A big thanks to Sue Stickly, program coordinator for Humanities North Dakota who led a workshop/series on memoirs and encouraged me to write the really hard stuff.

It was a godsend to meet Mack Schroer when I did. His art and avant-garde approach to cover design was brilliant. macklinart.com Thank you my friend.

Being in kindergarten with computers, I am indebted to John Geyerman and Leon Walter who offered help when I was in a panic.

Thank you, Lisa Thompson for editing the back cover blurb.

Thank you, Jen Fast for your unrelenting patience at formatting a finish product I'm proud of. www.thefastfingers.com.

Bless you Pastor Ross. Your example and constant up-beatness means more to me than you know.

And Jay Gordon, saying thank you seems inadequate to express my deep gratitude. After all these years nothing can separate us. Your insights and corrections and unending encouragement have been beyond helpful, not only in the process of writing this book, but in my life.

I thank the Spirit of God, who has been both a father and a mother to me. I'm still trying to figure out how it works, but I'm loved and that's what counts.

# 1

*I'll* call myself Dirk in this story but that's not my real name. Somehow it's easier for me to tell the story in this way, either out of vanity or regret. I chose the name because it seems to be fitting, based on one of the colorful characters in Clive Cussler's earlier novels that I enjoyed reading. My father put me onto his books forty plus years ago. Dirk Pitt was an explorer, a treasure hunter and always had the beautiful girl, invariably the hero by the end of the story. He'd get knocked down but always bounced back. I'm a daydreamer and would like to think there's a little hero in me; I've certainly been knocked on my ass more times than I can count. That's how I came to choose the name for lack of a better one.

I'm keeping most of the people in this story anonymous like they do in Twelve Step programs or witness protection out of respect for friends and family. This narrative is by and large true, although looking back sixty years and getting reacquainted with dormant memory cells is a bit fuzzy. Brain cells thrive and brain cells die and some are not working up to par like they used to. Some of the events and details from so long ago are hard to account for, as I strive to be entirely accurate, so please allow me the liberty to make mistakes and enhance here and there for continuity sake. I promise to do my best at being factual.

 ~

I'm the oldest of eight, and no, we weren't Amish or Catholic. My father was a dark haired, handsome hunk; letter jackets in varsity sports, a Marine who served in the Korean War, a strong and ambitious young man of scrupulous morals. Mom was a pretty redhead who was the top of her graduating class. She wore a cute apron while working part-time during high school at Parris's Pharmacy on Broad Street, making cherry phosphates and ice cream sundaes at the soda fountain section. They called them "soda-jerks" back then, probably not politically correct in today's world. She still makes the best peanut butter fudge sauce in the world. Their whirlwind courtship at a young age didn't go unnoticed. Dad's best friend, a high school buddy named Bezzer, broadcasted the news. Montoursville was a small town with a gossiping grapevine and still had some party-lines on the telephone, which lent to everyone knowing everyone's business. In November of 1954 they eloped and got hitched in Altoona, Pennsylvania. I was the result of their fiery courtship and have jokingly said I was conceived in the backseat of a '52 Chevy sedan. Dad bought a sizable lot and built a modest three-bedroom house on Bennett Street. The bedrooms soon filled up and a second floor addition was necessary by the time I was ten. Mother must have been very fertile; it seems that every other year she popped out another baby.

 ~

For me, growing up in a small town during the early sixties were peaceful times. The first day of elementary school merited wearing sporty new shoes and spiffy clothes. Thom McAn desert boots were trendy, as were Sears and Roebuck jeans (stiff as cardboard), that were actually blue as compared to today's pre-washed brands. I cuffed the bottoms like Elvis Presley did in the movies when he was breaking waves on the Victrola console in our living room. Back then, it seemed less stressful and more fun than the stuff kids growing up today have to deal with. The madness and tragedy of all the school shootings never entered anyone's mind in my generation. The times sure have changed.

I don't mean to be insensitive, but it seems to me that so many kids today are pansies and want to stay indoors with some kind of device exercising their thumbs and fingers, what I call an artificial exercise of eye to hand coordination. I grew up actually catching and hitting real balls, from baseball to getting knocked around playing sandlot football or our own version of rugby, mostly in my big backyard. I was fortunate to be among half a dozen kids in my neighborhood within a few years of each other and we sure did tear up the turf.

Our neighborhood gang consisted of Timmy Packard who was two years younger than me. His dad was a teacher and played saxophone in a jazz band that practiced in their garage caddy-corner from our house. I hung out and listened to them jam and it made me want to be a musician. *The Monkees* were hot stuff at that time, they were the first music videos on TV with funny backstories, and we created our own garage band called Going Ape. Of course, it was pantomimed, compliments of household brooms for guitars and cardboard ice cream containers from Hurr's Dairy for a drum set. We had it covered except for Peter Tork. He wasn't in the neighborhood. The Packard's house had a high stone front wall that Timmy and I bounced a tennis ball off of for hours like racket-ball that must have driven his mom nuts.

Stu Rennick was older than me and lived directly across the street. As I recall, he was one of the original hippies in town. Stu had a killer stereo system and record albums galore. He had a growing collection of albums labeled psychedelic music that I took a liking to. Frank Zappa was sure different than Neil Diamond. Stu's dad was a private charter pilot; they had money and an in-ground swimming pool. Stu showed me my first Playboy centerfold circa 1964.

Duck-footed Benny lived down the alley and trapped muskrats and an occasional beaver at Mill Creek before school. He skinned and stretched the pelts on boards and sold them for pocket money. Benny was also deadly with a .22 rifle and hunted squirrels. He trapped along Mill Creek that was across a cornfield behind the fire hall. I could see it from my second floor bedroom window. A carnival came to town every year around the Fourth of July. I can still hear the "carny" music and picture the Ferris wheel lit up at night, smell French fries and cotton candy from yesteryear like it was in the now. Benny and I wandered around the carnival, spending less than a buck on the penny-pitch to win an ashtray or shot glass and indulged our fair share of junk food that gave us a belly-ache. Neither of us particularly liked going on the rides. Benny had an unforgettable voice that kind of sounded like Sling Blade, especially when he grunted and chuckled and repeated himself.

Lars from Mars lived a few blocks away. He had a neat bike with a banana seat and ape handle bars, painted with spray cans in bright colors. My bike was a clunker, but we'd wrench this and that around, trying to modify my JC Higgins to make it cool. Lars was mechanically minded more than he was athletic, but he'd get down and dirty with us playing football and horse playing. His mom was like my second mom and I slept-over every so often. We'd read Marvel comic books or fiddle around with an acoustic guitar, giggling until midnight when his dad would bang on the bedroom door and yell at us to get to sleep. Lars's house smelled of cigarette smoke and wasn't as tidy as Mom kept our house, but there was always Fudge Royal ice cream and chocolate milk in the fridge.

And there was my kid brother (my best buddy), who was sixteen months younger than me. We nicknamed him Sparky because his hair was like the steel wool Mom kept by the kitchen sink and stuck out like he'd put his finger in a light socket. It'd get wiry and bushy until Dad sat us in the dreaded yellow chair on the patio and gave us the summer boot camp haircut. Sparky was clever and tough, a real bruiser and a quick learner. No matter what the season, we were never in the house.

The gang on Bennett Street got together after school and played some kind of game, making the best of what we had at hand. It'd be anything from tackle football in the mud to shooting hoops in a game called HORSE, or playing spies like the Man from U.N.C.L.E. with homemade gizmos and secret code words. Mom must have had one a hellova a time getting grass stains out of my jeans.

I remember smacking a flat stone like a hockey puck six blocks to second grade. The stone bore an imprint vaguely resembling an Indian Head Nickle. When I got to the Lyter Building it went in my pocket with my lunch money. That stone and I were inseparable until it went down a storm drain and ruined my day. In third grade I made an artful Plaster of Paris relief map of the state of Michigan where my favorite uncle lived and balanced it in one hand like a pizza delivery guy riding my bike to school. Not paying attention for whatever reason, I plowed into the rear end of a parked car and my school project broke in pieces on the macadam. When I got to school, knowing that making up an excuse that the dog ate it, wouldn't work, I made up a story about getting brushed by a brown sedan that knocked me to the ground, a hit and run accident. I faced an inquiry from the principle, my teacher and a brief round with my father, answering questions. Mr. Mazzani, one of the town cops wrote up a report but nothing came of it. I was able to redo my project and replicated another relief map of Michigan. I'm not sure why I made up such an elaborate story and lucky not to get caught lying.

Uncle Charlie lived in Grand Rapids where we'd visit sometimes over the summer vacation. Besides being my favorite uncle, who I resembled in appearance as a Fullmer and could have been the son he didn't have, he was an outdoors enthusiast and a camera nut. We camped along some river that swarmed with clouds of mosquitoes during the day and got fogged out in the evening with insecticide. The canoe trip was fun, but my brother and I looked like raw meat by the end of the weekend. We toured the Kellogg's factory in Battle Creek and got free samples, browsed the souvenir store that sold everything from bowls to mugs and keychains. Racks of T shirts marked toddler to XXX proudly displayed a face that made Kellogg's famous. I loved cornflakes but hated the goofy hat my dad bought and made me wear. It had a propeller on top, for crying out loud, and everyone wanted to make sport of me. "Grreeaatt!" I'm pretty sure that was when I dropped Tony the Tiger and opted for Snap, Crackle and Pop.

On another visit at Uncle Charlie's, sirens blared and a tornado touched down. We all found shelter in their basement and Dad made a game out of it with flashlights and a Kazoo. I don't remember it very well, but Mom tells the story that Aunt Margaret huddled nearly shell-shocked in a corner, wringing her hands until the storm passed. She worried about her fine china on display in a cabinet that I don't recall ever using it. I do remember getting a skateboard the next day. Sparky and I cruised down the church's parking lot next door to Uncle Charlie's house without sissy pads, weaving between downed tree limbs and debris from the storm like California surfers.

My brother and I were imaginative and rather industrious. We used dad's tools and some scavenged boards to make a fort in the old cherry tree out back with his help. Dad had a workbench in the basement well stocked with hand tools that had to be put back in place, and we'd tinker making simple birdhouses or toy guns. We road our bikes to Mill Creek or to a man-made pond we called the Lagoon behind Indian Park and caught suckers and catfish. Mom never complained that her pantry was raided; canned corn worked pretty damned good for bait. Neither did we get the reaction we hoped for at bringing home turtles or frogs and an occasional garter snake, which was Sparky's catch – not mine. I was scared of snakes. Mom would simply shake her head and tell us to keep our new friends outside without so much as a please or thank you.

One summer afternoon when I was in grade school, I broke my wrist swinging on a vine over Mill Creek that snapped off and landed (my luck!), on a log. My sister and her friend sang a jump rope ditty on the front sidewalk to tease me. *"The vine broke and the monkey got choked and they all went to heaven in a little row boat."* I was in a cast for six weeks. On a visit back home many years later, it was disheartening to find that our old haunts down by Mill Creek have since been rerouted, all but obliterated, and the landscape leveled for a Lowes and Walmart. I guess that's called progress.

As a youngster I had my tonsils taken out, and like Forrest Gump, the best thing about being in a hospital is the ice cream. It's the only time in my life that I've been in the hospital overnight until last year when I spent three days in the cardiac unit. It sucks to get old. My folks should have had stock in Big Pharma back then. Between us kids, we sure went through Mercurochrome and Band Aids, Calamine lotion for poison ivy, and my arch enemy; Iodine. Trust me, it does sting something awful.

Dad spanked my brother or me whenever we were overly mischievous; he never used a belt or a switch or a clenched hand. Mom used a wooden spoon to scold us like Mother Superior, but when we outgrew a slap on the wrist and made a joke about the spoon being a flyswatter, it was definitely a mistake. Her retort of: *"Wait until your father gets home,"* put the fear of God in us. The Beast of Bennett Street would arrive promptly on schedule at 5:15 from work to find one or the other of us duly awaiting the guillotine on the living room couch. The discipline we received was never excessive and I wouldn't call them beatings, they certainly didn't leave a lasting or internal scar that affected me later in life as the proponents against capital punishment says it does. I'm sure my folks had their hands full with a family growing faster than the crop of dandelions in our yard. I always deserved a spanking or a cuff on the back of the head whenever I got one. I learned quickly that it made better sense not to cry and take it like a man.

We grew up playing board games like Chutes and Ladders and Monopoly. Dad taught us boys how to play chess. I have that chess board to this day. I had a library card and read everything from the Hardy Boys and the Wizard of Oz books to Uncle Wiggly. Along with the comics (Jughead, Batman and the Archie's), Mom brought activity books home and reams of blank paper to draw on that kept us occupied. I read Life magazines and remember goggling over bare-breasted natives in National Geographic's, enamored and thinking it was a wicked secret I had to keep to myself because it aroused my interest. We watched Friday night fights on the TV in black and white while eating Hi-Way pizza when Mohammed Ali was Cassius Clay.

Summers were carefree willy-nilly times with weekend picnics wherever a picnic might take us. Dad had a Coleman camp grill that he'd load with charcoal briquettes and douse with a baby jar of gasoline to get it going. Kaboom! We'd squeal like hyenas. If anyone was in the same county they knew that my family was present and we were having a picnic. I have to argue that hotdogs on a grill are the best if you smother them with relish and mustard. If it wasn't on our backyard patio, we'd picnic at Roaring Creek Park or under the pavilion at World's End, where Sparky and I tormented chipmunks with marshmallows on a hook and string-line.

My favorite picnics were when we'd go to the grandparents on my mother's side. I affectionately called grandma: *Belle*, short for Isabelle. She was more down to earth than my other grandparents who were kind of religious and more proper. Sunday afternoon visits at their house required being on our best behavior. They had a small orchard in the backyard and the most enjoyment I can recall, if we got away with it, was climbing in the trees and picking whatever was in season. Grandma's basement was wall-to-wall shelves, stocked with canned vegetables from the garden and fruit preserves; her apple sauce was amazing and I can still imagine the cinnamon aroma in her kitchen. I remember being stung by a yellow jacket, they sure liked the rotten apples, and Grandpa knocked out his pipe, spit in his hand and made a tobacco plaster to put on it. The sting went away almost instantly. I recall an evening in absolute agony needing to take a pee long before our visit was over. As we walked home, Dad said to go behind the neighbor's bushes, but Mom put her foot down. "Hold it," she said sharply, "you're a big boy... we're almost home." I barely made it. It seemed taboo to use Grandma and Grandpa's upstairs bathroom, in fact, everything about "upstairs" seemed off limits. It was years later, as a young adult while visiting Grandma after Grandpa had died, that I used the upstairs bathroom for the first time. It was a bold request but what do you do when duty calls? I found it sparkling clean, painted bright yellow, bar soap as if just out of the wrapper on the sink basin and the towels creased, hanging perfectly. I quietly checked out the bedrooms and found them spotless, appearing unused, the beds made, shades drawn, and had the sense that I was looking at a museum or a mausoleum. Being kind of spooked, I wondered if Grandpa's ghost was around the corner or would jump out of a closet and never again went upstairs. Rule of thumb: pee before going to Grams, especially if she's talkative.

It was different at Grandma Belle's; I could go upstairs and pee anytime I needed to. I could wander around the bedrooms if my curiosity got the better of me. Belle had a plaque in her kitchen that was very apropos. *My house is clean enough to be healthy – dirty enough to be happy.* And so it was. We didn't have to take our shoes off inside the front door or sit up straight on the couch and mind our P's and Q's. There was always an ashtray on the kitchen counter with an L&M cigarette burning away beside her old coffee percolator; maybe the ashes were Belle's special seasoning in soup or sauces. She used fatback and lard, buttering up old cooking wares with Crisco that I'm pretty sure were clean but made me wonder sometimes. Her panty was a dinky little side room and kind of a wreck that slanted severely to the back wall. The old enamel sink was stained orange and chipped, dishes and coffee cups and an ashtray in a strainer. But everything Belle made was unforgettably tasty. No one can out-best her spaghetti sauce or chicken potpie.

She had a pair of canaries in a simple wire cage between the refrigerator and the stove, where seed husks riddled the floor. They were named Ralph and Alice from the Honeymooners and gave Belle a chuckle. She alone knew the difference. She could make them give her a beaky little kiss if she pinched a sunflower seed in her lips and coaxed them. Belle also had a cat called Cocoa that she kept on a leash outback. Talk about one mean cat! You got hissed at, attacked and swatted with raptor-like claws if you ventured too close; never a typical cat-like moment of purrs and beckoning to pet it. I wondered why Cocoa didn't chew the rope and go kill something like the grocer next door. Maybe I should try writing a novel about Cocoa like Stephen King's *Cujo*.

Grandpa was a retired carpenter and made lawn do-hickies. Mini donkey carts and whirly-giggies and wooden cut outs of gnomes and such cluttered the backyard between the croquet or badminton game. It was an obstacle course at picnic times that made playing yard games extra fun, but we had to mind not breaking anything. My brother has his paper patterns in an old trunk for safekeeping, but hasn't decorated his yard with Bertha-Big-Butt bending over. Grandpa liked his Carlings Black Label in returnable sixteen ounce brown bottles. Not every time, but every so often at a picnic, my brother or I would sneak a bottle floating in ice from an old galvanized wash tub and split it outback in the dinosaur boneyard at the rear of their property. We'd get dizzy and belch and think we were hot stuff. I'm pretty sure Grandpa knew that we snitched a beer but he never said anything, neither did Belle, and she had eyes like a hawk. By the way, of course, they weren't actual dinosaur bones. Sparky and

I loved dinosaurs. We had plastic figures on the window ledge from stegosaur to triceratops. T-Rex was badass. Along with getting my first real camera and a flashlight, I got an illustrated book of dinosaurs on my eighth birthday. We pretended to be Doctor Leakey or archeologists who found the missing link, but it was just a dilapidated chicken coop full of discarded bones and rusty treasures.

~

I think I was eleven years old the summer that Belle and my spinster Aunt Faye went to Bolivia to visit my other aunt. Aunt Peggy, mom's oldest sister, graduated from college and took an offer to teach English in La Paz. Aunt Peggy ended up marrying a Bolivian and had a family of two boys and two girls, my long-distant cousins. Carlos, who we call Spike is my age. We were cut of out the same fabric and had a rocky time finding our way as budding adolescent rebels.

I volunteered to mow Grandpa's grass that summer while Belle was away. He gave me a buck and there was always pop in the fridge. The day I finished and cleaned up the mower, sticking all the lawn ornaments back in place, I went in the backdoor to the kitchen and called for him but received no answer. Helping myself to an RC Cola and store-bought cookies, I wandered around and found a carton of Pall Mall cigarettes in his bedroom; Grandpa smoked like a chimney. I snitched a pack, making it appear as though I hadn't. A high overgrown hedge bordered the house next door providing perfect camouflage and I lit up like grandpa did. Not knowing about the effects of inhaling, I hacked and coughed and got dizzy. I shoved the pack of ciggies deep in my pocket and headed my loopy ass down the alleys back home.

That evening during supper, Mom expressed concern that she hadn't been able to reach Grandpa, calling every hour with a whiny baby either nursing or on her hip, or she would have walked to the old homestead. She asked Dad to go and check on him and told me to go along, as I was there most of the day. We rode bikes to 509 Cherry Street. It was a warm evening and usually a pleasant trip, but Dad didn't say anything on our ride across town. When we arrived at Grandpa's house, I was told to stay outside and sat on the back porch fidgeting and wondering why. Shortly after, he found my Grandpa in the upstairs bathroom, dead from a heart attack. He probably lay there all day. My father had had a premonition, although it was a shock none the less. He came outside and squatted on his haunches, mumbling the short version of what happened and I was sent on home. I ever so slowly pedaled my way home, scared and regretting that I'd stolen a pack of Grandpa's cigarettes and Juicy Fruit chewing gum from Belle's nightstand. I didn't understand death, especially when it visited my family. All I knew was that it made everything sad for the longest time. It still does.

Getting caught for anything was one of my greatest fears, not so much knowing that what I did was wrong, but the gallows at being found guilty. In my imaginative mind, I worried that Grandpa saw me stealing and the memory has haunted me ever since, silly as it may be. I'm thankful that I didn't go upstairs to use the bathroom. The bushes by the dinosaur boneyard worked just fine and spared me a nightmare.

∾

We took family vacations every summer that were probably hard on dad's salary and the budget to raise a growing family. We'd pile into our pale blue Ford Falcon station wagon and head for places like Valley Forge or Gettysburg or some other battlefield. Dad quoted Barbara Fritchie's famous poem when we walked around the sites at Frederick like a grand storyteller, amazing those within earshot. *"Up from the meadows rich with corn, clear in the cool September morn..."* I'll never forget the line; *"Who touches a hair of yon gray head, dies like a dog! March on, he said."* As kids we didn't just visit battlefields, Dad made them come alive.

My first trip to Washington DC to tour the Smithsonian and the monuments is indelibly etched in my brain. I have images of antiquity that you could touch back then before it became encased in glass or roped off. We spent an entire day at the National Museum of Natural History with my father as the guide. He corrected the "official" tour guide a time or two, knowing the actual facts, and unwittingly embarrassed the man to move on with the group. I recall being spellbound by the "Spirit of St. Louis" and the exhibit of Charles Lindbergh, daydreaming about being a pilot when I grew up. Another unforgettable vacation was at colonial Williamsburg, not just for the restored village and people wearing period clothing, although I did enjoy the blacksmith's stories, but because the Motor Lodge we stayed at had a swimming pool and a vending machine that dislodged a bottle of pop if you kicked it.

On the road trips, my brother and I usually opted for the way-back, sitting Indian fashion without a seatbelt in sight. My sisters sat in the middle with dolls or whatever, and when we got bored playing the alphabet game from billboards or Tic-Tac-Toe and got antsy as boys do, we misbehaved. Dad's arm was longer than a cartoon Gumby and could reach me with a cuff on the head clear in the way-back. "What..." he'd say in a voice that was more a statement than a question, one that didn't necessarily demand an answer. We knew what *what* meant. He said that a lot. It was usually Sparky's fault that brought it on, he was devilish at taunting me to a reaction but knew when to keep his mouth shut when Dad bore down on us and slinked off out of harm's reach.

My parents loved history and artfully combined teaching us kids' lessons with having fun. My brother and I wore Revolutionary tricorn hats and Indian feathers and beads and the blue and grey of Civil War soldiers. We had cap guns and muskets, swords and bows and arrows and bags of plastic soldiers from nearly every war. We'd strategically set up dozens and dozens of thumb-sized soldiers opposite from each other on the linoleum floor in the playroom, making forts and hazards from a book or rolled up socks, and shot marbles at one another's armies for hours.

Dad had a great affinity for airports. We spent hours while in DC watching big planes coming and going; Dad took pictures with his old Browning camera. He'd take us to air-shows for a daytrip to see Bi-planes putting on an aerial show like Snoopy and the Red Baron with skydivers doing crazy stunts. There were many Sunday afternoons watching twin prop TWA's and piper cubs, military planes and helicopters, whatever came in or out of our small airport across town.

We'd sit on a blanket near the runway licking away at a hand-dipped ice cream cone that Ms. June would load up from Hurr's Dairy before it melted. One of my favorite flavors was Teaberry. It was pink like Pepto Bismol my mom kept in the medicine cabinet but certainly didn't taste like it. I recall mentioning Lindberg and his famous plane from our visit to the Smithsonian and Dad giving me a funny look, surprised that I'd remembered the name. "They called him a Commie," he said but added nothing more. I wondered what a Commie meant and assumed it was a compliment.

We had a mason jar with a screw-on lid poked with holes and caught grasshoppers that hopped around us by the millions. I believed my dad when he said they spit tobacco juice because my hands sure got stained by those rascally critters. He also said if a frog peed on you it gave you warts. He had many such sayings; like where a bear shits. We used the jars at night to catch lighting bugs that flitted in our backyard. Sparky caught an orange and black salamander down by the creek that lived in a jar with grass and sticks tucked in to make life easy for him. We dropped ants and a thimble of water in the jar thinking it could be dinner for our friend. The salamander lived on our bedroom windowsill until school started after Labor Day. Sparky set it free where he found it with great ceremony. Its name was Stanley for some reason, probably from watching Laurel and Hardy every

Sunday morning.

We were certainly anything but spoiled, we were treated like little kings and queens, my sisters and brother and I. Christmas's and birthday parties were always more than we expected. Mom made the comment that a neighbor asked her if we had a rich uncle. I don't know how Dad did it, we had so many treats. I have fond memories of outings for A&W root beer in frosty mugs and foot-long hot dogs that were brought to the car and hung from Dad's opened window on a tray. We walked to Cellini's hoagie shop next to the library and had ham and cheese cosmos, Middlesworth Bar-b-que potato chips and Yoo-hoo. Sometimes Mom would give us each a quarter for penny candy and off we'd go to Ed's Market when a quarter went a long way. Ed's Market had a candy case that seemed to a kid like it was a mile long. Before being politically correct was an idea or a term, let alo ne a mentality, you could buy little figures of gummy black licorice coated with sugar that were called nigger-babies. I have no idea if you can still find them or what they might be called now, but they were sure my favorite, even though they made your tongue black. Belle had a tray on the coffee table over the holidays with a variety of nuts and a nut cracker. Back then, Brazil nuts were called nigger-toes. Thinking about this brings to mind an old black and white series we watched as kids on TV. *Spanky and Our Gang* was made up of an amusing cast; Alfalfa, the smart-ass with a cowlick, Spanky, a fat boy who wore stripped jerseys and a funny cap, and of course, Buckwheat, the black kid with a hokey southern draw and a natty afro. It was ground breaking for the times as an attempt to portray kids getting along as equals in the face of racism and having a hilarious time of it. I can't recall a black family living in my hometown. Looking back, residents seemed to have trouble with Catholics and Jews integrating into the community, but that was the Dark Ages, right? If only.

∽

Our backyard was the only one on the block that was set up like a playground. Our next door neighbor, old Joe Detch was generally a quiet man until we lit his fuse. If something set him off he stormed and swore like a sailor, holding Vic his German Shepherd on a short leash from attack. He had a huge vegetable garden we had to be careful of if a stray ball happened to land in it, which was usually his contention at having such a rambunctious tribe living next door without a fence. I was bit but not mortally wounded and have been leery of German Shepherds ever since.

Beyond mom's rosebushes was a basketball hoop on a post and the worn paths of a baseball diamond in the far back next to the alley. We had a swing set under the maple tree, a ten by ten sandbox with plastic shovels and buckets, die-cast toy cars called Hot Wheels by the dozens and Tonka trucks and bulldozers that were made of metal. I recollect a time when Dad set traps in the sand box because we discovered cat crap and were too young to know what it was, innocently loading it into a bucket like Lincoln Logs. I don't think he ever caught one, but it must have sent a message to whoever's cat it was.

A large forsythia bush grew under the kitchen window where a hose hung on the basement wall that we drank from on hot afternoons or sprayed one another with cold water. We had a portable knee-deep pool and a four-man army tent set up in the backyard during the summer months. I can still smell the musty odor of that old canvas tent. Sparky and I sometimes slept out and we'd sneak canned beans from the cupboard, wolfing them down and singing the musical fruit song. We nearly caught the tent on fire trying to light our farts with kitchen matches. Where in the hell do kids learn such things? Dad built a porch cover over the patio with green translucent fiberglass roofing that made everyone gathered under it and sitting on the wooden porch swing look like Martians. Our backyard was a magical grand central station.

We never went hungry, a troop of kids around the kitchen

table and one in a high chair. There was always more than enough including seconds, but we had to finish our plates at suppertime. Dad was the king of the castle and his word was law. It was futile or fatal to ask why; "Because I said so," was uncontestable. Perhaps it was his Marine Corp training or the way he was brought up. His parents, my grandparents, lived through the Great Depression and you didn't waste or throw anything away. I wasn't a picky eater but I hated what mom called goulash. Almost predictably, come Wednesday evening for supper, it was on the table with bread and butter. Stewed tomatoes are nasty and impossible to make vanish like my sister Pissy-Missy could do with food she didn't like. Learning that it wouldn't get any easier to sit defiantly at the table until it got cold, I ate it. Mom would say, "You're going eat it and like it." *Wrong, Mom,* I'd say in my head, we didn't sass back, and make a face in objection; *Okay, I'll eat it, but you can't make me like it.* Sunday dinner was tops; roast chicken and stuffing or a big fat meatloaf, occasionally roast beef or a ham dressed up fancy with pineapple rings and cherries, and all the mashed potatoes and gravy you wanted. After meals we were shooed outside while Mom and Dad washed and dried dishes, their time to bond as I look back, and told to find found something constructive to entertain ourselves. All those wonderful years without Game-boys or an IPad, geez, how in the world did we survive?

Mrs. Ludwig was my second grade teacher and loved our class like we were her own kids. There were twenty-two of us, I think, and we sat alphabetically in rows at one-piece wooden desks bolted to the floor that had a lid on top with a cubby for our books and sundries. The hard attached seat made my butt go numb within an hour after first bell and I looked forward to recess. I may have been the teacher's pet, as Mrs. Ludwig was very complementary on my report card, at least that's how I understood it. *"Dirk is a delightful student but he daydreams. His vivid imagination is*

*quite entertaining - his grades could be better."* I think that's what the textbooks call a brilliant underachiever. Mrs. Ludwig loved us so much that she moved to the next grade and remained our teacher. But third grade was a difficult year.

It was 1963, the year JFK was assassinated; also the year that death visited our home. My baby sister, Susy was in morning kindergarten and pleaded with Mom to stay home because she didn't feel well. Her head throbbed so much it made her sick to her stomach. My brother, who was in second grade, followed me out the door to the Lyter Building for school. No doubt we talked about how Susy always got special treatment, obviously being mom's favorite, but who could fault her. Susy was a beautiful little blonde haired, brown eyed China doll and mom's first girl. It was an off the cuff stupid thing to say, careless and childish when I said, "I hope she dies." I don't think my brother heard me. Was I jealous at Susy getting all the attention or just that I had to go to school?

Later that afternoon we were called out of class and my father took my brother and I home in utter silence. I don't remember much but knew that something was really wrong. The house felt different, Mom was nowhere in sight. My brother and I were ushered to our bedroom where we sat on our beds, numbed, curious and frightened. Unbeknown to us, Susy had died suddenly from an undiagnosed brain tumor. When Sparky and I were informed of her passing, I think it was an uncle or maybe the Methodist minister, I rolled on my side to face the wall, barely able to breathe, and for the rest of my life have carried the guilt and shame that it was my idiotic comment that stole away her life. I felt that it was entirely my fault.

A few years ago, Mom gave me a copy of a photograph of the three of us in the backyard. We're dressed up as Indians posing for the camera. I'm pulling a bow and arrow at whoever is taking the picture, paper feathers sticking up from a band around my head, the summer pool is in the background. Sparky has a headdress of sorts, which he had to have to keep up with his brother no doubt; feathers drooped and stuck out sideways. He wore some kind of draping skirt, probably a towel tied around his waist, kind of like Apaches might have worn. His look seems uncertain, the bow hung at his side. Susy is standing between us in a one piece sundress with her hands on her hips looking off in the distance as if saying, "Can we please get this over with? I'd rather play with my dolls." I've stood before the framed collage of miscellaneous old photos hanging on my bedroom wall under a plaque that says *Pennsylvania Avenue*, always drawn to that picture among the many pictures from a scrapbook album. I've talked to Susy a hundred times and told her how sorry I was about what I said that morning on the way to school. I still tear up and feel deep guilt. I've heard Suzy's soft voice reassure me. I can't wait to hug her.

~

I got into serious trouble that year as a third grader, more than the kind of trouble from talking in class or sneaking a look at Kim Crosby's paper for the right answer and getting caught. Sometime after Christmas break I had my first ride in a police car, and let me tell you, it wasn't all that fun, nor was it ever afterwards, but I don't want to get ahead myself. My best friend, who we called Murray might have dared me that wintery afternoon and I couldn't turn down a dare. He and I were walking home after school, pitching ice balls at streetlights when Chief Early happened to come around the corner in his cruiser and caught us red-handed. Dad was anything but pleased that I had a pitcher's arm and got my tail warmed but proper and grounded for a month.

Murray was a bit slow in school but certainly not stupid. One day he was called to the front of class and instructed to circle the nouns in a simple sentence on the blackboard, which I wasn't totally certain about either. He choked and froze like a Popsicle and everyone in class laughed. His face turned a deep shade of red as he shuffled back to his desk. Murray was one tough son-of-a-bitch, hell on wheels at recess, but that really hurt him. I sat beside him across the aisle and probably didn't know what to do or say. I felt bad for him but glad it wasn't me.

I met up with Murray nearly fifty years later at a Starbucks when I went back home for a visit. After we hugged and complemented one another on how dashing and debonair we looked, kidding ourselves that we were beating the odds at showing our age and making a joke of it, Murray asked me what my first memory was of our friendship. Good question. He vividly remembered his and recounted that day at the blackboard and how embarrassed he felt when everyone laughed at him and told me, quote; "Dirk, you were the only one who didn't laugh at me. I'll never forget that." I felt self-conscious in the crowded room, wiping my wet cheeks with a Starbucks napkin.

It's funny what we remember. In answer to his question concerning our friendship, what popped into my mind was trying to stand on my feet like a skier going down the big slide in the school playground at his taunting. I fell part way down and caught my jacket on a bolt or something and nearly ripped the sleeve off, no blood was drawn. So many adventures and misadventures happened between the two of us that it was hard to narrow it down to one incident. As we parted ways from Starbucks I hollered, "Hey, Murray, I can still pack a mean snowball and knock the lights out."

～

I was blessed with a better than average IQ, certainly the result of my parent's genes, and did well in school. I never really had to study that I can recall and got by without much effort. I was happy with B's. An F would mean being shackled in chains and put on bread and water. My easy-happy-go-lucky mentality grew along with the inseam of my jeans, sneakers and jock strap. I hardly took a book home and skated by with homework. Average was good enough for me, but I kind of took some slack for it. My parents and peers thumped me on the head, so to speak, to apply myself and do better. It went in one ear and out the other. Taking their good advice could have made a difference, but at the time it didn't seem to register. I balked at authority and joked that perfection wasn't my thing when those counselors only meant to steer me in a better direction for my future success and wellbeing. It was an emerging pattern as I look back in retrospect; just getting by was my outlook on life in general. Even though I was connected with good friends and sports and a solid family, I began expressing myself as a rebel without a cause and took on an identity that would alter the successful future everyone said I was so gifted for. I'm not sure to this day what in the hell I was trying to prove.

Junior High came with the rage of hormones and peach fuzz, the pitch in our voices oddly changing like sucking helium or sounding like Bela Lugosi. Pimples weren't a problem for me, but puberty brought questions and confusion complicated ten times ten. Masturbating like it was my last day on the planet and the only thing to do felt good, but it also made me feel like a freak, thinking I was the only one hiding an obsessive secret. I'm convinced that all of us, my classmates and me at that age, were in the same peculiar bubble trying to figure out what was going on inside our bodies and how to fit in. It was an awkward time. Along with the fashion police, who all of a sudden turned up and scrutinized what you wore, cliques began to form. The in group - the not in group, Jocks and Band, cool-cats who grew their hair long and those in the model train club, definitive lines of demarcation were fast becoming evident. Being a freshman changed everything.

We had no middle school to transition to as kids do now; you went from the elementary building to the big school. My education was taken to a new level. The upper classmates enlightened us on the finer things concerning girls, such things as blow jobs and 69 and French kissing. I heard the hokey come-on lines they used on the girls who were outgrowing training bras, especially those who were stacked and didn't wear falsies. Some of the girls seemed quite proud to advertise their goods with tight sweaters, or would nonchalantly bend over in front of you revealing some cleavage knowing full well what they were doing. All I can say is: Hallelujah!

I sprouted like the magic beanstalk almost overnight between sixth and seventh grade to five feet eleven, which was kind of tall in seventh grade. My growing surge stopped and I am still five feet eleven fifty years later, if I stand up straight. I played basketball and was a starter on the Jr. High team, meriting me a certain amount of popularity. Among my idols at the time were John "Hondo" Havilicek and Dave Cowens; obviously my favorite team was the Boston Celtics. I had posters scotch taped on my bedroom walls. Coach Felix, God bless his soul, put us through the drills. I can still see his big buck teeth and feel his excitement as we huddled before tip-off time. "Teamwork and hustle equals win!" He was a good coach who took a personal interest in his players and had high hopes for me, but I was ill equipped to interact comfortably on a social level off the court. I was shy and didn't know what to say to a girl until an hour too late when some great line would dawn like the cartoon light bulb in my head. But I did kiss my first girl during a tournament in Renovo when our team was in the top bracket.

*Hanky-Panky* and *Dizzy* were among the popular songs at the time. I preferred *Crimson and Clover* or Steppenwolf's *Born to be Wild*. The hometown cheerleaders did a dance routine at halftime in their blue and gold short skirts and pom-poms, shaking their booty and smiling like a sunbeam to *Build me up Buttercup...* There was ice on the river, a short walk across the parking lot from the gym, and you can probably guess who went with me to explore between games; Murray. He was our starting point guard and he and I were thick as thieves.

We horsed around the river's edge and ventured out, skating on the ice in our loafers. A couple of cheerleaders from our rival district wandered over, bundled up in their school colors of maroon and white (the Lancers), and hung out on the bank with the sole intent to tease us. Murray and I were excellent show-offs until the ice broke and I crashed helplessly. Fortunately, I wasn't in deep water and landed on my feet, shocked and standing waist deep in ice cold water, totally mortified. I had one hell of a time crawling to shore. Murray luckily landed on solid ice. I was soaked to my skivvies and freezing to death when I heard a girl who I came to know as Karen rooting for me when everyone else was hooting and laughing. Her voice was the only one I heard, though Murray was pitching a fit. Karen had a pretty oval face, a button nose and freckles, dazzling green eyes and strawberry blonde hair to her shoulders held in place by earmuffs. I was taken by the most beautiful smile on planet earth.

After retrieving a sense of dignity and some dry clothes from my duffle bag, I found Karen waiting for me outside the locker room. We walked around the grounds, holding hands, and took shelter in a dug-out beside a snow covered ballfield. We could see our breath, mine was sputtering like a steam locomotive pulling a grade. Butterflies stirred in my stomach more than at tip-off time on the court. Karen giggled at my stories. I think her favorite question was; "And then what happened?" She told me the guys in her class were all jerks and was glad to have met me. In the course of conversation, Karen said she often daydreamed about running away and I wondered why. Maybe she'd runaway to Hollywood and become an actress. If it wasn't that we were in a strange place away from home and the ice providentially broke under my feet, we would have never bumped into one another.

Words sort of piddled out and we cuddled together to get warm. Karen looped an arm around mine to squeeze tight and touched my face to brush some snow away with her mitten. It smelled nice, girly like lavender hand cream. Awkward moments passed stargazing into each other's eyes. Words would interrupt the feelings that rose, breathless, curious. We tentatively leaned in and kissed as if testing the water. It didn't take long to warm up and get it ever so right, me being the novice, as our mouths melted into one. It was like a furnace blazed between us, heat flushing my face, my heart beating like I'd run a hundred yard dash. Karen was a really good kisser.

If it'd been summertime I might have tried for second base, if you know what I mean. It seemed ridiculous at the time and I wasn't really so bold. She wore a thick ski jacket zipped to her chin. I was smitten and certain that Karen would be my girlfriend, but when the tournament was over we each went our different ways. I saw her at a keg party a few years later and she remembered me. We spoke casually but she seemed preoccupied with the college guys hawking for her attention.

At the end of that weekend in Renovo, I rode the team bus back home with a trophy from the tournament. We lost by three points in the finals to Karen's school. I also took with me the lingering memory of my first kiss, the taste of her Chap-Stick on my lips and how our tongues played a slippery dance neither of us wanted to end.

~

Identity and self-worth are items one can neither buy over the counter nor send away for a crash course like in a Charles Atlas advertisement in the back of magazines. There's no magic wand or miracle pill. Knowing what I know now, I wonder if I wasn't bipolar. One day I felt like I was better than everyone and secretly, or maybe not so secretly, looked down on lowly geeks and stupid ball-hogs who took all the glory. Idiots. I couldn't help it if I was right all the time, brighter or more agile, suave and Mr. Da-Boner. But the next day would come around like the entire game was turned upside-down. I was a joke, a loser, less than average and the jerkiest jerk ever born. I had a way of camouflaging my insecurities with buffoonery and artful dodging. None of my friends talked about their feelings and it made me wonder why I was different. Of course, we all felt the same way. Hidden under the veneer of invincibility was a frustrated, displaced and confused kid who overcompensated with antics like snapping a wet towel at some poor soul in the boys shower or taunting the class nerds in the cafeteria. Bullying is still bullying even if it's joking and seemingly harmless. I rarely joined in and should have stuck up for Keith Aultson instead of laughing and going along with the crowd, which makes me guilty of bullying as well. That kid took it on the chin every day. The crowd... huh? Which one did I really fit in?

This is in hindsight, but maybe the reason for my impulsive choices to crash the gates of the status quo was that the requirement was all about "fitting in." No one was going to tell me what to do. My Dad had a phrase I often heard growing up whenever he got totally exasperated with me. "By God boy, you have a wild hair up your ass," and then the lecture would begin. The thing I didn't see coming were the consequences of my rash choices. I started getting into trouble, a rogue wild hair I'm guessing, but at thirteen going on fourteen it was heady stuff. I got noticed beyond the basketball court.

# 2

*To* tell you of the upcoming events is certainly not to boast. Frankly, much of it embarrasses me. They were not all the glory days that Bruce Springsteen so aptly sang about in his gravelly voice; his anthem about the days of baseball, girls and High School. Some of my story is like a bad flashback and hard for me to relive, let alone making mention of.

There were good times, many pleasurable, memorable, fun-filled days. Fond memories are etched on my brain that I can still picture. Summer afternoons riding my bike to our swimming hole out on the Loyalsock Creek to Slab Town and Shore Acres. Hunting for fossils at the sand pits with my buddy Lutzy always proved entertaining and successful. I wish I still had some of those amazing fossils. And there crazy times when the gang played Army and we actually shot at each other with B-B guns on Beatty's hill at a place we called Devil's Den. Making snow forts and sledding down cemetery hill entertained us on winter days. My chest would swell with pride at hearing my dad rooting for me from the bleachers when I scored. Yes, some of my memories are indeed glory days and what I want to impress others with; those things that I did right and made my folks and coaches hold their heads up high. But the beginning of my life-changing events is tricky. I hope to maintain a positive narrative, but it means sorting through the dark and crazy times, travelling back on a road that was hilly with switchbacks, potholes and detours, but never hit a dead end.

~

Last year a writer friend (who I'll tell you about later), said that I had a life story to tell and should write it. Really? Jackie was persistent and I humored her. I was never one who could remember much of the past let alone have the know-how to write a book. My past wasn't something so distant that it was unreachable, but more as though my recollection button didn't work up to par. It amazes me to have written this much past history with something I hope has clarity. At hearing stories among my family or friends when they walked down memory lane, I could see it, feel it, and be part of my past by proxy. Left to myself, yesterdays were shrouded in a fog. But something remarkable happened as a result of my writer friend's prompting. She said life was like going to the library and browsing the labyrinth of spirits, sitting under green shaded lamps illuminating a mystery to be solved. Parchment and words when connected had power to heal. I began making notes.

This story began by stumbling upon a door. The door is imaginary and figurative, not the result of drugs or dream therapy or induced hypnosis. Perhaps it's a vision, or maybe an answer to an unasked prayer. A door appears totally involuntarily without warning. I never know how or when it will turn up. The lettering above the door is puzzling: "Lost and Found Department." Is this the kind of place I think it is? Misplaced random and forgotten items left behind to collect dust? The door itself is a bit of an anomaly, maybe it depends on my frame of mind, but it appears within my periphery, gradually coming into focus, no two times the same way. A better way of putting it is that of a portal to another place. It beckons to me, whispery, other-worldly, a veil blowing in the wind, and I hear a voice or sense a presence that gives me pause to pay attention.

I see an outline of a door, sometimes surrounded with prism-like flashes in surreal colors as on a sunny day like a promising rainbow, or shrouded in grey patina on a cold and windy evening, haunting and ominous, and I'm enticed to venture closer by childish curiosity. I've seen the door appear sturdy yet blistered, ancient and mysterious, peeling layers of washed-out red paint, bloody just as life can sometimes be. I've seen it ramshackle and beaten by weather and time, yet standing firm in the framework, looking as though it couldn't endure another gale force assault of life as I know it. And then again, it appears like a common steel commercial door, windowless, dented and rusted at the hinges; the kind of door you wouldn't want to be locked behind. There isn't any way to predict its appearance, when the door shows up, or what it might look like and what it might speak. The door is an entryway, the back panel of the wardrobe in Narnia, the magic carpet ride to Kashmir or the gateway to Hades. Subtle warmth may allure and welcome me in as in a pleasant fairytale, or a flashing barricade warning me to proceed slowly. "Enter," the door seems to beckon, "Come on in; take a deep breath. Give it a shove if it sticks." I've never found it locked.

The room is well lit once I'm inside. I know this is all in my head, but before my wide-open eyes there's a labyrinth of aisles, a veritable maze with shelves upon shelves and cubbies from the floor to the ceiling. I've seen the Yellow Brick Road lead the way back home and I've seen the rocky pathway to the depths of Mordor. An array of boxes are stacked one upon the other on every side of the aisles, labeled by dates or a single bold word in crayon or marker, some taped and still sealed, others partially opened or torn completely apart. I can spend hours, if I chose to do so, sorting through files and files of memories organized like the old Dewey Decimal System the library used back in the day. My preference is to sit back, look around, mindlessly shuffle this here and that there, not feeling hurried to do any real concentrated exploring, but maybe unhurried isn't the right word. Perhaps a better word is apprehension.

Something always grabs my attention in the Lost and Found Department. There's so much to entertain me. I'll pick out a reel of Super 8mm from the teetering pyramid of hundreds of canisters of home movies that my Dad took, enticed to watch them again or for the first time, often amused, but sometimes convicted by viewing the disappointing failures of such a zestful and promising kid. Occasionally it's unnerving to watch him growing up and I don't stay very long. I much more prefer the times when it's rather enjoyable to linger. Making the connection between me now and me back then with so many gaps in the time-line, to be honest, that's kind of my current conundrum. Memories lost – memories found; a blessing and a curse in the trickledown effect.

Getting in touch with my past and presently writing it down is supposed to be healing, or ramp up the positive to circumvent the negative as gurus and faith-healers propose. The surprising disclosures of forgotten or hidden memories, many deliberately buried and shoved back on the shelf, are certainly revelatory when revealed. I think of Bill Murray in *What About Bob*, baby steps. They're coming back to me; the circuits are slowly connecting and the light is dawning. These distant memories that have been lodged in the cobwebbed corners of my mind have been speaking to me. I feel a sense of promise, not so much fear as to turn and run away, and have adapted a new mantra: "Don't deny the truth of what you have yet to understand."

I never played it safe, nor do I remember ever bunting. I always swung for the fence - for the homerun. If there was one lesson my old man taught me growing up it was to be the best at whatever you did. It could have been basketball, getting good grades and a college scholarship, but no, not me. I don't mean to make light of my father's advice or mock him, but I did try to do my best. Unfortunately, I excelled at making a mess of my life. I ran recklessly with abandon, those young and promising years

I can never retrieve, like a hound dog on the trail of an angry porcupine that gave me a face full of horrible regret.

~

A dirt alley ran a straight shot from my backyard on Bennett Street to the high school, six blocks with grass still growing in the middle like it did fifty years ago. Benny, my muskrat trapping friend, lived a block from my back door. We'd meet up and walk together to school while shooting the bull, have spitting contests and torment the dogs along the way. Mr. Hessler had a lush grape arbor ripe for the pickings in season. The Toole's had a large garden where we pilfered cherry tomatoes when old man Toole wasn't hoeing or standing guard. Among our many adventures, Benny introduced me to smoking. I'd had a short-lived experience with stolen ciggies from Grandpa Fullmer, but it wasn't a habit. Ed's Market was a mom and pop grocery store and a routine stop, a quick side trip off the beaten track. They still had nigger-babies, along with Bazooka bubble gum, three layered watermelon taffy and Mallo Cups in the candy counter, just to mention a few of my favorites. They also sold cigarettes. Benny smoked Kool filters and I got a taste for them. A pack cost thirty five cents at the time, which was my lunch money for the day. This was before you were "Carded." A pack would last me a week or better, hidden under my mattress so as not to get caught. I guess I thought I was cool and took to smoking. Benny and I would puff our way down the alley to within view of the high school auditorium to a place we called The Red Barn. It was a leaning out-building with roof cover where fellow smokers gathered before first bell. Smoking on school property merited two days suspension if you got caught, which I did several times. One of the second floor boy's restrooms had large, hand crank casement windows we'd crack open to catch a draft, but as clever as we thought we were, inevitably a male teacher would wander in like a cop and drag our ass to the principal's office. Getting busted meant the dreaded pink slip, and trouble at school meant trouble at home. It wasn't that I hated school so much as I loved cigarettes more. Smart, right?

~

On a spring-like February day, Murray and I decided to skip school. It never took much of a reason or persuasion on each other's part to dodge and run and find some kind of amusement for the day. The alternative was sitting through English Lit. and algebra class. We banked on the hope that when we got home on schedule, the phone didn't ring and wind up getting us into a hassle with the folks. It seemed harmless. Murray and I had gotten away with playing hooky before. Call our impulse to run off the touch of spring fever or the call of the wild, but that particular day all hell broke loose.

We wandered the railroad tracks down by the airport. There was an abandoned silica sand mill across the runway we called Ghost Town; an old factory that was sadly collapsing in ruin as the years went by. It had a reputation that hobos frequently camped there as it was shelter and close to the railroad tracks. I saw a fire ring blackened by use, ratty blankets and discarded tin cans and empty bottles of cheap wine, but never ran across a hobo. I'm not sure what I would have done if ever I encountered some codger travelling the rails or what he'd make of me if by chance I wandered into his space. Maybe I'd join them. They were probably just local stories that got better by the telling, but exploring Ghost Town was the best entertainment boys could imagine, despite having No Trespassing signs posted everywhere.

Murray and I trotted across the runway, luckily not getting run over by an incoming plane, when a jeep that looked military started after us with sirens blaring and a light bar flashing like a nuclear disaster was occurring. We shifted into high gear. I thought we'd go to jail. Murray thought we'd get shot. We didn't stop running until coming to the river and hunkered down, hiding in the bushes. Don't ask me why or how our reasoning worked out the way it did, but Murray and I agreed we were in serious trouble and decided to keep running. It seemed like there was no turning back. If the law didn't hang us from a tree, our parents surely would. With a combined amount of a dollar forty and a pack of Kool filters, we thought Florida looked pretty good. We crouched in the bushes and fantasied about hanging out on the beach, drinking ice cold beer and checking out bikinis. It wasn't a well thought out plan.

My dad harped like a broken record not to hang out with Murray because he was a bad influence. Murray's old man told him the same; "That Dirk is nothing but trouble. Your mother and I would prefer you keep better company." I'm not sure if either of us was necessarily a bad influence on the other. I think we just thought alike in some kinetic way and were drawn to break free of the spoken or implied boundaries that we had to accept. Rules... aren't they made to be broken? We thought so.

Murray and I followed the river until noon and came to a town called Muncy where we spent fifty cents on peanut butter crackers and Cokes at a gas station. We hitched a ride with an old coot in overalls that smelled of cow manure and whisky, crowding against one another on the bench seat of his pickup truck with the stick shift nearly up my butt. He stopped at a turn off, wishing us luck, and pointed to a four lane highway where Murray and I stuck out our thumbs like seasoned hitch-hikers. I don't recall the details, but somehow we ended up in Lancaster, over two hours away and well after dark. It may have been our guardian angels who led us, for we found ourselves at a downtown Rescue Mission. There was probably a sign-in sheet to fill out, if so, we obviously lied. We were assigned a bed and lined-up for soup and sandwiches and a four pack of Oreos, along with the drifters, the homeless and county drunks. At lights-out, Murray and I laid side-by-side, whispering and giggling about all the crazy people. An old man lay in a bunk beside me who looked just like W.C. Fields in the old black and white movies. He had a bulbous nose and greasy black hair slicked over his forehead and wore a rumpled black suit, a stained collared shirt and a bow tie, ornery and sour smelling with a disapproving attitude at life in general. He constantly hacked a harsh smoker's cough and kept repeating a scornful tirade as if it was directed at me. "I've got asthma you asshole, and you think that's funny? I oughta box your damned ears." I clenched my face into a knot, trying to stifle the impossible. When you get bit by the laughing bug you can't stop, it's sometimes embarrassing. In the morning, Murray and I had oatmeal and toast and got the hell out of there, thinking that maybe the police were informed about two young boys with just the clothes on their back.

Later that day we wound up in Washington, DC. Don't ask me how we got there, but I do recall when a VW van picked us up. Two long-haired hippies engaged us in friendly conversation saying something like we were free spirits, part of the brave new world. They passed a thin cigarette back and forth that didn't smell like any cigarette I was acquainted with. "Have you ever been experienced?" I had no clue what that meant. "Like Jimi Hendrix, man. Do you get high?" Murray looked uncomfortable. I said, "Yeah man, all the time," and reached for the joint. It was rolled in red paper and tasted at first like strawberries. I smoked it just like a cigarette and inhaled. Murray told me later that he didn't inhale. He was scared that he'd freak out or something.

We'd watched the film documentaries in school about marijuana with the droning voice of a commentator putting fear in your mind; the graphic depictions of people going looney and winding up in strait jackets, shadowy faces behind jail bars, junkies shooting heroin as a result of smoking weed. Murray was very impressionable and the images must have stuck in his head. I saw it as government fear tactics, total bologna and propaganda even back then.

I felt emboldened, casting a glance at the hippy's reflection in the rearview mirror and handed the joint back after several tokes. My head slowly lifted from my body like a balloon floating weightlessly on a dizzy, spinning breeze. A song by Jefferson Airplane played on the radio when we went over the Potomac River, something about a rabbit and Alice. I wasn't sure what was happening, reality had changed, but I wasn't scared. It was trippy in a disconnected way and everything made me giggle. I was totally relaxed. Many acquaintances I've met since have told me they didn't get high the first time they smoked marijuana, but I sure did. I'm fairly convinced that what I smoked was laced with something.

We were dropped off on an on-ramp and found a suitable position along the guardrails to stick out our thumbs. I can't piece together the exact events, but a compact car pulled over. A friendly young guy, maybe a college student, opened the passenger door and called to hop on in. I went for the backseat, still stoned on my ass and rolled the window down, watching the billboards and landscape fly by on Interstate 95. I must have dozed off until Murray shook me awake. The road signs were perplexing, we'd come to the city limits of Richmond, Virginia with a million exits. The guy said he had to pick up a friend at the airport and dropped us off at a major interchange of crazy, fast moving traffic and gave us each twenty bucks. He encouraged us to call home and check in with our folks, knowing, of course, that we were runaways. We walked across the highway and found a cheap motel, bought some hamburgers at building that looked like a white castle. It felt great to stretch out and watch TV as our T shirts, socks and underwear dried over the heat unit after washing them in the sink. Murray was antsy, looking worried like he should call home. I felt like Christopher Columbus discovering the New World. It was all dreamlike, but dreams don't last and they're certainly not for real.

We had a rude awakening the next morning when a Richmond City Police car came up behind us on a major highway. We tried lying to him that we were students going back home to Florida and our car had broken down. When Murray answered the officer; "Janesville instead of Gainesville," the gig was up. Of course, we no more looked like college students than the policeman looked like Barney Fife. We spent our third night since running away from home in a cell in the Richmond City Jail. Our parents were notified. I'm not sure which scared me more; the murderer in the next cell who played head games with us, or how my Dad was actually going kill me.

It's uncanny what you remember and what you forget. Our brains are complex, but my hard drive is messed up. I can't remember what I had for supper last night, but I can still see my mom's face when I stood in the living room at fourteen going on fifteen years old, freshly released from a jail cell that seemed like a foreign country. It's still vivid in my mind. My mother stood in the hall archway in her housecoat like she was in a trance. Her eyes were haunting, shadowed by sleepless nights, and peered into mine with an imploring look as to ask why without a word. There was such sadness and disappointment in her gaze that I should have fallen to my knees and pleaded for forgiveness.

Andy Warhol said we all get fifteen minutes of fame, or something like that. I think he may have been right. Easy come – easy go, like a flash in the pan, the perfect Kodak moment, a headline with your name in bold letters. My celebrity status was short lived, but what attention Murray and I got when we were back in school. We may have embellished telling our story, but why? Truth was stranger than fiction. The fiasco of running away should have been a wake-up call and turned our heads around to batten down and straighten up; instead, it kind of backfired. Coach Felix and my homeroom teacher, Ms. Springman pleaded with me to see the light. I tried, I really did. Their efforts to reach me were so emotional and they seemed to genuinely care, but my attempt to reform only lasted a little while. The experience of being my own man with a taste of freedom, being on the road like Kerouac and smoking weed in DC was like a springboard that catapulted me into deeper, murkier waters. Maybe my dad should have left me locked up in Richmond.

My hometown wasn't very big in 1969; three red lights on Broad Street from the bridge to the cemetery and you were through town. It was pretty much blue collar, nice lawns and good church people, nothing like Compton or Southside Chicago. There weren't gangs or drive-by shootings or stabbings in the school parking lot. If there was serious crime it was going on somewhere other than our little borough. The rowdiness when I was growing up was burning rubber with a hot car, raiding Browning's fruit market for a watermelon when you slept outdoors in the summer, or streakin' buck naked in public. "Don't look Ethel!" The only tattoos that I was aware of were worn by veterans who served in the military. We didn't have Crack or Meth. What we did have was the garden variety of cannabis and blonde hash and I knew where to get it.

Our school's signature image was the Warriors with proud colors of blue and gold. The logo was the profile of a chief in full head dress. My gym bag in ninth grade was pro-school except for the contents zipped inside, which were nickel and dime bags of grass along with my hi-top Converse sneakers and gym clothes. My buddy's and I pooled our change together to cover the cost of a twelve pack of Schlitz or Rolling Rock or a few bottles of Boones Farm Strawberry wine on the weekend. A guy lived down Bennett Street who I called Mr. X and bought alcohol for us under-agers with no kickback.

The high school hosted a Saturday night dance in the gymnasium that was always a party. There was a grove of pine trees behind the Ag building where the 4H Club met that made a cave-like cubby, safe from any curious on-lookers who might blow the whistle. We'd hang out to chug brews and pass around a joint before going into the gym. I never danced, but I did enjoy watching the girls dancing among themselves, with sparkly lights from a disco ball that made everything magical. Local bands played covers of what was rocking on Casey Kasem's Top Twenty Count-down. Grand Funk Railroad's *I'm Your Captain/Closer to my Home* was among my favorites. A local guy we called Stink was the lead vocalist in a band and sang just like Mark Farner.

The parents of a friend of mine had a garage opposite the west end of the football field, a short walk from where the dance was held. You had to sneak around the back under parental radar. The garage had an upstairs loft covered end to end with mattresses. Black lights illuminated day-glow posters plastered on the walls and ceiling with rock icons, magic mushrooms, dragons and wizards. It was a destination you could take a girl to if you got lucky at the dance. Rodney's garage should have been called "Hotel Hickey." Remember those mock turtlenecks called Dickies? Handy cover that saved the day if you ask me.

I paid for my exploits, if you can call them that. The word exploit makes me think of noble men, pioneers like Dr. Livingston in the dark heart of Africa or Lewis and Clark trekking the Missouri River; but honestly, I was just a dumb kid wandering lost without a compass.

The sixties were tumultuous times in general; the Vietnam War was in full swing, protests from coast to coast and the horror at Kent State were reported by Walter Cronkite who shared the nightly news of the war and Civil Rights leaders blazing new trials. A mass exodus to Haight-Ashbury introduced us to the counterculture, and, of course, Woodstock. I was too young to be a part of the scene, but had I been a few years older I'm sure that I would be playing guitar and singing Bob Dylan songs. I think my brother would have enlisted and said give me an M16. I would have lamented being drafted.

As to the price I paid for my rebellion, at the top of the list is alienation from my family. When I was at home it felt more like I was a visitor, graciously given permission to eat at the table and get my laundry done. Another small cost my so-called exploits cost me was paying the fine of $37.50 for getting caught numerous times for under-age drinking. I'm sure the magistrate had a steak dinner on my dime. The police car rides weren't exactly like a well-worn path but the local cops knew where I lived. Chief Early had it out for me ever since our little run-in involving snowballs in third grade.

My dad wasn't amused whenever a cruiser parked in front of our house. Looking back, I don't even know what to say about that. He worked in the bank and saw people from town every day that read the paper and heard the gossip. At one time my brother and I were the talk of the town with sports awards, but the latest news was different. Was my father embarrassed? Angry? Distraught? I know he was and much, much more. I'm sure that I made him so livid he could have snapped me in half like balsa wood. I was testing his patience to the outer limits and started spending nights away from home to avoid the confrontation, more times than not, too drunk to find the front door.

⁓

I haven't mentioned my other brother who is number six in line among us kids, but it's fitting to do so in keeping with my story. I'm sorting through memories in the Lost and Found Department and came across old photos of Kenny, my autistic brother.

In a household that was upbeat with kids playing and making a racket, my folks dealt with the loss of two children almost in the blink of an eye. As I've mentioned, Susy died suddenly at age five. Chris never left the hospital, He died a year and a half after Susy's passing at four months old in St. Christopher Children Hospital in Philadelphia from an unsuccessful operation to correct an undeveloped heart. He was buried at the family plot in a casket not much bigger than a pair of men's work boots. Parents should never have to live to see the day their children die before them, but I don't make up the rules. An atmosphere like dim candlelight could steal in and shroud an otherwise happy occasion, but we were bolstered, shielded and cared for. Birthday parties still happened, toys for the sand box and a new swing set got added in the backyard. Mom made brownies. In spite of the grief and pain, my parents endured and made us feel like everything was okay. They give true definition to the word resilient. I was too young to comprehend the pain they went through and how they managed to keep us all secure. And along came Kenny Jr. who changed the dynamics in our house in an atypical way.

Kenny had dad's chiseled chin with a dimple like Kirk Douglas, jet black hair and deep set dark eyes with the build and potential of being a linebacker. He grew to the age when he started saying simple words like dada and momma and the like. Stu's mom had a fat black cat that sat on their front porch across the street, and Kenny would stand at our screen door for hours watching him. He called, "Pook - Pook." The cat's name was Spooky. Suddenly, the best way I know how to describe it, a switch got flipped. Kenny never out-grew diapers. Everything went in his mouth. He ran instead of walked. Cabinet and closet doors were fixed so he couldn't get into things and make a mess. Mom's pretty knickknacks and anything breakable and of value within Kenny's reach were put in storage. Instead of the homey feeling of welcome and warmth we knew so well and were accustomed to, you came in the front door to a kind of starkness, uncertain about the atmosphere, wondering what kind of day it was for Mom. It seemed like a battle for peace in an on-going war-zone.

Kenny was extremely hyper-active and kept Mom on her feet running to mind him, to restrain him so he wouldn't hurt himself, changing his clothes and cleaning up poopy messes smeared on his face and the walls. My sisters, who were little and played with dolls or playdoh making colorful cookies, instinctively tried to baby Kenny and take him into their fold. Missy was only a few years older and a tremendous helper with Kenny and mom's stability. My folks cared for Kenny until he grew big enough they couldn't manage him, and with broken and weary hearts, sent him to a country institution in Laurelton for the mentality handicapped.

Laurelton Center looks like an old college campus or an abbey for religious orders; ivy covered stone buildings with porches and weathered gables were tucked in a wooded area with picnic tables that seemed like a safe place. It was Kenny's home for twenty plus years. As I recall from visiting, the staff was compassionate and very accommodating.

Autism is the buzz word, although I don't really know exactly what his diagnosis is. Do the doctors or any of the experts really understand the scope of autism? Kenny is now fifty four and in a group home, needing full-time care. I visit whenever I get back home, but Kenny doesn't know who I am. I hold to the hope that he knows me somewhere deep in his subconscious DNA. There's a day coming when we pass across the divide and we'll sit together, each of us with a new body and mind, and swap stories while having a milkshake.

Kenny was around eight years old when I began screwing up. If our house on Bennett Street wasn't already drastically altered, I didn't contribute anything more than added chaos. I was oblivious to the complications that I caused. It's no wonder my parents were frazzled.

You know how it is when you're the oldest and basically it's required of you to set a good example for your siblings? If that's something you've experienced you'll feel my pain. In all that was happening under our roof during Kenny's evolving, Sparky, my kid brother was following my not-so good example. Stories were told of our childhood days referring to us as Pete and Re-Pete, double the pleasure - double the headache.

We both played Little League. Mr. DiRocco was our coach for Carey McFalls, a local factory that sponsored the team. Dad was an assistant coach. We wore real-to-life baseball uniforms and caps. I played first base because I was tall and lanky and could stretch with my foot on the bag to snag the ball. My mitt had webbing like a good-sized lobster. I was a hit or miss batter, but parked the ball over the fence for a homerun enough times that I batted clean-up. If you don't know what that means, I was fourth in the batting line-up with the hope there was someone on base.

Sparky is a southpaw and was one hell-ova pitcher. He could throw any kind of pitch; a fast ball, curve ball or a knuckle ball, the surprise sinker that made a batter swing and miss. He came at you from the opposite side of the mound with such accuracy and ferocity it was intimidating. He's still in the Little League record books for strike-outs back to the sixties. I'm sure if he had keep at it and had the proper training he would have been the second baseball player from my hometown to make the majors. Sparky was every bit as good as Mike Mussina. He surely gave the old man a work-out in the backyard, burning pitch after pitch into dad's old leather glove that had to burn hot when they'd call it a day. We grew up learning how to slide into home base, but somewhere along the line we started sliding down a slippery path.

I was pretty much failing every class except art class because I chucked studying aside, and skipped school regularly. It was as though everyone had turned a blind eye and I ran unfettered. The new destination was across the street from the corner grocery on Montour Street only a block from the high school called: "The Eight Ball Pool Hall." Pop Tayler, an old veteran of billiards, opened a low ceilinged pool hall with six tables of fine green felt and racks of good cue sticks. You paid by the hour and could smoke, but never-ever put your ciggy on the rail. I learned how to rack and break and shot fairly well, though I was no shark like old man Remalley or Indian who could run the table. In the back were several pinball machines that took a beating without always tilting. There was also a jukebox, three plays for a quarter, my favorite was J3; *Ramblin Man* by the Allman Brothers. Those of us who indulged would huddle at the backdoor and inconspicuously pass a joint around. The pool hall was one of my homes away from home; Lars and Benny's house were the others. I never wanted to go home to Bennett Street unless it was necessary because I felt like an intruder. I suppose that in my mind it was a long, long way back home if I could find it, metaphorically and yet for real, but it took too much effort. I wasn't disowned, I abandoned them. I lost something of great value by my cavalier and foolhardy rebellion, values called stability and support, a nesting place of security with my family. I didn't see it as being all that important at the time. Dropping out of school was the last straw and there seemed to be a mutual understanding that I was on my own.

So, how does a kid get by? What about money? There was Grants Department store for one, also my grandad's Woolrich hunting coat that I'd somehow inherited, with a game pouch and deep pockets. Before the days of security cameras and electronic scanners at the doors, a smart shoplifter could get away with carrying the cash register out. Among the easy pickings were 8Tracks and they sold like hotcakes. I feel that I need to interject and briefly define what an 8Track is. It's about the size of a VHS tape, which may also need explaining if you're under twenty years old. 8Tracks were entire vinyl albums on a ribbon like reel-to-reel in a hard case that you shoved into a player either in your car or home stereo system. It played continuously until you ejected it. If I didn't hear Jethro Tull's *Aqualung* a zillion times! Anyway, you get the point. I stole impulsively; the lazy man's way to get by without working and paying his way. Sad, but true, I got away with tons more than I ever got caught for. Open garages were also fair game, whenever I wandered back alleys. It's amazing how many people kept cases of beer and wine in their garage.

My first car was a '63 Plymouth Signet, basically a compact Valiant and in mint condition. I bought it from Stu's mom for four hundred dollars that I actually worked for, washing dishes at the airport and delivering newspapers months before I was old enough to drive. It was copper in color with bucket seats, an automatic slap-stick with a slant six, more of a granny car than my dream car which would have been a shiny black '55 Chevy Nomad. Unfortunately, it didn't last long. Two months after getting my license and cruising back roads with friends and my brother, the 8Track cranked full volume, passing a joint and drinking tall neck Budweiser's, needless to say when car versus guardrails, guardrails usually win. After another run-in with the law I was assigned to a Friend of the Court, a kind of court appointed guidance counselor. Records were kept and a once a week visit was mandatory to play by the rules, but I must say, I liked the man that I was assigned to.

Mr. Sullenberger owned the Sonoco gas station on Broad Street down by the A&P and specialized working on foreign cars. He told me to call him Sully. His demeanor was soft spoken and anything but overtly forward, but he engaged me with a common sense approach that touched a nerve. After getting together several times I warmed to him and started opening up. He was a keen listener and seemed to hear my inner thoughts, knowing just the right questions to ask. I swept the garage floors and emptied the trash cans every other day after school and made $25 pocket money for the week. Sully was patient and taught me the way around the shop and I'd bring the right tool (hopefully), when he called for it from under the hood of a car.

We went out for lunch, his treat at Fox's Family Restaurant for a burger and Cokes and he bowed his head to say grace. It was the first time I ever saw someone pray outside of church. I felt a twinge of embarrassment as some people looked at us with raised eyebrows and wanted to hide under the table. Sully shared a little bit of his faith whenever we took a break in the garage and gave me an updated, illustrated copy of *Pilgrims Progress*. He was the first one in a long line of people who touched something inside me to rethink what I was doing and I wish I would have paid attention. It could have saved hundreds of hours with so many other well-meaning counselors who showed a little interest and tried to talk sense and hit a sensitive nerve. I went through the revolving door, in and out of trouble time and again, shaken but not awakened.

I'll spare you the long version and skip a stone across the pond. This story was never intended to be a tome of thousands of pages. Good Lord, I don't want to relive all that bad shit. It's enough to do this much. I'll be as succinct as possible, but there may be some long sentences, so take a deep breath.

I was the first in my immediate family history to drop out of school and also the first to stand before the judge. I was seventeen and back in front of Judge Greevy again, with the threat, or shall I say, the promise of jail-time at Camp Hill Detention Center on charges worthy of a year sentence. My dad stepped in and signed papers so that I could join Uncle Sam's Army and avoid juvenile corrections. The Army didn't work out. I know, that's a short sentence so save your breath, but it just didn't. I returned home after basic training and AIT with a general discharge (disciplinary), and a new game plan. *"It's time to get your act together!"* I wasn't home but a few days and followed a man, at his request, from Alby's corner sub shop across the street from Shannahan's Used Car lot. The allure of a basement bar with Harvey Wallbangers and a pool table drew me in. Maybe I could snitch something of value. I could hold my liquor, but when he put porn on the TV and tried to get frisky it was lights out. I don't play that game. He could have ended up in the ER had I not come to my senses and charged me with assault. It's amazing the damage a mop handle can do. I felt like I had to get out of town and stay out of town and asked myself who the real victim was. Why I was I the one running and why did I feel that I had to make excuses and lie for a guy I thought I knew but was a sicko in disguise?

Jimmy was older than me by a few years, I knew him from the pool hall. He had an ongoing screw-fest with one of the hottest girls in my grade, Teats describes her well. Jimmy lived in the Jordan Street neighborhood which had a scurrilous reputation, but I'm not one to judge. So what if it was down by the railroad tracks? Jimmy was a scraper; he and Buggy's gang had a reputation for being hooligans and a winning record at fighting. Jimmy was in violation of his parole and looking for greener pastures. We hooked up in an equal quandary at a party and took off. He had a cache of stolen money from a mutual friend of ours, who I should have been loyal to and said something, but you can't squeal on someone like Jimmy without serious consequences of bodily harm.

We caught a Greyhound bus from Williamsport to Salisbury, MD to Rehoboth Beach, following a "make-it-up-as-you-go" pathway. Sitting on the boardwalk at Rehoboth we concocted a plan. Easy money was at hand, and after some practice we pillaged our way down the coast from resort town to tourist trap to West Palm Beach. I drank enough cold beer and checked out thousands of bikinis that would have made Murray jealous. What Jimmy and I did was ruin many family vacations, which grieves me to write this.

We'd watch the parking lot for incoming Cadillacs, Lincolns and sport cars with an eye on rich men dressed flamboyant as a pink flamingo with a fake swagger; the sales rep at a convention or trade show at Myrtle Beach or St. Augustine or wherever, some voyeur screwing around on his wife back home. Fat bankers, real estate tycoons or lawyers or anyone that appeared rich and stupid flashed like a target in bright neon that they were easy pickings. We were like Robin Hood, spying out the crooked and wealthy, wasn't that all right? The sad and sorry mistake was robbing a family man by mistake. We watched as they'd park and invariably cranked the car window down an inch and stow their wallet and valuables under the front seat before heading to the beach. Back then, the locks were old school, no alarm systems, no key pad; a coat hanger or slim-jimmy did the trick. Take for example a white assed, pasty, beer bellied, hairy chested bung hole wearing Speedo's and a New Jersey wife beater T shirt with gold chains and a buxom Italian wife wearing jewelry in tow buried the family fortune in the sand under the beach blanket, they were easy prey when they went into the surf to frolic. Take a breath. I warned you about long sentences. It made me wonder if I'd gone to college and met so-called A-holes daughter, he may very well be my father-in-law and I'd be living in Newark in a split-level on a cul-de-sac as an insurance salesman. Why did I picture things in my mind like an artist drawing caricatures on the boardwalk? Yeah, I was doing my fair share of hallucinogens, but that wasn't being fair.

Jimmy and I traveled up and down the Atlantic coast. Money was indeed easy. Living the life was crazy. And then, the crap hit the fan at a Ramada Inn in West Palm Beach. We'd run-up a tab exceeding the stolen credit card limit, living it up and partying through the night, and were awakened with hammering on the door. When you face the Sherriff, two cops and the hotel manager on the fifth floor in your BVD's and still drunk, there's nowhere to go but follow and hope for the best.

I was fortunate; it was a slap on the hand to do five months in West Palm County Jail after being charged for fraudulent credit card use and passing bad checks, the spoils of lifting wallets on the beach and thinking I was so clever. When I was a free man, I hitchhiked home, lonely and forlorn, thinking long and hard about starting over. Jimmy was held for extradition on his parole violation.

During that time, I sent my mother a postcard every once in a while when I was on the run. I didn't want her to worry like when I ran away with Murray. It'd be a fifteen cent card with a scene of palm trees or an alligator and always; "I'm fine, wish you were here." I meant well.

The few months back in my hometown were a whirlwind of

Quaaludes, mescaline, blotter acid (LSD), and vodka. The times demanded drastic measures to get money, so breaking and entering and petty crime was a night-time routine. I fashioned a long tool to pop open doors and started a side business called Quick Call Crowbar, looting small businesses around the area. If I was hungry, it'd be breaking into a deli. If I wanted smokes, pop the grocer's backdoor open, when it came to booze or liquor, wait until after two a.m. when the bars and liquor store was closed. Unlocked cars were always fair game if something glimmered and looked promising. When I broke in a small business and stole a ledger of blank company checks and the desktop printing machine, a brilliant idea dawned on me. It was time again to get out of Dodge, as heat was on my tail. The Painted Desert in Arizona always intrigued me, and Mexico was close if I needed to make a run for it, hopefully having a sidekick. I could be Sundance Kid with Butch Cassidy as a partner. Like an idiot, I wrote payroll checks in my own name easy enough to cash, thinking I would simply vanish in the desert and never be seen in my hometown again. It was another ridiculous plan. I was busted in a strip mall trying to pass a check before leaving town, charged with breaking and entering and several counts of forgery; not a petty crime. I was eighteen and meant that if I was convicted I was looking at State time. Now I was scared.

I was in the county jail on Third and William in Williamsport for months during the preliminaries. No one in their right mind would sign for my bail. I read every Louis L'Amour and sci-fi in the rinky-dink library and played a lot of cards and chess. My cell number was (I kid you not), 13 on the first floor. One afternoon I was called out front for a visit. It was odd because it wasn't normal visiting hours and I never got visitors. I was taken to a small room where a rather large man awaited me. He wore a suit and tie and a big black leather book lay open on the table. The man was a total stranger. After introductions were made and idle chit chat ensued, he began sharing the gospel with me. I was somewhat acquainted with the story of Jesus and how he died for my sins, but I took exception to Pastor Brazzer. Who did he think he was telling me I ought to beware and repent? I asked him; "How did you come to see me? Who am I to you?" He said that my name came up at every Sunday service during prayer requests and he wanted to meet me. Mr. Parris, the man who made mention of me, was a family man who ran a small brick and mortar pharmacy that I'd broken into and robbed. I didn't steal drugs, but helped myself to miscellaneous merchandise, candy, Zippo lighters, rubbers, stupid stuff that made no sense. For some reason, I kicked displays and wreaked havoc that left the cost and time to do repairs. How Mr. Parris could request prayer for my forgiveness when he probably knew I was the one who robbed him makes me feel like a worm. He should merit sainthood.

I didn't pray the "sinner's prayer" with Pastor Brazzer, saying that I really wasn't ready in so many words. It was an honest reply, for in a knowing way I knew that if someone gave their life to Jesus it had to be lock, stock, and barrel. You had to give him everything, and frankly, that notion scared me almost as much as going to the penitentiary. He left me with a KJV bible and a study guide on the Book of John that I half-heartedly worked through. What I couldn't shake off was how someone who was stranger could be so concerned about me to pay a visit.

I had a court appointed counselor who didn't have to scrutinize my record too deeply to see that I was in deep mire. Everything until my current charges were misdemeanors, simple B&E and vandalism, nearly all of them included drunk and disorderly, along with two charges of resisting arrest and trying to punch a State Trooper. That episode worked out pretty good; I woke up the next morning in the designated drunk cell fairly beaten to a pulp. Miraculously there was nothing on my record concerning drugs. However, my current charges merited serious consequences. My court appointed counselor suggested rehab. I balked. He said the judge would look favorably on it if I went. I reluctantly relented.

The stories I heard about White Deer Run Rehab spooked me but I was painted into a corner. Wise old Judge Greevy deemed I go to rehab, and I was bound for White Deer Run for a sixty day period before sentencing. I hoped to skate through it as painlessly as possible and almost did. All I wanted to do was complete a program and stand before the judge with a halo over my head and get back on the street. Hopefully my girlfriend would wait for me.

∼

My days at rehab were tightly regimented with community sessions along with approximately fifty other people doing what I was doing, most of us court committed. Maybe some of them were serious about addiction and recovery, but I wasn't convinced that I had a problem. I attended the meetings after breakfast for lectures, then lunch, followed by more lectures, afternoon work details, supper, free-time, volleyball, and evening small group sessions. There was nothing to read from the library but Twelve Step Books and the like, not even a magazine from the outside world. We were on complete black-out, no phone calls or visitors. I'd sit along the wall and people-watched, staying pretty much to myself or wandered around the grounds, scheming and daydreaming about freedom beyond the invisible borderline, which would land me back in jail if I ran away. I saw people wearing signs or their clothes on backwards, a few with finger painted belittling words on their foreheads; Dopey or Bashful like in the Seven Dwarfs. White Deer Run Rehab, in my mind, was a low budget cult movie about a crazy house. I coasted along without drawing much attention and dodged the bullet on being one of those who were made an example of. As hard as I tried to stay invisible, on day fifty-five of a sixty day stint, my turn had come to be under the spotlight.

The community was divided into co-ed groups of maybe ten per group with an assigned therapist. In my group, we all knew each other in an odd way, but there wasn't anyone I'd particularly be friends with outside of White Deer Run. Allen, a black guy who shared my bedroom in dorm C was from Chambersburg and a double-bubble like me; drugs and alcohol. I was acquainted with the few women in our infamous little group, who roomed on the upper floors of the main building and brought variety to the group sessions. A chair sat in the middle of a circle at every session that we called the hot seat where all hell was paid. I'd seen men and women openly break down and spill their guts in that damned chair. The group, as well as the therapist, would fire questions, comments, insults and a barrage of cruel things at the poor soul whose turn it was to endure the dreaded hot seat. Maybe the idea was to tear a person down so they could be rebuilt. It seemed extreme to me and I never engaged very much. So, as I was saying, it was my turn to be under the spotlight.

I sat and squirmed on the hot seat past midnight, past three a.m. The sun started to break when the group wearied of breaking me. I lied and told them stories, was sarcastic and nasty in return. Marty, my therapist was an unassuming young woman with good looks and a colleague meriting obvious respect among the other therapists. She monitored our group session and took notes, chewed on the end of her pen, and vacillated between adding stormy frustration and expressing her advice in a subdued, venomous, accusing, no-nonsense kind of way. The breaking point in the grueling ordeal was admission to being powerless over alcohol (or drugs), and that life had become unmanageable, but I wasn't ready to make that admission or take what they called the first step. When finally someone asked; "Isn't there anyone in this group who you think can help you?" I matter-of-factly said no, I can help myself.

Rita B was a short, stocky girl with wild spikey dark hair and an attitude expressed in a Philly accent colored with expletives. She jumped in my face and lambasted me up one side and down the other. Rita was tired and pissed and merciless. I said, "Well, maybe she can help me. I'll make a reservation for breakfast and we'll get to know one another." Sarcasm has always bit me in the ass. As the fates would have it, I was tied to Rita, symbolically as it was just twine, and untied at night to go to our separate dorms. Honestly, I couldn't imagine ever sleeping with her. I thought she was mental. Rita talked me to death all day long and it was such a relief to be done with her haranguing at the end of the day. She bought the program's ideas as if her life depended on it. It probably did. Besides being tied to Battleship Rita, I also had to wear a sign around my neck for the remainder of my time at White Deer Run. The sign said; *I'd walk a mile for a cookie.* Childish? Embarrassing? Of course it was. My little group deemed that I needed to learn a lesson. The implications were that I'd go anywhere and do whatever it took, however far and at any cost for a pat on the back. In their collective mind, I was starving for approval. In spite of my objections at the time, maybe they were right.

Judge Greevy was persuaded by my therapist's testimony concerning my rehabilitation and took pity on me. My halo hung askew on thin hopes as I made my personal plea in contrition. I narrowly escaped going to Rockview State Correctional Facility on the agreement to relocate and maintain parole stipulations to a T for two years. No exception to the rules or it meant finishing my time behind bars. I had to meet with my Parole Officer once a month, pee in the jar, go to AA and NA meetings and keep a job. I moved to Sunbury and shared an apartment with two other recovering addicts. It wasn't so bad. My roommates were cool and I hardly saw them except at meetings. Being in a new town; working at a new job and navigating it as best as I could, the bright spot was seeing Cassie at AA meetings, a woman who I'd met at White Deer Run.

Cassie was knock-your-socks off beautiful, petite and curvy with shoulder length auburn hair and hazel eyes. She was a bit older than me with decorum and maturity and a witty personality. Cassie was way out of my league and I could only hope to beg for her affection and interest. She was vivacious and cheerleader fun on the volleyball court and caught my attention. We had a flirty thing going on towards the end of my time at Camp Crazy. I remember her wearing a pair of faded Irish green men's corduroy pants, maybe XX, tied with a belt around her waist to keep them up. Apparently, she, too, had landed in the hot seat and her group or therapist thought it best to minimize her beauty and teach her the lessons of humility in such a crass, demeaning manner. It was during that time when we had a good laugh about the "Uncle Bill W. Pants" while putting away dishes in the kitchen and crossed the bridge from being strangers to being friends.

I attended nightly AA or NA meetings around the area and looked for Cassie, as she did for me when she was out of rehab and back home in Lewisburg. We crossed paths often, and after a while started going out after meetings for endless cups of coffee and pie and talked all night in some greasy spoon restaurant. She was running away from something, or blindly running toward a dream she couldn't put into words. Cassie was in an unhappy, unfulfilling marriage and would escape to the bottle whenever the last straw broke the camel's back. That damned camel always lurked in the corner. Cassie would eventually grow weary of the excuses and lies her husband fed her and come unhinged, going on a binge for a couple of days to escape. She'd blackout from drinking and smashed up the sport car on one incident; another time getting rescued by a farmer combining his fields who found her passed out at the steering wheel. Every time she came to her senses, Cassie hobbled back to her unfaithful, philandering rich husband, trapped and miserable. She left Billy and divorced him within a year after rehab (truly the last straw), and walked away from prosperity and ease. Was she rehabilitated? Was Cassie really an alcoholic in the first place? I don't know. She said that she felt free for the first time in a long time; that AA was like church and she'd found salvation.

They say opposites attract and I happen to think that sometimes they do. We dreamily believe in fairy-tale stories whether we're children or adults, stories about a sleeping beauty aroused by a kiss, or a kiss transforming a frog to a prince, of a little mermaid feeling loved and becoming betrothed, Aladdin-like magical moments that transport us beyond the mundane. God help us if we get too old to believe in it.

Cassie and I cruised along country roads during the day whenever we had the chance, freely talking about life and listening to cassette tapes. We joined along with Elton John singing something about love that was a little bit funny. I can't begin to tally how many gallons of coffee we drank at Dunkin Donuts, or how frequently we sat in a booth at truck stops sipping sweet tea and eating yummy Amish-made pie. It was a natural thing when we began holding hands like a couple, and watched a sunset at R.B. Winter State Park. Our friendship deepened. Whatever else could be said about our relationship, there was passion and openness. I finally worked up the nerve to kiss her. Cassie probably wondered why it took so long. I actually apologized and said I couldn't help myself, which she teased me about for years. We were an item among our social circle for a rollicking year before getting married, finding something fresh in one another's arms, a cocoon of safety, comfort and fulfilled desire. It was indeed liked Elton John's song, these feelings inside.

I was working at Selinsgrove State Hospital at the time; a mentally handicapped facility in one of the all-men's buildings. My shift started at 5 a.m. to prep and serve breakfast. One morning as I was staging pans of oatmeal and scrambled eggs in the heat-steamer, feeling woozy from an all-nighter with Cassie, the fellows marched in, guided by aids corralling them to get in line and pick up a tray. I ladled the morning fare at my station and greeted every resident. Some of them had become familiar to me and rather friendly. The reason I bring this up is because of what happened that morning. Unexpectedly, I was taken for a loop like getting shock-treatment that changed my brain about so-called reality.

One of those young men waiting in line, that I recognized as having Down Syndrome, eyed me up with an unblinking stare. He wore a bright orange sweatshirt and had a beaming smile on his cheerful face so early in the morning. He politely stood across from me seemingly uninterested with food.

"Hiya mister," he said, "do you love me?"

I smiled back and said, "Yeah buddy, 'course I do. Eggs and taters?"

"Do you really love me?" He was being rather loud. "Do you really-really-really love me?"

I gave him an extra scoop of hash browns and said, "Yes... I really love you, cross my heart."

His grin widened, wrinkling his face, and giggled a childish twitter.

"I love you, too." And with that, the lad moseyed on in line.

I can see it as clearly as if it was yesterday. How unashamedly and innocent, how blatant and audacious that boldly asked question was; how honest his imploring! It rattles me that if – if we could ever be so simple and so uninhibited to ask that very same question; *"Do you love me? Really-really love just little me?"* ... and be so real and pure, would it not be life changing?

# 3

*Cassie* and I rented the sunny-side of a Victorian house on Third Street in Lewisburg. It had turn of the century charm and nice landscaping with lilac bushes and daffodils; the first place in a long time that felt like home to me. We knelt on big pillows on a beautiful day in the backyard on July 26th, 1975, as an Episcopal minister performed the official duty of a simple wedding ceremony with a small group of family and friends in attendance. Cassie wore a frilly white dress and flowers in her hair, my attire makes me chuckle as I look back. A gay friend from my dorm at rehab did my hair in a way that I never styled; swoopy with the part on the opposite side, and I wore a flowery print silk shirt with a wide collar, very 70's. My folks were at the ceremony in full support, my mother really liked Cassie. I'm not sure if she ever voiced the words, but Mom was relieved that a good woman was making a difference in my life.

Harry and Joann, who we'd met in rehab, rented the other side of the house. They stood in as maid of honor and best man. You could have cut an archway in the common wall between the duplex as we shared an open and connected lifestyle. We were all staying sober and going to AA meetings. One weekend, Harry and Joann went to visit her relations near Philly. Cassie and I minded their woodstove so it wouldn't burn down the house, eventually letting it burn out, and took care of their dog, Misfit, a cocker spaniel mixed with who knows what. The Sunday evening when they returned I was convinced they were high. They not only acted strange but actually looked different, behaving like they were keeping a sinister secret or an inside joke between them. Joann stood behind Harry and made eyes at me when I stammered to ask, "What's up?" Harry said he was starving and had to check on the dog. Joann shook her head to convey; "Not now, I'll tell you later." I would have bet everything I owned that they slipped and got high.

Joann was an attractive woman that made you wonder if there was some Native American in her bloodline. Dark brown eyes and high cheek bones masked a warrior's seriousness and attentiveness just behind her gaze. She was manic depressive, institutionalized for a brief period, and lucky to be alive from suicide attempts. Rehab saved her life from years of the love-hate relationship with barbiturates and hard liquor. Although she seemed hardened and worn down, a softer side eked out on rare occasions, exposing an inner beauty drugs hadn't entirely stolen. Joann was on the quiet side, a home-body and an artist with talent. Harry was a recovering amphetamine and heroin addict whose personality bounced off the walls like a superball. His name fit him rather properly, Harry had a five o'clock shadow by noon with eyebrows and ear hair that needed pruned with a weed-whacker. He was animated, funny and loud in his thick Philly accent, and could captivate a roomful of people with his stories. Harry missed his calling to be a salesman. I often thought he stretched the truth to spin a good yarn even in AA meetings. Being another relocated court appointee, Harry was going to trade school on a government program to be a welder. They were an odd couple, but people probably said the same thing about Cassie and me.

I was working at a Leer Topper factory across the river and was gone all day. Cassie had a part-time job, which was something brand new as she never really had to work before. She made minimum wage and good tips waitressing at a local Perkins Restaurant. I went there on occasion to have breakfast and batted eyes at her, and one morning she left me a Valentine's heart with a short lovey-dovey note on a red napkin beside my pancakes. Waitressing seemed natural for her, interacting and chatting with patrons, it gave her something to do. She said it was okay, working for tips and extra money; *I need to learn humility*. Maybe the "Uncle Bill W" green pants she had to wear at rehab sowed a seed. Cassie faithfully worked the Twelve Steps. If it was okay with her, it was okay with me. We hardly, if ever had disagreements, but out of the blue, one popped up from the quiet surrounds of our sublime world like the burst of a Jack-in-the Box.

When Cassie's shift was finished she'd come home and often spent the afternoon with Joann, drinking tea and crafting in Joann's dining room. During that time, Cassie listened to Joann share about her experience with Jesus. *That* was what was so different the Sunday evening when I thought Joann and Harry were high. Jesus came upon them in a thunderbolt and lightning kind of way. Cassie and I as a rule would cuddle in bed and talk about our day before making love or afterwards, but a new subject seeped into our daily stories that made my stomach clinch and gave me lockjaw. Joann was slowly poisoning my wife's mind, or maybe Cassie asked for it. It became Jesus this and Jesus that before I turned the lights out. I reacted in subdued stubbornness, sometimes not willing to even talk about it or in total disagreement. Then, there were times that things weren't so civil, voicing my angry protests and became demanding. I drew the line and told Cassie to stay the hell away from Joann. She wasn't welcome in our home, and if I got my hands around Harry's neck I'd... what? We didn't need that nonsense in our house, but did Cassie listen to me while I was gone all day at work? Yeah, right. Religion? You can have it. I didn't need it. Period. I had no clue that two trains were fast approaching from opposite directions on the same track. A head-on collision was unavoidable.

~

The day came when Joann's persuasive message of grace and forgiveness, or perhaps it was the idea of getting a new life and starting over, that Cassie literally knelt in her dining room and prayed to accept Jesus. When I got home from work and came in the backdoor, Cassie was sitting at the kitchen table reading a bible, a cup of tea poised to her lips. I knew within seconds what had happened and blew a fuse. This "I Am" that Joann espoused had invaded my world. Joann didn't often refer to the Savoir as Jesus or the Lord. She called him "I Am," which sounded kind of spooky to me. Suddenly, I was odd man out in the only circle of friends that had made sense. I was livid.

Conviction is part of the process of being convinced, or as I see it, like being painted into a corner. It may or may not be about something one does not yet know or understand. Guilt is often part of the equation. Conviction burrows like ringworm and gets under your skin, irritating at times, uncomfortable and troublesome, persuasively seeking deeper lodging against your will. At least that's how it was for me. There are things you just know to be true, things you're convinced of deep down inside if only in a vague sense, but for whatever reason, you fight it stubbornly and often rather foolishly. I was acting like a jerk with everyone living under our roof, Cassie and Harry and Joann. They were annoyingly pleasant. Joann was the boldest and told me I was on her "icky prayer list." I supposed that to mean she prayed for something bad to happen to me that'd serve as a wake-up call. I told her to stop it in no uncertain terms and called her a witch. I worried that her prayers had secret powers. If I remember the scene, she just smiled at me and said, "Jesus loves you." Did I know that Jesus loved me? Yeah, I sort of got that. Did I know that I needed saved? The very idea troubled me. If anyone needed saved it was me; but the word repent made me gnash my teeth.

~

I was raised Methodist in the traditional way and wore a clip-on tie and a collared shirt for Sunday school. I sang in the boys' choir, went to youth group regularly, and sat in the balcony drawing cartoons with a stubby pencil in the bulletin during the sermon. My dad would drop my brother and me at the side door and come back after service to pick us up. I think we attended until around sixth grade and then we weren't made to go unless we wanted to. We'd rather play slow-motion football in the backyard or watch Sunday morning TV shows like *The Roadrunner* or *Johnny Quest*. But somewhere along the line I had the conviction that there was a God. It was never a questionable issue. We didn't play with Ouija boards or attempt a séance and stuff like the wicked witch in Oz and those devilish flying monkeys scared the living crap out of me. I had a tender soul. I remember getting a white leather Bible that had a zipper to keep it snug like a little satchel; the page edges were red with thumb tabs. I received it from Sunday school for good attendance and read it in the corner of my bedroom, but I don't believe I ever read it all that much after Genesis. It was probably because it was something new and had caught my interest. At that age, my greater interests were looking at squiggly things under a glass slide through my microscope on the windowsill, dissected worms or bees or the smear of a booger.

My dad's mother; my grandma, grew up as a Methodist in the days of the old sawdust trail of fiery evangelists. After grandpa died, she watched the TV version and was a faithful supporter of the likes of Jimmy Swaggart. Her well-worn Living Bible was always open on the kitchen table, full of ribbons and marked with colored pens from cover to cover on verses she must have liked. It's funny that she also read smutty romance novels. Gram didn't harp about the Lord but wasn't bashful to talk about him either. She loved Old Testament dramas like Elijah's flaming chariot and Job being sorely tested, but the miracles in the gospels were her favorite go-to stories. I remember sampling her apple sauce fresh off the stove, its wonderful cinnamon tartness dissolving on my

off the stove, its wonderful cinnamon tartness dissolving on my tongue while she shared the story of Lazarus. Picturing Lazarus coming out of the tomb wrapped in tattered grave clothes made me think of Boris Karloff in the Mummy. My father grew up under her wings and had to have been influenced by her upbringing. He did his best with us kids to give us at least the foundation of belief, so I'd say I had a normal upbringing on the religious end of things. I didn't get preached at and thumped on the head with Bible verses while slathering peanut butter and jelly on my bread. However, religion was part of our family morals. I grew up in an environment with an awareness that God was present in a subtle way, kind of like an all-knowing ghost we had to watch out for. Mom didn't allow us to take the Lord's Name in vain as a swear word. That merited a good crack across the knuckles with the dreaded wooden spoon.

~

I was sober for two years, eight months and some-odd days. Those of us in the program kept count of our sobriety. I didn't go to AA meetings every night as in the beginning, maybe only three times a week. I was off parole but still kept my nose to the grindstone. One evening when Cassie was away, I received a phone call from my old friend Lars. He and Gene Thomas known as Indian, a pool shark from the 8Ball in my hometown, were in town shooting pool at the Blue Cue. They knew I lived in Lewisburg since getting married and found my number in the phonebook. I was excited to hear from Lars and met up with them.

Our visit began like old comrades sharing war stories, an innocent and fun-filled time shooting pool and getting reacquainted. I don't recall giving it much thought when they invited me to go to the bar, and I lead the way to Bull Run Inn. Long story short, I had my first slip since getting sober.

I woke up on the couch in Indian's apartment the next morning, alone and hungover, miles from home. I was disoriented, feeling heartsick and sort of lost and abandoned. It took debating for the longest time, pacing the floor in a strange apartment, a few cups of instant coffee and a handful of saltine crackers, but I had to call Cassie to come get me. My slip was tantamount to the second unpardonable sin. But as a storm does, the dark clouds disappeared in time. For once I was thankful that Cassie knew Jesus. She was very gracious to forgive and forget... if one can actually forget being wronged and hurt. It seems to me that wrongs are like a seed; it's just a matter of time until they germinate and sprout like a perennial. Cassie had a way of bringing things up from my past failings to figuratively slap me in the face, many I had no adequate way to give an answer to. I shrugged my shoulders and said, "I got drunk and screwed up. It's on me, not you. Why can't you just let things go?" If she was keeping a mental ledger, I, too, kept one.

We didn't have our own washer or dryer at the time and I was doing our laundry at a coin-operated place near the college. Someone had left a gospel tract along with the outdated magazines. With nothing better to do while I waited out the spin cycle, I read it. It was a colorful, cartoon-like pamphlet written for street people and quite catchy. The simple, non-churchy dialogue was well written and touched something inside me; a lonely man hiding in a cave and fighting the whole world. That silly gospel tract stirred nagging questions that plagued me ever since Sully prayed for me in his garage, and of late, had resurfaced with Harry and Joann and my wife. How many times had I heard this story? It was as though I had a target on my back that said; *Come and tell me all about the gospel.* I was marked, and in an uncanny way seemed to draw God's unfailing attention even as I ran the other way.

I'd encountered the gospel message many times. I'll never forget the time when a Teen Challenge bus painted with flowers and Jesus stuff in bright colors turned up on Vero Beach in Florida when Jimmy and I were on the run and laid low for the weekend. I was hungover from an all-nighter of mescaline and Sambuca, sitting on a boardwalk bench not sure where to go, kind of like Otis Redding's song *Sitting on the Dock of the Bay*. Indeed, it was as if I had nothing to live for. Two hippy-like guys walked toward me. One of them offered me donuts from a sack. They were down to earth, engaging me in conversation, and at some point hit a bullseye while relating to my current demise. They were my age and well acquainted with drugs and alcohol according to their testimonies. I felt the heat of their passionate determination trying to help and reach out to me. They pointed the way to the promise of a new beginning. The only condition was to surrender to Christ. I thanked them but declined.

There were others who'd crossed my path, and in so many words shared the same idea. I remember a Good Samaritan who gave me a lift from Augusta, Georgia to Fayetteville, North Carolina. I was headed home after a stint in the brig at Fort Gordon as a result of going AWOL when I was in the Army. Uncle Sam said here's your hat – there's the door. The stranger pressed a crinkled twenty dollar bill tucked in a gospel tract with a handshake, offering sound advice and a prayer. There were times on the road when the only station that came in clear played gospel music and some corn-fed country hick preaching on AM radio and I entertained it. What about Pastor Brazzer and Mr. Parris, or the sweet hippy girl on the city bus who shared her testimony of Jesus with me? I deliberately pulled the cord and got off the bus at a Howard Johnson's restaurant on the Golden Strip to dodge her penetrating words. She read my mail like the dudes from Teen Challenge. Were they signposts along the maze-like path I was travelling, offering me direction? Fellow runners who were passing the baton saying or implying to consider giving my life to the Lord?

I was glad no one was in the laundromat or I might have chucked the whole deal aside, but it made me wonder why I was fighting so tenaciously with this Jesus message. Why was I having such a problem with this alleged "good news?" The only reason I could come up with is what I now refer to as ownership. It seemed to me like Jesus invaded people's lives and took over. What worried me was that if I gave everything to Jesus what was left of me? Would I cease being Dirk and become a Jesus freak lead around on a leash saying praise the Lord all the time? The image of Jim and Tammy Faye Baker came to mind; not the kind of image I particularly cared to emulate.

I remember having a messed up time of it in my head, battling with this Jesus stuff. After changing a few dollars for quarters and tossing wet clothes in the dryers, the gospel tract went into the trash bin with the notion to forget about it. I wanted to argue that Jesus wasn't really for real, yet here I was debating with a faceless being that I couldn't see or hear, yet felt like someone was watching and listening. I felt off balance, but oddly, I also felt an arm around my shoulders like coach JD would do when I was woozy during football drills in the hot August sun.

"Take a knee. Take your time. It's okay. We'll get you back in the game."

I wondered if this might be my last chance; had I worn out my welcome with God after praying a hundred times if he got me out of this fix or that, promising I'd never do it again? Had I used up all my chips? Unquestionably, I exhausted the patience of many well-meaning people over my lifetime that washed their hands of me. Was I hopeless? I hoped not. What I know today is that was never the case with Jesus. He will love me forever and a day regardless of my best and worst behavior. Jesus wasn't a parole officer checking the registry line item upon line item to make sure I kept the law and pissed clean, or a harsh teacher recording whether I passed or failed, or a judge with the gavel poised over my head anxious to pronounce judgement. This Jesus wasn't like my father either, as good-hearted as my father tried to be whenever I screwed up. The infamous word: *What* didn't hang in the air, tense and expecting an explanation on my part to God as to what I was doing. The "I Am" that Joann shared about wasn't sitting on a cloud, all-knowing and exacting like a scrupulous bookkeeper perturbed that the numbers don't balance, ready to squash me like a bug with his big thumb for some mishap. It was dicey in my head, this back and forth volley of hope and questions in a game of Tug-of-War. I wanted so badly to believe that I could be accepted and find approval. There. I admit it. The cookie that I'd walk a mile for was within my reach.

There's no real way to put into words what happened next except to say that I was finally convinced to give Jesus a chance. I was sick and tired of holding back the tide like the little Dutch boy with his finger in the dike. I walked outside and lit up a Kool filter and paced the sidewalk, musing over the spin of thoughts in my head, questions and objections and bitching, and then, I just let go as though waving a white-flag. I let go of my stubbornness and the flimsy facade of how well I'd done being my own man since getting sober. In a word, I let go of control and laid down my weapons. The arguments I had about the bible message seemed lame, and all the many witnesses who touched my soul made sense. Was it a divine epiphany or the culmination of pieces falling in place? As the door to the Lost and Found Department turns up by surprise, all that I could do was be daring enough to open the door. In one sweeping gesture, I surrendered.

As best as possible, I tried to purge doubt, hostility and pride aside. I said to Jesus (who was present in my mind), that if he could make something new out of my life he was more than welcome to try. It wasn't a dramatic experience. The heavens did not part like the Red Sea, nor did I see some vision of Jesus in a robe with his heart glowing on his chest, waiting for me when I opened the door. But something changed, or should I say, I began to change. It was like I did an about-face from somewhere deep in my being and walked in the other direction, a new direction yet to be revealed.

I butted out my smoke and went back to the laundromat to fold clothes, deciding to keep what happened (that I'd be hard pressed to explain), my secret, as if testing the validity of my experience. I suppose that I was a doubting Thomas. I trust that you recall the interaction between Thomas and the resurrected Lord in the gospels. I felt the same way. "Lord, I believe; help my unbelief."

Everyday things started to look and feel different. Inappropriate conversations and raunchy jokes offended me at work. An old lady struggling to reach canned goods on a high shelf at the grocery needing help made me turn back to offer assistance. That wasn't so odd, I helped old ladies as a rule, but my parting words to her shocked me. "Jesus loves you." It just sort of slipped out. My normal reaction at being impatient and angry with the likes of slow drivers began to soften, waving someone ahead of me or offering my cart to a stranger at Walmart. There were times I caught myself whispering a prayer instead of judging on outward appearance. Lord knows, people can test you. I finally worked up the nerve, swallowing my pride, and told Cassie what had happened at the laundromat weeks ago. She was overjoyed and we were one again, not only in bed but in every way. We happily jabbered while making pancakes and pulling weeds in our garden and walking downtown, our openness and dialogue was infused with the spirit of budding newness. Harry and Joann prepared a feast to celebrate my coming into the fold. Be it ever so humble, a meatloaf dinner shared with my closest friends was better than any high I ever experienced. Jesus was our special guest at the table, and how he made us laugh.

The four of us started having a home bible study. We'd sit around the kitchen table drinking coffee, cigarette smoke hanging like a low cloud, and engaged in lively discourse about spiritual things that none of us really knew anything about. We tried doing a study on the book of Mark, and I think God humored us. If you ever wondered if you can smoke and be a Christian, I happen to think you can. Perhaps the Holy Spirit coughs a bit, but revelation and blessing is a gift bestowed graciously to any seeker. As to smoking and going to heaven, you'll just get there quicker.

Joann and I began speaking out in AA meetings, thinking the idea of a Higher Power named Jesus was conducive to the program. We were ostracized, not so much persecuted, but viewed as troublemakers and were somewhat snubbed. The icing on the cake was a heated interchange with Don W. (the Great Puba), who chaired the meeting with something like twenty years sobriety. He took exception to me, arguing that he was a Catholic in good standing with God, and made a derogatory comment that included something about me being dumb as a mother... I can't repeat it or type the rest. I told him if he insulted me again I'd grab him by his scruffy goatee and make him kiss the Pope's ass. I had a lot to learn about sharing the Good News of Jesus. Soon afterwards, there was a natural parting of ways. I took a giant step back from AA and NA, thinking it wasn't all that necessary anymore. I had Jesus and friends, even if it was just us four and no more.

We continued sharing our daily lives together over a meal or just hanging out on the couch. Our discussions were fun, often relating the latest "aha" moments that we were certain were Jesus moments. After a while, Cassie and I started having difficulty with Harry and Joann. Our comfortable norm began to get a bit strained, it seemed like we were spinning our wheels without much forward momentum. All we wanted to do was grow and learn, but none of us knew where to find the next step. We were familiar with steps (as in the Twelve Steps), but we had embarked on a new journey without clear understanding. I suggested church, that it would be a whole new support group. Joann's reaction was voiced with attitude and bated breath. Organized religion was out of the question. She was adamant. Harry tried to interject but was cut short with a scolding look. Even Misfit cowered and ran for cover to the back porch. Church, Joann said, was man-made and suffocated true spiritual growth. Looking back, she may have been correct.

# 4

*It* used to be that my desperate search was to find alcohol, weed or pills, the next high and a party where people would fill the void and somehow I'd find it. Yes, I'll admit that wherever I found acceptance and approval it always gave me a sense of ease being among fellow mindless stoners. My life began to change after rehab in subtle ways. AA was a new circle where I found company and support, and the many recovering druggies and alcoholics who I met were great. But, it had spiraled round-about the same things; nose first to addiction one day at a time, least ye forget, with a sense of never really being healed or free. I listened to re-runs of the same stories meeting after meeting, speaker after speaker; that nothing in my "nature" would change. I was doomed to be an addict for the rest of my days. That idea wasn't really all that encouraging to me. If AA works for you: Be free – Be sober – Be blessed. At the time, I needed more than grabbing for the same brass ring on the Merry-Go-Round. I desired friendship from those who would support my new experience. They were out there, somewhere, with something to offer. I wasn't exactly sure what it was I needed or was seeking, but if there is truly a sense of destiny, it had a hand in my life.

Cassie and I visited a church across the river aptly named Crossroads; a Nazarene Church. It was Christmas Eve, a candlelight affair with something called a cantata. I remember thinking it was like tripping on acid, sitting in a pew surrounded by subdued lighting and candles, shadowed faces in the sanctuary, the choir draped in diaphanous red robes singing four part harmonies. I basked in the most amazing aura of peace for an hour and a half, captivated by the Christmas cantata *On This Shining Night*. I drank it in to my very marrow. Such magnificence has to touch you unless you're dead. I was new in the faith and didn't understand the strange feelings welling up from somewhere deep inside. When the choir sang a moving crescendo my heart raced and I tried to conceal my weeping. It would be a while before I understood that my feelings were the tender nearness of the Holy Spirit.

Friendly greeters and so many people shook our hands and seemed genuinely glad that we were there. The tall, soft spoken pastor welcomed us and took time to chat awhile. We had holiday punch and goodies in the social hall afterwards, easily mixing and mingling. It was a meaningful and happy Christmas Eve, one I shall never forget. For the first time since I lived at home as a kid, Christmas actually felt festive.

Harry and Joann didn't exactly disapprove of our report when we returned that evening, but they weren't enthusiastic about it either. There'd been no convincing them to come along regardless of Cassie's pleading with Joann. They were happy being lone mavericks. For the life of me, I can't remember the details of how or what happened when they left Lewisburg, but have a sneaking suspicion that it had to do with church. They left an empty place in my heart and a lasting impression of survival against all odds. Cassie's tear-stained cheeks expressed a deep sadness to lose Joann's company. I'd miss the insights she'd share about "I Am" and Harry's bombastic stories. I vaguely recall that they moved somewhere near Chester outside of Philly, setting up a booth at flea markets and consignment shops, selling Joann's pottery and paintings and Harry's welded abstract sculptures. They were both very imaginative and creative. I hope they prospered and are still sober. Above all, I hope they've kept the flame of faith alive that burned bright in our hearts when we were babes in Christ under the same roof. Maybe some prefer to fly alone or fly as a couple, as they chose to do, but that seems kind of lonely to me.

I think that all of us are stumbling and groping half-blind on this terrestrial ball and need each other. My heart's cry was to be a part of the flock, sheltered and surrounded, never immune to temptation or pompous to think I could make it on my own willpower. God, I'd done that way too long and failed miserably. No matter how strong and independent we think we are, we all need support and a shoulder to cry on, or be a stalwart companion for another who's in need. The new normal for Cassie and me was finding a community where we'd fit in, somewhere we could find our place to learn and serve. Crossroads seemed like the perfect fit.

～

We were embraced in the arms of kindness; love was passed back and forth giving us a sense of belonging. My testimony of being an alcoholic and a drug addict with a criminal record seemed to have its perks. Who woulda guessed? Between singing hymns and the sermon a period of time was set aside for prayer needs and testimonies. It was probably during such an allotted time when Mr. Parris requested prayer for me when I was in jail. I was not so bold to stand up and give God praise when I knew that I should without the friendly nudges of those around me. We were invited to people's homes for meals and found our niche. It wasn't long until we began attending new member's classes.

I recall the evening when Pastor Clayton handed out a form to sign having a check-list of twenty plus requirements to be a Nazarene. It was mostly things like regular attendance, tithing, modest "Christian" appearance including dress code (there were no hippies in the church), and miscellaneous items. It read like marching orders; don't drink – don't chew – and don't run with boys that do. I jokingly said that Moses only had ten. Although the class chuckled, the pastor didn't see any humor in my comment. I think it was things along this line that put Joann off about church; the *man-made rules*. She probably would have put the pastor on her "icky prayer list" or unleashed the flying monkeys. Anyway, Cassie and I became members and were applauded and welcomed along with the other newbies at a special Sunday service.

The church had a bus ministry that reached out to the surrounding communities. A fleet of half a dozen school buses were painted white with the church logo, a team from youth group served as stewards on Sunday mornings. Each bus had a Captain who was responsible for leading the program. The idea was to engage in outreach on the various routes on Saturdays that involved talking to groups of children, teens hanging out at the park, someone walking their dog, whoever, if they were a minor, meet the parents and invite them to church. The Captain and an assistant walked together handing out church flyers and gospel tracts. This was before the landscape became hyper-sensitive and suspicious of strangers walking around neighborhoods and parks approaching kids. I was recruited to join the bus ministry. Cassie joined the choir.

A man named Leon Parrish introduced himself at Crossroads Church. He took a shine to me and became my mentor, and in a way my second father. Leon was the bus Captain in the Milton area that I joined up with. I cannot say enough praise for this man. He made a huge difference in my life then and forever. Leon and his wife, Sandy became our new best friends. Leon resembled Paulie Gualtieri in the Sopranos on HBO but opposite in character. He was humble in his approach, down to earth. Leon's heart overflowed with genuine love for those we encountered.

We walked many hours and miles together those Saturday afternoons, sharing bible-stories with kids and visiting with moms and dads. We were invited into people's homes when solicitors were turned away and shared coffee or iced tea with many families. I witnessed hardship and poverty I didn't know existed in our area, heard the sordid tales from troubled mothers with juvenile sons or daughters doing the same things I'd done. My heart would fill to the brim and I'd want so badly to help. I wasn't eloquent with the scriptures; I shot from the hip and said whatever came to mind that seemed prudent, and our visits often became a heart-to-heart dialogue. What an honor it was to be part of their healing, walking with them toward salvation. It doesn't often happen in one visit. I shared my testimony and prayed from my heart and God gave me favor with strangers.

Saturday after Saturday, Leon and I followed up with families we came to know. Patty Cope, the mother of a middle-school age daughter who rode the bus was the first one to pray with me and accept Jesus. We sat at her kitchen table and I caught Sally spying on us from the living room. Sally knew every chorus from riding the bus and must have been very happy that her mom would be joining her in church. Patty could have driven to services but she wanted to ride the bus. Trish, a college drop-out lived in a trailer park on our route, another searching soul who we encountered. Her testimony about looking in all the wrong places until she found direction in Jesus was a blessing every time she shared it. Trish went back to school and made new friends in the youth group. She always thanked me and gave me a hug, parting ways with the peace sign. Multiplied scores of kids discovered it was cool to know Jesus. I had a blast being part of their journey and hope they continued walking in the faith for the rest of their lives. May we meet again someday and sing: *This Little Light of Mine* on God's heavenly bus.

The church board decided to split the Milton, New Columbia route. A used school bus was purchased, serviced and painted up to match the others and I was asked to be the Captain. I wandered around neighborhoods with a silly homemade puppet named Zippy, or dressed up like Noah when it rained for days, swallowed a live goldfish when the story on the bus was about Peter the Fisherman, sang children's choruses and acted crazy on their level because Jesus is fun. By the end of the summer we were nearly full.

If you ever wondered if you could get into trouble doing the right thing, you can. After a Wednesday evening service I was called into the pastor's office. I dutifully listened as he spoke about my track record since being part of the church as verbatim. I wondered if he kept notes. With no little praise for my zeal, he strongly criticized my "unorthodox" ways. They didn't reflect well on the church's good name, he said, to have one of its members traipsing around neighborhoods in outlandish costumes and funny hats. Neither did the children's Sunday school appreciate some of the kids I unloaded on them that were rowdy or not all that well dressed, maybe a bit dirty, and if given the chance; misbehaved. The pastor didn't only allude to it, but frankly told me that those kind of families wouldn't make good tithers and I should seek other mission fields for the betterment of the church. I was aghast. Was I being called on the carpet for reaching out to the poor? I guess there are politics and ways to run every business, even churches. I silently refused to compromise.

At the time I was working for a road construction company setting concrete forms for curbing and run-off culverts, it was a really good paying job. Looking back, perhaps I was naïve, as I wore my Jesus badge on the outside unashamedly. I had Jesus stickers on the bumper of my car, on my lunch box and hard hat, and read a pocket New Testament on break whenever I got the chance. In a short while, and not by choice, I was eating lunch alone. I soon realized that not everyone was so enthusiastic about the Good News. The workdays were long and lonely, I was mocked, and had it not been for the good wages I would have quit. But a day came when my suffering turned to joy.

A guy named Red who was at least ten years my senior, a brute and a bully, joined me at lunch break. He hem-hawed a bit, said that he'd been watching me with a close eye for some chink in my armor and told me I'd earned his respect. He went on to tell me his wife had kicked him out of the house for his drinking. He loved his wife and kids and knew he'd screwed up. Red wanted to straighten things out and go back home but didn't know what to do. I shared how Jesus changed my life, that I used to be a bona fide alcoholic and a screw-up, and if God could do that for me, he could do it for anyone. We talked a while and I ended up praying with him to accept Jesus. For such a brute of a man, he cried while mumbling along in prayer. Red was undone, God touched his heart in a way that was emotional and real, and he thanked me in a way I felt so unworthy of.

We had a brainstorm and asked the boss if we could bug out early. Red wanted me to meet his wife and tell her the things I'd told him. Given our leave, I followed him to a sub-development in Middleburg where we sat in the living room of a prefab ranch house with his wife, nervously sorting things out. It took tip-toeing and easing into a comfortable conversation, but after a while she softened to the idea of reconciliation and prayed the simple prayer Red had prayed. She opened the door not only for Jesus, but embraced Red to come back home.

I was in the first cut to get laid off when winter rolled in, you can't pour concrete when it's freezing, but the last I heard they were together and doing fine.

～

Every summer the church had what was called "Revival Meetings." A quest speaker would come for a week to preach and get us all in tip-top shape. The message was always about something called sanctification; a major doctrine that Nazarenes hold to, and the altar was full of repentant folks every night. I went forward thinking I needed to be saved when I already was, but it seemed I should do it in public and in an official way. What did I know? One night, the evangelist preached a message on having a family altar, a place in your home where you had devotional time. If you had a spouse and kids - all the better, make it a party. I took the evangelist's message literally and set about making an altar.

We had a small barn behind the house in Lewisburg that tilted a slant, full of old treasures tucked among cobwebs, crates and moldy boxes of miscellany from another generation. Weathered boards were ranked against an inside wall that probably helped hold the barn from collapsing. On a humid day, the residual odor was reminiscent of it being a chicken coop at one time. I salvaged good boards and put together a fine altar, recycling the rusty cut nails to tack it together.

The east wall of our second floor bedroom had a bay window where the morning sun streamed in. It was idyllic. Cassie had a rocking chair and an end table set up that was a good reading sanctuary if clothes weren't piled on it. I repainted the walls and set up our family altar, complete with an antique bible I found at the flea market that I lay opened to Psalm twenty-three on the back rail. I hung a cross made of the same barn wood from the ceiling on fishing line that made it appear to float. When we had friends over from church, I'd usher them upstairs and show off our family altar, fairly tickled with my creation. I got funny looks; "Oh, isn't that nice," a few chuckles and a pat on the back. I came to find out some time later that the concept of "family altar" was quite different than my idea. I assumed that everyone in church had an actual kneeling bench and prayer rail for such an occasion. Cassie and I did indeed kneel for prayer in the light of the bay windows at my humble, barn wood altar, but after some time it collected dust. It's a shame to lose one's innocence and crumble to church ideology.

∾

Cassie and I struggled through the winter of '76. I was laid off from the concrete company on unemployment, drawing a whopping $104.00 a week. The next spring, Leon decided to start his own business as a home builder whose forte was framing and I was his first employee. He worked out of his old four-door Pontiac, the trunk loaded with tools and bungeed down. The backseat had enough room for his two teenage sons, Todd and Michael to squeeze in. Saw horses and ladders were tied on the roof. If we didn't look like the Beverly Hillbillies! I started work on my birthday, turning twenty two and full of vim and viv, or so I thought. Leon didn't wear a watch. His routine was to work hard when you're fresh, take a break mid-morning for a snack and a cup of black coffee at a good stopping point which was ambiguous. We'd shoot the bull at lunch about the Lord or something happening at church and banged nails until the sun went down or he felt satisfied to call it a day. Needless to say, I learned how to work, not only the ethics but the trade. Leon was a patient man and taught me how to be a carpenter. It's all I've done vocationally going on forty-five years and with success, not that I'm rich or anything.

I told you that as best as I could this would be an honest account of my days. There were times when I indeed walked on water, those miraculous moments when God just showed up, and there were times I took my eyes off of Jesus and sunk like a rock. I'm not sure what the reasons were that I'd misstep and tilt like a pinball machine. I remember my dad saying I'd get a wild hair up my ass. Was that it? Just push the pedal to the floor and blow out the carbon? Slam the mallet down and ring the bell? An impulsive urge to tear shit apart? Whatever the reason was among countless and daily trials, I'd backslide and slip once or twice a year to satisfy my craving to let loose. If I'm not mistaken, that's a handful of days out of three hundred and sixty five, so maybe I wasn't a total screw-up.

I took off on another hair-brained urge on a rainy day when I was off work and drank enough to make up for lost time. I'd been at the corner bar in Watsontown since noon; the sun was setting and I was slumped askew on a barstool, too drunk to drive home.

My guilty conscience nagged at me after the first beer, which was many beers ago. I kept to myself in a cloud of cigarette smoke in a darkened room with depressing people; country music played on the juke box that added to my demise, some game show was muted on the TV. I felt like I was drowning in a thick soup and was ready to swim ten thousand miles back home. I called Leon from the pay phone, not wanting to deal with Cassie just yet, and, of course, he came to get me. On the way home he pulled over and put the four-ways on. I was ready for a lecture, Lord knows I deserved one, but Leon simply put his hand on my shoulder and said, "Let's pray."

There was no judgement as I'd expected; no diatribe about taking my eyes off the Lord and how could I do such a thing. Leon wasn't a man of many words, but what he spoke found deep lodging in my confused mind. Love is not particularly a tangible thing, you can't hold in your hand per se, but love washed over me like a gentle rain as he prayed, a sorrowful love but a true love. We sat along the side of the road for I don't know how long, crying and steaming up the windows. Even though I was drunk, I felt the presence of God. Leon never brought the occasion up afterwards.

I have to say that I was spoiled rotten. Cassie kept a clean house and had dinner on the table within an hour after I got home from work. I never sat down to a Stouffer's frozen dinner; it was salad fixings from the market to a full-course meal, some kind of dessert and all the sweet tea I could drink. I started getting the "Good Living" pot belly. One evening, Cassie brought home a flyer she'd picked up at the bookstore, thinking it might be something I'd enjoy and we discussed it over supper. "Fishnet 76" was billed like Woodstock for Christians. Was I interested? Are you kidding me? How cool.

We loaded up our Pinto hatchback with a pup-tent, sleeping

bags and gear. Cassie packed the coolers so at least it promised to be good eating while we camped. I had no idea what to expect. The event was held in Front Royal, Virginia, beautiful country in the Shenandoah Valley. It wasn't half a million like Woodstock, but over 25,000 Christians camped around the rolling hills with a pond, a mainstage, several large tents for workshops and speakers, vendors and an air of vibrant excitement. I saw vehicles and RV's and VW vans plastered with Jesus stickers, hippies and families with kids around campfires, everyone smiling and waving hello, calling; "Praise the Lord." For two wonderful days, Cassie and I interacted with a community from all around the country from every walk of life gathered together to celebrate Jesus. I heard Christian music unlike what I'd become accustomed to. It wasn't southern gospel like the Bill Gather Trio, some of it was rock and roll or progressive folk music. This was in the days of cassette tapes and I loaded up on Randy Stonehill and Larry Norman. The evening speakers preached new revelation to my inquisitive mind, as did the teachers in the tents during the afternoon sessions. I took notes and bought more cassettes. The line-up included CJ Mahaney and Larry Tomczak, who I particularly liked, and many others. Their message was different, relevant and challenging and ignited an interest in my hungry soul with exciting possibilities. The worship was different as well, lifting me up so high it was sometimes hard to breathe. I was like a sponge. I was drunk on the new wine. A fresh wind was blowing across the land and I couldn't wait to get back home to Lewisburg and share it with my friends at Crossroads.

I wasn't prepared for the reaction I received. Everything that I shared with friends at church about the weekend festival was scrutinized and questioned, pretty much discarded with the wave of a hand, implying that I was foolish to go in the first place. My pastor gave it a label: "The Charismatic Movement." He said they were in extreme error and it was dangerous to go beyond the borders of our safe church. That's what he said. Dangerous. Were those wonderful people our enemies? He went so far as to call it false teaching and a cult, and once again I stood in his office feeling like I was being categorized as a nonconformist and a troublemaker. I stood my ground. The inference wasn't subtle in his smooth voice as he made it clear that I was someone who didn't want to conform to church by-laws. He read me right. Okay, I do have an authority issue, but I believed that Jesus saved me to be me. Was I really being rebellious? Misguided? I didn't think so. The man I came to trust and learn from - our shepherd, turned a sour face at me. I read disappointment as he shook his head, but it also made me realize a paradigm I hadn't seen before.

There existed in the mind of the church, not just at Crossroads but across the board, an endemic flu strain called: "Judgement." It became all too clear to me that it was *Us and Them*. Everyone who went to a different church was categorized and had a labeled. I just assumed it was the flavor of gum they liked. Christians outside our circle that had their own preference or background and went to wherever they assembled were somehow flawed if they had a different theology. Judgement was spoken in hushed tones, sometime disguised with a disclaimer; "I only bring this up so that we might pray for them." Innuendos, sarcasm, the sly wink and a quiet nod didn't disguise the gossipy suggestions. Folks that believed differently were judged with certain proclivities based on doctrine that put this one here – that one there. Debates about Free-will verses Predestination boggled my mind and made me wonder why there was even a debate; another one was how you were baptized. Charismatics were a heated topic in general, tongues being the focal point that main-line Evangelicals objected to. The issue of whether you talked in tongues or not or how you were baptized wasn't what I found problematic; it was the attitude behind the words. It dawned on me that majoring on minors wasn't what God wanted in my life to get real and personal and walk with him.

I loved singing the old hymns. I embraced the idea of having a close relationship with the Lord as in, *"...and he walks with me and he talks with me and he tells me I am his own."* I made a comment that God wanted intimacy and was still speaking if only we had an ear to hear, something one of the speakers at Fishnet taught about. My pastor and associates reacted rather uncomfortable with the notion that God actually talks to us. But that's how it happens, each individual hears their name called whether it's an inner voice or a thunderbolt and embarks on his or her unique journey to follow a supernatural leading.

Lutherans, Seventh Day, Catholics and so on who heard God's voice in a different way were under the magnifying glass, including that blue jean, folk guitar fringe group meeting on campus at Bucknell. It seemed to me that those who didn't fit our pattern of being true Christians were eyed with scrutiny and misgivings.

Not knowing prejudice other than the racial kind in my blue-collar hometown, I didn't have a clue that church people looked down their noses at another just because they had a different label. Apparently they thought it was okay because it seemed that everyone ignored the biblical warnings of gossip and hasty judgement. In my pea-brain, I thought if we're all going to sit together at the Lord's Table in the sweet-by-and-by, why not start practicing now? I admit that I have utopian beliefs and wish we'd all just get along, but we don't and that's unfortunate. When my pastor told me I'd be "dis-fellowshipped" if I continued my current path, my heart sank. I made my choice against conflicting emotions not wanting to compromise what I felt was the Lord's guidance. It meant I'd have to leave my church family. Leon, bless his soul, stuck by me.

Feeling like we were exiled, Cassie and I floundered in a quandary, sorely missing the fellowship of precious friends at Crossroad's. The years we spent together were wonderful and a valuable part of my life-story. Instead of going to services,

I listened to the cassette tapes from Fishnet, rewinding and replaying teaching series over again, and great tunes by The Second Chapter of Acts and Phil Keaggy. But it was time to find a community. That was how I thought of it; believers of like mind who walked beside and with one another. We decided to visit the blue jean, folk guitar fringe group on Bucknell University's campus. Perhaps one of the reasons they were labeled fringe was because they met on Saturday night and not the traditional, sanctimonious 10 O'clock service on Sunday morning. I worried about being smart enough to fit in with a college group, which I thought I was if you didn't count studying and earning degrees.

I was relieved to find that it wasn't just students, although the majority was, but there were also "townies" like us. The group was a blend of migratory birds from here and there, some from a rich family in New England with a major in chemistry or engineering, and those working locally in the chair factory or the hospital. Everyone roosted in the same tree seeking the same thing: the manna of heaven; or as someone put it, *God-sent trail mix*.

Lamb Fellowship met in the auxiliary room of Rooke Chapel, an iconic landmark on campus in our area, consisting of a small group of 30 or so. First impressions are crucial and I was taken by their welcome and acceptance. I was also enthralled by the guitarists and choruses, some of which were written by those among them. The worship aspect of the meeting was my favorite time. It was free-wheeling, unrehearsed and spontaneous. I'd get lost in the Spirit, being touched by the feathered breath of God when the worship was just instrumental. I saw things in my head (and no, I wasn't taking LSD anymore to expand my mind), images like dreamy pictures carried me high and away with a thought or a word playing in my minds-eye. I'm hesitant to call them visions, but God was near and "spoke" to me as he did with David in the Psalms. Selah; the fresh spring breeze, fragrant with nectar and pregnant with life was intoxicating. I didn't know what to do or how I should respond to the things God showed me, those heavenly images and phrases, and tucked them in my heart of hearts, often making note of them in my journal.

The ambiance at Lamb Fellowship was laid back without formality; no bulletin with the order of service, no pews or a pulpit, you sat on folding chairs or on the floor or wherever. One felt free to share openly of whatever God had put on their heart. A rotating schedule of leadership shared a teaching after worship, and it didn't take long to become friends with the co-leader, Randy Welch. The messages weren't like the routine of preaching the gospel to the choir as I had become accustomed to at Crossroads Church. Their words were charged with meaning, organic and seed-like, provoking questions in my mind, questions that made me delve deeper to understand God's word. My introduction to this kind of teaching found birth in my soul at the "Fishnet Festival" and I felt a sense of comradery at Lamb Fellowship.

I bought an old Gibson acoustic guitar for $100.00 from Battleship Rita when she was in halfway house and needed money. Yes, we stayed in touch for a while, how could I not have a fondness for Rita? The guitar was weather checked and kind of battered like Willy Nelson's but it was a solid investment. Being inspired by the new music, I dug it out of the closet and had a friend put on new strings and tune it up and bought a simple chord book. I was never what you would call a musician. The two or three lessons I took always began with music theory, which I couldn't for the life of me retain. But major chords and a minor could play anything, so I practiced until I got calluses on my fingertips.

Solomon of old said that there's a time and a season for everything under the sun, that life turns-turns like a song by the Byrds, and in 1976 it seemed like my time had come to take a turn. It was certainly a crossroads, offering an exciting change of redirection, another chapter in my life to be revealed. I cashed in my King James Bible for a New American Standard Version and sold all my southern gospel records and leisure suits at a yard sale. I decided to be real Dirk and not a Christian caricature, and devoted myself to learning more in-depth truths. I was a disciple, if you can still be called that, and fell in love with the Word of God in a new way, devouring the written page like a hungry bear out of hibernation.

≈

Cassie and I moved across the river to Milton and rented a storefront on Main Street with a five bedroom apartment upstairs. I was still working for Leon and salvaged lumber and borrowed tools along with donations for materials and converted the storefront into a Christian coffeehouse. We christened it: *"House Upon the Rock."* We built a stage in the back half of the building and rigged overhead lighting, not exactly the Fillmore East but catchy and functional. Added to it was some Peavy sound equipment I begged from a neighbor who had a Polka Band and didn't use anymore. We plumbed in a basic restroom per code, built a service bar for refreshments and had a coin operated Coke vending machine delivered and stocked monthly. I made eight round plywood tables and we borrowed folding chairs from the funeral home to seat thirty to forty people.

The doors opened Friday nights at seven o'clock for contemporary Christian bands; some rock, some folk, some really good and some not so much. I networked with other coffeehouses in the state, all of us sharing great artists and talent. On occasion, we'd show a Christian movie for kids or have an evening with mimes and puppets. Cassie had the idea to start our own drama group and the *"Rock-House Players"* were born. The cast was made of six to eight good friends, surprisingly gifted, and worked really hard to be theatrical. As God opened doors, the group performed in churches and parks and events and had a pretty steady schedule on weekends. I bought a VW camper bus, and with Bob's help and his pickup truck, we shagged gear for the *"Rock-House Players."* On our return trip home after a service there was always a mandatory stop at some family restaurant where we gathered around tables and had a party of how God blessed and touched those we were invited to minister to.

With all the extra bedrooms upstairs, we started taking in people who were just out of rehab or down on their luck, a few new converts from a Friday night gig at the coffeehouse. Cassie went to retrieve a young woman who stayed with us for several weeks but had slipped and wound up back in Chicago. Marala's choice of poison was cocaine. She was a charming woman of color and we loved her. The phone rang and Marala cried, pleading to come back, promising to really try this time. We felt her pain but didn't trust sending money for bus fare. I wasn't happy about Cassie driving halfway across the country let alone try and find Marala in some all-black neighborhood in Chicago, but we couldn't let anyone down. Marala was rescued and came to stay with us for nearly a year. She'd join us for Lamb services, but she found her home at Brother Reeve's Pentecostal Church and blossomed. I enjoyed visiting with them. When they got to singing you could feel the floor moving under your feet, the whole building seemed to shake in rhythm while the pigeons in the attic were going bonkers. Boy, could they sing! Brother Reeves and I became friends and met often at Dunkin Donut to share vision and ideas for reaching out to the city with the gospel.

At one point, every room in our place was filled with someone who turned up at our door. Andrea, newly relocated from I don't remember where, came upon us one Friday night at the coffeehouse and ended up staying for quite a while. She was a social-worker and probably a lesbian, which didn't matter. She was a new Christian, very sweet and polite and thoughtful to help keep the place tidy. Her story was one of being like a leper, set aside and pushed out of sight, almost nameless. Andrea struggled through horrible mayhem with her family and drank to escape. I think the sign caught her eye and drew her in; *"House Upon the Rock"* was a beacon, or at least I hoped so. Maybe she saw the promise of a home with a solid foundation based on love.

And there was good ole Lewie who was an unforgettable character. He happened to be one of Lancaster's town drunks who we went to rescue when Joann called out of the blue in a panic. We hadn't heard from her for over a year. Lewie was her uncle and Joann loved him through years of alcohol abuse. He was a slobbering-fall-down but jovial drunk knocking on heaven's door. I found him deliriously singing Irish ballads, sloshing a pint of ale and wearing most of it in a peacock rattan chair in a crap-hole downtown apartment. After calming him down, I bundled Lewie in a blanket for the journey back home. Honest to God, he looked just like a Leprechaun. He was very short and rather thin, wide-eyed with tufts of reddish grey hair and a semi-groomed beard. All that he lacked was the proper hat bearing a shamrock and a pipe, but he did joke about his lucky charms with women in a rather colorful way. He was always humorous, bouncing on his toes at the punchline of longwinded tales. Lewie stayed sober for several months and worked part-time for me, but disappeared one day. He probably caught the bus back to Lancaster being drawn like a moth to the flame and left without so much as a note. He left a pair of worn but polished leather shoes tucked under his bed. They may have been size seven at a stretch with up-turned pointy toes.

A guy named Brad who drove a Subaru Brat and drove me crazy stayed a few short weeks. It was quite appropriate that he drove a Brat; he whined about everything. And that, my friend, lest I weary you, is just to mention a few. Our door was opened to hitch-hikers, breakdowns and broken people. Some were just overnight and not particularly interested in the gospel, which they heard, and moved on after a hot meal or a bed. I'd like to think some seeds were planted that helped them down the road. Who knows?

*"House Upon the Rock"* was a non-profit ministry. My partner, Dale Wolfe was a trucker whose wife had savvy accounting/legal skills. Beyond the "Cheerful Givers Bowl" for freewill offerings

of crumpled dollar bills and change, which helped cover the expenses for goodies and coffee on a Friday night, the ministry survived on faith. We gratefully received modest donations from a few local churches to stay afloat. God provided. There were more mouths to feed, personal needs to be met from someone just getting sober when they didn't have so much as a toothbrush and we became home for them, at least for a little while. Furniture had to be bought and was found at secondhand stores. Weekly surplus from the local grocer's over-stock and kindness was picked up on Wednesday morning before the store opened. Jim Brown, a student in pre-med at Bucknell who I'd met at Lamb Fellowship worked the graveyard shift at Dunkin Donuts and made sure we had a sizeable bag of free day old donuts on occasion. We managed, amazingly, with one bathroom for 5-6 people.

*"House Upon the Rock"* sponsored such things as a community bonfire at Halloween time in the downtown park after getting favor and permits from the city. The venue was free cider and donuts around a huge bonfire that the local firemen stood guard over. We rented a truck trailer for a stage and offered an evening of music, skits, puppets and testimonies and ministered to a good size crowd. On a funny side-note during the coffeehouse days, I dragged a youngster from church to do a bit of street out-reach. Gary Reigle was game to tag along. We walked downtown and hung around the corner where the Stettler Hotel was located, a bar of sleazy notoriety and brawls, and came across a likely suspect we thought needed the gospel. I was armed with a four-point programed lead-in and pulled it off in a casual way, sharing the gospel in a nutshell. When I asked the obviously inebriated gentleman what would happen if he died right now, thinking we were on the same page about eternal things, he said: "I guess I'd fall down." Gary got the giggles that set me off and we patted him on the back, hoping our hilarity was a blessing.

The weekend of July 7, 1977 was approaching, adding to the magical number of 777 as compared to 666 which would have bothered me, and an idea dawned for another outreach. I don't think it was coincidence or the planets aliening. And by the way, I'm not one of those Revelation quoting doom and gloom, end of day's anarchy Antichrist kind of guys. At the time I happened to be reading about the biblical mandate on Israel's calendar year. Trudging ever so slowly through Leviticus, which is not the most interesting of Old Testament books but something you had to do it, right? The Torah is kind of important. I read Moses' account of the coming of years when seven times seven times seven occurred, a rare time in Israel's history they awaited and looked forward to. The coming of days for the generation whose lucky numbers came up meant that every man or woman who was exiled could return home, the foreigner reinstated with his birthright and reunited with his or her family. Along with that promise, every man's debt would be forgiven and start with a clean slate, as well as slaves set free unless they chose to continue with their labors. Moses called it the Year of Jubilee. Today's nightly news on Fox would call it socialism, opening the borders to illegals and giving handouts to those who didn't deserve it. How sad. I don't think Moses had a fake tan and orange hair. We set about planning our own version of the Fishnet festival calling it: *The Day of Jubilee.*

There were many hoops to jump through but the pieces fell in place, which seemed to be confirmation that we were on the right track. The West Milton CB Club volunteered their campground at no charge. It was a perfect fit. The area was several acres in size, semi-wooded with modern restrooms, hook-ups and water, having the capacity to host several hundred campers. The plus was a band shell with rows of wooden benches in a semi-circle to accommodate a sizable crowd. We prayed and fasted for good weather.

Posters were printed and circulated county-wide (I wish I still had one), soliciting churches and restaurants and any willing window or bulletin board, even free public radio announcements to spread the word. I wonder what might have happened had there been internet. It was a free jamboree; a weekend family event with camping, uplifting entertainment for every age, music, dramas, puppets and teaching ministries scheduled on the main stage. Vendors set up; hot sausage hoagies from Gunzy's food-truck, volunteers grilling hot dogs and burgers, kids with lemonade stands, a bake sale from the combined efforts of the Four Square Gospel Church and many others. An artist friend from church designed *Day of Jubilee* silkscreen T shirts and sold out on the first day. The event was very well attended. I booked a converted Hells Angel as the keynote speaker. He towered over me when I met him at the airport, a hulk of a man with a deep intimidating voice, but he had a soft heart for Jesus. Ron DuPriest shared his testimony about being a sergeant of arms for the L.A. Hells Angels and preached a strong word that brought the roof down. Over a hundred came forward to pray at his invitation. It was a glorious, climactic, supernatural ending to our *Day of Jubilee*. I don't think I slept the entire weekend. I didn't want to miss a thing.

# 5

*The* voices in my head are making make me dizzy with a weird sense of vertigo. It's all coming back too quickly now that the flood gates are open. I'm not sure if remembering is a blessing or a curse. Maybe I've been the proverbial ostrich all my life, sticking my head in the sand when I'm overwhelmed or perplexed, but I asked for God's help to remember my past and write this story. Needless to say, he took me up on it.

I stretch my weary bones and get out of this chair, my mind reeling, and wander around the house puzzling all the random pieces beginning to fit together. A therapist would have a hey-day with me. Is this how it is? Are memories like rows of dominos triggered in motion that when one falls it causes a chain reaction? I stop at my reflection in the bathroom mirror and see a face that is me and ask, what's in a face, the one we all look at every day? Is it the canvas of an inner work of art put on display, just the surface, the skin, the distillation of an on-going painting on the fabric of our soul? A Rembrandt? A Picasso? Finger paintings by God? I'm suddenly caught like deer in headlights.

I'm still that renegade kid with a cocky grin, and it surprises me as he grins back at my reflection. The expression on my face changes like changing the channels on TV. There's a face laughing his ass off in an "I don't give a goddamned care," a juvenile risking all for another crazy escapade, then, it's an older and wiser face, caught off guard by buried secrets brought to the light, shutting down joviality like hitting the main breaker. Layers and layers of the past both distant and near as yesterday flash by quickly. I feel vulnerable and naked and grip the edge of the sink, leaning my forehead against the mirror and breathed a prayer. If you're lucky you have an anchor to grab ahold of, my steadfastness is holding fast to the promise that I am a work in progress, a priceless work of art fearfully and wonderfully created, but still quite unfinished.

I was once a sandy-blonde with clear blue eyes, a smooth faced youth with my father's chin and my mother's nose with a good deposit of their intellect and creativity. It makes me grateful for good genes. I'm still trim and agile (sort of), it takes me longer now to recover from taking a spill or getting up when I've been kneeling or sitting too long without the old-man groans. Presently, I'm looking at the infamous: will you still need me - will you still feed me number sixty four. I'm silver haired but still have a good head of hair, not like my brother who's nearly bald. He wears it well, me, it wouldn't be pretty, too many lumps. I'm a bit weathered from time and working physically outdoors for most of my adult life, not a bad looking man with deep laugh-lines and crow's feet around my eyes as if the whole murder of crows danced on my face. As I study this face, I see someone behind my eyes still lying and hiding, certainly clever and elusive. It's only a glimpse, but he's there; that kid who tumbled and was trapped as though stuck in a Whirlpool dryer trying to get untangled.

I should have told you my deepest secret when it would have fit better in the chronology of my story, but was afraid. I've never spoken of it in my entire life to a living soul. I don't know if I've come to terms with it even with God. I'm battling against reason to make mention of it now, but I feel compelled if for no other reason that it might heal something within me by making a confession. It may also help you, my dear reader, if it rings true in your experience. If a deep wound that you've carried all your life can be healed, then I'll be brave and bare my soul, kind of like show me yours and I'll show you mine. As it happens, I've once again entered the door into the Lost and Found Department and cannot escape what comes to mind.

⌇

I've had some bad trips, as in the LSD kind, when I imagined demons chasing me and voices clawing at my mind to torture if not to kill me. It wasn't all amusing mind altering trippy games and giggles. There were long, dark nights wandering the streets around my hometown or some strange place, anxiously looking over my shoulder, certain that at any moment I'd be pounced upon and devoured. I had a propensity to be paranoid when I was high, but kept my fears under control and dodged the bullet from totally cracking up and ending up in the Funny Farm.

Back in the day, some buddies and I built a primitive cabin up Beatty's Mountain to party, a place where one could find shelter and a friendly face. When it was night-time and I was tripping on acid, the path was twisty and scary and whispered to me like a haunted forest in fairytales. When I made it to the cabin, the Black Forest behind me, I wouldn't want to leave until my head was clear. Sometimes I'd drop another tab of acid, and another, and it'd take several days to get straight and walk back to town. We had a stockpile of Graham crackers and canned goods pilfered from home, tins of sardines that Whitey insisted on having. Stocked in the corner was usually a twelve pack of Rolling Rock or a few bottles of Boones Farm wine. If you used it – you replaced it. After squirrel season a pot-belly stove kept the place toasty. Someone drew a picture on cardboard with colored markers of a mutant, dimpled orange surround by tentacles of wavy sunbeams that hung over the stove, indicative of acid named Orange Sunshine which is very potent. When I was tripping out of my gourd it grew faces that changed and talked philosophically to me. I don't know why I continued taking hallucinogens, it was fifty-fifty odds that

I'd either freak out or have a good time. What I'm about to tell you is not an acid trip, not even close. This is unquestionably the worst nightmare of my life and my deepest secret. With a lurch of heart at this memory that is real to me still, I suddenly come face to face with something from time beyond time.

$\sim$

It was the summer of '73 when Jimmy and I were running the coast stealing from beach-goers and partying like tomorrow would never come. We were at Virginia Beach in a pub on the boardwalk, drinking dark Michelob by the pitchers and shooting pool. The place began getting crowded and a black guy approached us, asking if we were in the market for some weed. We were, and he offered us a ride to score. He seemed harmless and unassuming, so we paid our tab and went along. He took us around the business district and down the coastal freeway, soul music playing on the radio as we passed a joint around. We turned off the highway and went beyond the streetlights of residential sub-developments outside the city limits, a side road took us to a rundown motel. Several older cars were parked in front on the broken macadam, weeds and cigarette butts and rubbish cluttered the sidewalk; it was a shady affair that should have caused the alarms to go off in my head. A small party was going on when we entered the room; two black guys and a white dude were sitting in a cloud of blue smoke with the TV tuned in on rabbit-ears to a ballgame. I don't remember much after the bong went round and round and drank quite a few strong mixed drinks of Black Velvet and Coke. The black guy, who gave us the ride, kept plying me with drinks and offered Jimmy and me lines of cocaine which I declined. I could barely keep my eyes open and enough was enough.

I awoke the next morning disoriented on an air mattress on the floor, still woozy and seriously hung-over. Jimmy was in the bathroom. I was wrapped in a blanket and needed to piss, struggling to find equilibrium to make a mad dash for the door hoping that no one was outside. My underwear was tangled around my ankles. I was naked. Suddenly everything felt wrong. My butt was sticky with something greasy and my crotch was caked with dried semen. I had absolutely no recollection of what happened, but instantly realized I'd been drugged, raped and sodomized. I should have been glad to be alive, but the horror was such that I wished I was dead.

There was no one else in the crap-hole room but Jimmy and I, and I ventured to ask him what had happened last night. He said that he'd passed out and shrugged his shoulders; "Just another night of suds and shots. Those niggers sure had some killer weed." He went about shaving and humming some chipper tune and showed no signs of being any wiser than I was. I didn't say anything. I hated Jimmy's casual melancholy and wanted to scream; "God-damn-it, why didn't you come to my aid?" He obviously didn't have a clue. I showered for an hour and cried like I never cried before.

The black guy left our wallets, although much lighter with around $80 between us, and a bag of weed on the nightstand. I insisted that we leave Virginia Beach. The parking lot was empty as we backtracked our way toward the freeway in silence. I turned my back on the whole affair and tried to forget it, but obviously haven't.

≈

I've been through a lot of ugly, painful and lonely times. I know what it's like to be on the street and have money or be flat broke. I've seen stuff in jail cells, back alleys and flea-bag rooms where people shot up heroin that would make you shake your head, and this was the life I chose? If you walk close to the gutter, eventually you'll lie in it. An ancient wise man said to every yin there's a yang. The gospel says that you reap what you sow. My dad said you sleep in the bed of your own making. To put it bluntly, and if you'll please forgive me for saying so, looking back, I was one fucked up kid. Since then, there's been a little black spot on the sun.

$\sim$

Of the many things I've realized over the span of my years is that we must come to terms with our past. The Twelve Steps includes one that suggests taking a fearless moral inventory. Smart advice from Bill W. If the past is not forgiven we carry it like a weight and limp or stagger rather than soar effortlessly like an eagle on the winds. It might be just a small thing, or huge nightmarish things, but in my experience even a pebble in your shoe can hobble you. Oh how we over-compensate and hide our handicaps! A cripple can appear quite normal with enough practice. My pain may not compare nor my experiences relate to yours, but all of us carry something that hinders us.

As an adult, I've heard a plethora of horror stories, and although the commentary isn't short I'll try to keep it brief. I've met people who seem to value suffering as if it were a badge to be proud of. "And you think you've had it rough... you ought to be me." Ever hear that one? It makes me wonder if somehow it was to my advantage to hear someone else's horrific story and feel better about my own. It can be wearying to hear about cancer or infidelities, PTSD and countless hardships when the person sharing them is almost bragging, otherwise I'd feel empathy. There are others who've been so deeply wounded that they've adopted a whole new personality; Jekyll or Hyde on any given day. It's a crying jag pleading for sympathy, but on the next visit its accusations and aggressive words, mocking, scornful, shot at you like poison darts from a blow gun. Still others are locked behind barred doors in a safe room with gun towers positioned at every angle, guarding against anyone getting too close.

Pain lurks in the corner like a ghetto conman with an accent; "Just-forget-about-it", but we don't. All it takes is an obnoxious family member dissing you at a holiday meal with a "joking" comment about the pickle tray arrangement that reminds everyone how screwed up and haphazard your life is. At times it's a friend's insensitive comment about losing your job or breaking up from a relationship. The innuendo is that you've failed and it's your fault. It's sort of amazing how powerful spoken words can be. Pain comes in all sizes, but one size does not fit all. A Band-Aid may staunch blood from a minor cut, but other times the wound is so deep major surgery is necessary.

No matter how ornately we dress it up and try to casually pass off being offended, the rising heat of anxiety at feeling like a victim chokes the very breath out of us. It sucks to get hurt and the damned Band-Aides rarely stick right. The cocktail of self-pity and rage is a bitter drink to slug down. Most of us deserve an Academy Award for putting on a sterling performance when shaking off a hard blow, letting it roll off like water on a duck's back when our insides are bleeding. An adage from childhood days rings in my ears; "Sticks and stones may break my bones but words will never hurt me." Really? Who the hell said that? I'd rather take a stiff shot on the chin and have my teeth knocked loose rather than get insulted verbally and emotionally.

Perhaps you're like me and have shared something so often that you're pretty sure it actually happened but aren't entirely certain if it's really true. Has some event or story gotten to the point that it sounds make-believe in your own ears? In a way, turning facts to fabrication is a mechanism we employ to deceive ourselves and feel vindicated. We're all so very guarded, aren't we? Our past, the parts we want to forget, becomes shadowed as we pull the shade down to block out the light of truth. But every once in a while, the shadow stranger sneaks in and visits us as a familiar face, invading our intimate place and touching a sensitive nerve. Keeping misery as a comforting bed-mate isn't the kind of nostalgic lover that ever has our best interests in mind. I wonder if we don't all play the game of hide-and-seek. If you've been jolted alert by a buried nightmare of some distant memory, feeling raped, robbed, ridiculed, entertaining fantasies of suicide or fear of eternal imprisonment in solitary confinement, take heart. Someone is paying attention and cares very much for you.

We wouldn't be human if we didn't have pain to some degree, but I want to shout good news from the rooftop. We don't have to carry it alone. Ever! Yes, taking a fearless moral inventory as the Twelve Steps suggests is helpful, even necessary, personally or with a confidant, but isn't the purpose of laying our past and all its afflictions on the table in an effort to reveal the naked truth meant to be a means to an end? Isn't our honest disclosure intended to set in motion some wild hope of a breakthrough and the exorcism of Legions tormenting and mocking us? Freedom, for crying out loud, freedom and healing is what we are called to; not rehashing painful memories that galvanize us into some kind of warped identity.

I'm not an authority, nor am I educated to sit in the seat of a psychiatrist to offer clinical guidance. I'm just a simple man who has learned by trial and error. What I offer is without charge, so take it or leave it. I happen to believe that our lives *can* be whole and healed, free and strong and vibrant to the fullest extent, even as victims or victimizer who seeks a new way. I have hoped and continue to hope for that reality to be true for me in real life for many years. The prospect of discovering freedom takes more than crossing your fingers and counting on luck. Sorry, hate to burst your bubble. Luck has nothing to do with it. I think healing is possible through making a conscious personal choice to seek healing and approach it head-on like a damned torpedo, a determined way of reckoning to get closure regardless of who or what blows to smithereens.

Having a relationship with someone who loves us deeply in spite of all our quirks and scars and lies, a dear friend who joins along-side on the trail and hikes with us over hills and plains is unparalleled. I find that when I take the time to vent or converse and unburden my soul with a friend, it's like reevaluating and processing the very words that pour out of my mouth and it helps me find centeredness. Choosing to believe that somehow and in some way, by God's grace, there's Flubber under our soles to get us over our jumbled mess. Choosing hope sounds easy, like a solicitous quip on a Hallmark card, but it's not. Choosing hope takes courage. Every step thereafter takes vigilance to keep on believing for tomorrows. Risk is involved, for we must continue to be open and hope even in the face of further hurt, but light will shine on the next step and the next step, however daunting.

I've said this to myself as I'm sure you have; "But if you really knew me... the true essence of what's buried inside, my deep down ugliness and hypocrisy and suspicions you probably wouldn't or couldn't accept and love me." That's a huge wall to scale over, how well I know, but quite simply, we can't go it alone. To find forgiveness or the grace to forgive and rest in being loved and loving are cornerstones of life and the pathway to healing. Without it we are lost. The age old adage that none of us are islands unto ourselves is quite apropos.

I think of Tom Hanks in the movie *Castaway*. His beckoning cry for companionship and his conversations with Wilson (the soccer ball), when he was marooned, wasn't just witty, humorous Hollywood entertainment, it echoed real life. What thrummed in his soul and kept him alive was the hope of "knowing" someone and being "known." Thus, the tender dialogue with Wilson emerged. Keeping an unfailing dream alive no matter how hard pressed and trying paid off in his being rescued. It was gut-wrenching to hear his cry when Wilson was lost at sea, the soul companion who'd kept him sane, but deliverance was his reward at a great expense. Tom Hanks' character was drastically changed by getting a fire started against all odds, of enduring unfathomable isolation and circumstances beyond his control, yet he survived by keeping hope alive. There's a well know bible verse that says; "...faith, hope and love will never fail. But the greatest of these is love." Faith gets headlines and love has become a household word, but what about hope? Hope is invaluable and part of the divine trinity that's declared in the verse. Maybe it's like a three-legged sack race to cross the finish-line.

At the risk of sounding naïve, at long last I've come to believe there is such a person who is a constant companion and has my best interests in mind. That person is Jesus Christ, who loves me for who I am regardless of being adrift or marooned. I believed that I am undeniably loved even in my tattered, impoverished condition. I fail at times and falter, but I've gambled my hopes on an imaginary person such as Wilson, but for me, Jesus is real. I am forever grateful to be rescued.

Cupid directs arrows not a bouquet of roses to lover's heart. We are not only smitten by a kiss but penetrated. When that thunderbolt revelation struck me I was undone. I'd been a Christian for seven or eight years at the time and never really "heard" that message in church like when I "heard" it in my own soul. If you're a Christian or not, you probably already have a clue that God loves you, but for me, it got buried under a lot of other stuff, even church stuff.

I found clarification at Dayspring Retreat Center on a personal weekend retreat in the mountains not far from Gaithersburg, Maryland. After finally getting Internet, I tracked the lead from the back of a book that proved quite interesting. I was trying to access the allusive "quiet-time" that Christians talked about. Being pragmatic, I thought that maybe there was more to this thing called "quiet-time" than spending fifteen minutes with a verse for the day and a one page devotional, putting in the mandatory visit with God before getting busy with the important business of the day. I figured that if you're getting a quote for a new electrical panel to upgrade an old one you'd call someone who knew what they were doing, right? The shelves at Barnes and Noble and my local Christian bookstore offered little help. I debated about investigating Zen. I mean no offense, but books similar to authors like Max Lucado or Charles Stanley didn't scratch me where I itched. So I sought wisdom from the ancients; the Desert Fathers for example. I read Thomas Merton, Richard Rohr and Brennan Manning's book titled *The Ragamuffin Gospel*. I wanted to learn and felt that I had to go outside the box of my comfort zone, my acceptable theological way of seeing things to lay ahold of what it was I was seeking. I became intrigued by Catholic mystic writers and their simple lifestyles, the history of saints, divine miracles and visitations, of their prose and commentaries which was beyond suspicious and borderline heresy with my evangelical friends. I weathered their criticism and stayed the course, tuning an inner ear in a different direction to hear the "Voice." My goal was selfish; I wanted to learn things about contemplation and the essence of genuine quietness and inner peace to satisfy my thirst. I saw glimmers, however dimly, as I sorted through their writings, some that I set aside, much of it deep and hard to understand. Yet I was compelled to find answers to questions that I had no words for. To say that I was hungry does not express what my hunger was like.

I made reservations for a weekend at Dayspring, enrolling for a silent retreat without big-named speakers, expectant to explore the possibilities and discovery as a result of my reading. I knew that I was in the right place while sitting in my truck in the parking lot. Before venturing to the main building to register, I felt welcomed and breathed in the peaceful solitude, the rustling of a warm spring breeze. Leaves were budding and crocuses peeked from the ground in colorful piety. It was a good way to begin my endeavor.

There were twelve other retreatants doing the same thing I set my bearings upon; meditate and find God. We all took a vow of silence after Friday evening's opening session and allowed each other the space and respect to seek God in his or her own way for the remainder of the weekend. Each of us had a monk-like cabin with a single bed, a wooden chair and writing table etched by use, a lamp and a simple wash basin. We rarely saw one other except at common meals, which was tricky because we'd taken a vow not to talk. We communicated between one another quite easily in the silence. All it took was awareness and kindness to pass the bowls and pitchers to one another, always bringing a warm smile and affirmation in return. We became a close-knit community of fellow seekers bound by silence.

I'd picked up a guide book by Henri Nouwen at registering and meeting Elizabeth O'Connor, the author of *Eighth Day of Creation* and other publications. It was only after returning home and doing some research that I found out how significant a role she played in DC's inner-city needs. She struck me as a unique and wonderful grey haired woman, humble and soft spoken who'd warmly greeted and pointed me in the right direction. The book was titled: *Life of the Beloved*.

After a monk's breakfast of porridge and bread, I hiked to a point on the map called *Merton's Pond*, so named for the Catholic mystic, Thomas Merton. My plan was to try out this thing called meditation. I found a log beside the pond on a grassy bank and parked my butt, where I sat for a long time unsure what I should do. But doing is what trips me up. I tried practicing the breathing technique I had read about and inwardly empty my mind with a mantra: *Be still and listen - be still and listen - be still and know.* Those old monks knew something I sure didn't. I was restless and crazy-bored within an hour, ready to head back home and work in the shop, start doing something. There was always work calling my attention, but I endured. An hour passed and then another. Work could wait. Doing anything seemed ridiculously counterproductive.

When my spirit was finally still and expectations evaporated, of all things, the dragonflies returned and birds cheeped, frogs playfully splashed around the muddy shoreline. A good sized snapping turtle emerged from under a stump at my feet and headed nose first into the water. The pond resumed its normal vibrancy. Apparently I'd become lost in the background and all the critters forgot that I was there, or maybe I'd become one with them. I felt connected like our worlds weren't all that different, the diversity of this pond and my busy mixed up world. A calming rhythm beat in my soul, silently embracing an alliance with my surroundings. Our sustenance and very life came from the Creator. We were together in our worship as one body. Merton's Pond was heaven on earth and sang in secret code to my soul as a grand choir.

Sometimes I held my breath for fear of squelching the spirit by any untoward activity. I was vulnerable and receptive, waiting beside that ordinary small pond in a wooded grove, when I heard a ringing in my soul like hearing a telephone. I actually turned my head toward the woods to ascertain if what I heard was perhaps real. How strange. I was far removed from anywhere a phone would be and cell phones were not yet on the market. I tentatively answered in my mind; "Hello?"

A soothing voice whispered in my ear, conveying welcome and a sense of quizzical interest that nearly rocked me to my feet. It was as though I was greeted by a friend with the invitation to join in, and share a casual, chit-chat conversation. I recognized the voice. I think it was the shock at hearing my name called like when you're daydreaming and awakened to the moment that caught me off guard. It dawned on me that someone cared and was reaching out, as I waited with an aching back, sitting on a log for hours, and that someone was Jesus. He wanted to be my friend and not just my Lord. I felt deeply loved in such a way that dispelled any fears of being accepted. I felt like a bird released from its cage, a fish set free from a net, a man given the ticket to walk away from prison and breathe fresh air. I began to believe that the crux of true healing was a gift, pure and simple, totally gratuitous.

I'm having a difficult time trying to find the words to describe my experience so you might understand it, for was it not an earthly love or physical arms that enveloped me, nor was it just poetic idealism or allegorical imagery. What I felt was real, something beyond words that seemed to fill me layer upon layer, drowning and infusing me, fundamentally changing my nature. What I felt was the Holy Spirit in a myriad of ways. A nearness and tenderness brushed against me, fiery glory and a holy hush descended within my trembling being, tantalizing tickles of the spirit caused outright belly laughter. I had a lump in my throat one minute, weeping hot tears the next, goosebumps danced as though electrified on my flesh. In as much as my "Born Again" experience on the sidewalk in front of a laundromat was unassuming without great emotion, this was something, if I dare to say the word, supernatural. Some would call it being filled with the Holy Spirit. As I said, words cannot do justice to express what happened, but I was touched by an overwhelming, endearing, unending, undeserved sacrificial kind of love. In that unexpected holy moment of being utterly overcome, I realized that Jesus was offering me hope and healing with open hands. Dare I believe that it meant everything past, present and future?

I bid Merton's Pond farewell for the day and headed back to the lodge for supper, carrying with me a conscience sense that Jesus is the ultimate optimist, an ever present companion who believes in us more than we believe in him. It'd be very difficult not to talk about my day with my fellow retreatants during our evening meal, I was so excited. I sensed that others around the table had some kind of spiritual experience as well. In our silent fellowship, a palpable atmosphere of great joy prevailed.

Jesus is still calling person-to-person and available for the fortunate ones who hear his voice and answer. It's really as simple as picking up the phone when it rings and not second guessing, but if you're in therapy, maybe you ought to keep your appointment.

I retrieved a flashlight from my truck after our meal and wandered back through the woods to Merton's Pond, humming a

Bob Marley tune. Reggae has been a favorite style of music for me; it puts bounce in my step. *"Don't worry... every little thing's gonna be alright."* I knew it would be. I wrote furiously in my journal, trying to record words and revelation and visions cascading faster than I could keep up with. Merton's Pond was a magical place and a story grew out of my experience that I'd spend years writing. It was my first attempt on the road to becoming a novelist. The pond told the story.

For me, I couldn't be a monk or celibate, but I learned from the mystics. I came away from that weekend of silent retreat realizing a profound truth. What's primary is hope, that and being in harmony with Jesus, cultivating an intimate and divine love affair in everyday life.

# 6

*I* went through my first recession in 1980-1982; the not-so-wonderful Reagan years. Housing plummeted with high interest rates and Leon struggled as long as he could but had to fold his cards. There just wasn't enough work to keep a crew busy. I applied for a painter and wallpaper-hanger position at a huge Methodist nursing home complex and was hired. Along with the job description to refurbish rooms was an expectation to interact with the residents. I fell in love with many wonderful seniors. I put on weight from eating cake and casseroles and goodies the aids brought in, usually spending my break-time in one of the nurse's lounges because it was convenient and more comfortable than the breakroom at the shop.

There were seven of us in the maintenance department; the mechanical guys, lawn care and general repairs. I learned to be a bit wiser about wearing Jesus as a label on the outside, but I didn't hide my light under a bushel. I paid attention and was getting to know the fellows. In a short while I was eating lunch alone, again. Sometimes the guys would leave the breakroom when I walked in or get uncomfortably quiet. It was confusing and difficult and I wondered how I'd offended them. One afternoon I was pulled into a mop room by a guy named, I kid you not, Rick Nixon. He was on the grounds-keeping end of things and flat out told me I was causing problems and made them look bad. Huh? Tricky Dick told me that before I showed up it took two guys a day to paint one room. I was painting two rooms and stripping wallpaper and rehanging like a seasoned pro on my day-shift. Good old Leon taught me well; you put in an honest day at work. I made some adjustments, spending more time with the residents while on my shift, and was rejoined in the breakroom with my coworkers.

Fall of 1982 promised an economic rebound and I decided to start my own contracting business. It was as if being outside in the fresh air and sawdust called to me. Leon had big shoes to fill and I was often with him at Shuler and Alder's model home office picking up blueprints and taking care of business. I'd met the general manager, the salesmen and the building inspector, so they all knew me. I secured a position as the number two framing crew, hired four men, and off we went swinging hammers. There was always one on the crew who I worked with as a mentor; an exceptional worker with the right attitude that had a knack for carpentry. Most the crew, which changed regularly, were so-so carpenters or total greenhorns. I learned the ropes on hiring and firing. I find it crazy how many men in the trades are drunks and have hard luck stories, many without a driver's license for DUI's and other baggage. Several times I had to pick up one of my men from work release at the Union County Jail if he was worth keeping. In the mix were those with a good attitude, hopefuls that learned and hustled who got bonuses, a few became friends after work. Anyway, I did just fine and ran my business for twenty six years, though never making tons of money. I'm thankful to have engaged dozens of men over the years with the gospel message and practical help, spending time in their homes and bailing some of them out of trouble. Oh the stories I can tell of tobacco chewing Rodney and Nate the Snake doing a great Wallenda act while setting trusses, as well as many other colorful characters I'll never forget.

I met Gladys Coleman in Riverview Manor, a semi-independent

part of the nursing home complex I worked at. During an ice cream social on Memorial Day I had the pleasure of getting reacquainted. The social/activity coordinator would call me to fill in slots on the schedule even after I left. I never ventured far from the nursing home and dropped in occasionally on a weekend to see how my favorite old-timers were doing. One notable gentleman named Henry was on the list to visit. His character resembled that of a circus announcer, loads of fun and engaging. I met him on B-wing while doing drywall repairs in his bathroom, and couldn't help but notice 2X4's glued on the bottom side of his toilet seat. It was an ingenious way to keep his schlong from getting wet when he sat to take care of business. His jokes and witticism often reflected his endowment. Okay, back to Gladys Coleman who was a nun by comparison.

Gladys was a retired school teacher pushing ninety. She was a charming woman of wit and sharp intellect who still liked her hair colored, a weekly manicure, and insisted on wearing make-up and jewelry. You'd have thought she was a Vanderbilt. Gladys was independent and stubborn, always wanting to do everything on her own, but she needed assistance getting in and out of her wheelchair.

That Memorial Day was unseasonably warm, as sweat ran down my back while playing the old Gibson guitar and singing gospel and folk songs to entertain the ladies. During refreshments, Gladys shared stories with Cassie and me; her knowledge of local history was most entertaining. During our visit, she mentioned having a house that hadn't sold and was ready to take off the market. Gladys seemed stressed about it and made me wonder if she knew she'd never be able to go back to it. Something clicked as she described the house and location.

Mifflinburg was only a twenty minute drive from everyday life in Lewisburg, a town worthy to explore. Wandering a few blocks in any direction you'd find homemade Pennsylvania Dutch pasties, an old hotel and bar, antique dealers and local crafters, merchants selling clothing and handbags. If you browsed and picked up a brochure, one of the highlights was the museum. Mifflinburg is dubbed Buggy Town after a major manufacturing business in the eighteen hundreds that provided buggy's of all variety.

Cassie and I went to look at the house and fell in love with the turn of the century brick Victorian two story. The house had history and charm with a detached two car garage located on Chestnut Street in a great neighborhood. Gladys apparently loved gardening. Along with the beds of mature perennials and shade trees, irises bordering the south wall were absolutely stunning. Gladys left us the grandfather clock on the stair landing as a house warming gift. I had a full-time second job remodeling the magnificent 200 year old house back to its former glory.

Our church didn't have a midweek service; we had home-groups for worship and bible study. Cassie and I hosted a group on Wednesday night with people from church who lived in our neck of the woods and invited the neighbors. During that time I met two Gordons who impacted my life; Gordon Barnes, called Gordy, and Jay Gordon.

~

Gordy Barnes was a big gentle bear you could barely get your arms around when he hugged you. He had a full salt and pepper beard and a jovial demeanor, a contagious laugh and eyes that sparkled whenever he testified about something the Lord was doing in his life. We instantly became friends. Gordy was a state rep for Prison Fellowship, and upon getting to know me, asked me to come on board.

Prison Fellowship is the result of a man named Chuck Colson who was one of the Watergate conspirators. He was Nixon's "Hatchet Man" and did Federal prison time where he discovered saving grace in Christ. Reading C.S. Lewis' book *Mere Christianity* was pivotal, as was a man that visited Colson who offered to do his prison time. Colson was a brilliant man and pioneered new legislation on prison reform and after-care, not only nationwide but globally. Cassie and I where extended an all-paid package and went to Colorado Springs for training where we became certified In-prison seminar instructors. The venue was hosted at the Navigators Headquarters at Glen Eyrie Conference Center, not far from Pikes Peak. On our breaks, Cassie and I wandered the canyon, seeing golden eagles and big horn sheep and amazing landscape. Watching a herd of elk grazing on the lawns in the evenings was breathtaking for a guy acquainted with white tail deer. Little did I know I'd come to live in that beautiful city years down the road.

We were in a county jail, a state institution or federal facility statewide, fifteen to twenty weekends a year, ministering on a variety of topics provided by Prison Fellowship. It was a major part of my life, maybe the best part. For twelve years we shared living water and interacted with inmates. Perhaps I've done more time as a volunteer than many who've served time. Cassie actually bought me a leather briefcase. Didn't I look important!

A team of local volunteers (those countless, wonderful, caring people), would join us as small group facilitators. We sang choruses, did skits, had the inmates do skits, taught the lessons with creative means and reached out to hundreds and hundreds who happened to be incarcerated. I made some close friends who were doing life sentences. On occasions, Cassie and I would assist someone we came to know who was released and looking at the monumental task of reassembling his life on the outside. Of all the many weekends we ministered behind concrete walls and bars and razor-wire, there's one in particular that comes to mind.

I felt more useful, if that's the right word, doing county jail seminars, although addressing big crowds at some state or federal prison was gratifying. My thought was that if you could reach someone in those early stages of crime and addiction, sentenced to short-time, perhaps he or she could be spared going to the penitentiary. We were conducting a seminar called "Life Plan" in the Clinton County Faculty near Lock Haven, Pennsylvania. The meetings were held in an educational room and a small group of men came out on Friday night, maybe six or seven. They were wary, cocky and street savvy, but they were respectful. Perhaps it was the idea that if they completed a course it would reflect well in their file. If they were disruptive and I reported it, that was a check mark in the wrong category. I never had occasion in twelve years to give one inmate a bad report. I think a lot of them came out just to break up the monotony and not to heckle.

Opening sessions were critical, you either won their interest or lost them from the get-go. Their participation was completely voluntary. I have no way of really framing into words what happened that Friday night but to say it as simply as it can be said, God took us by surprise in Clinton County Jail.

I opened with an introduction and some choruses, coaxing the men to join along, loosen them up with a few jokes, but not having a very good response. I played the Eagles song *Desperado* and began to share a little bit of my story. Being one who followed the syllabus outline, I was also given to improvising and going off-script. I sought for an open door to reach these men, when out of nowhere a memory came to mind, blind-siding me. I was walking through it as they were eyeing me up and leaning in with interest, so I pressed on. And then, the damned emotions flooded in and I kind of lost control. I think that's when God showed up.

In my mind, I walked down the dirt alley to Benny's house and circled around my old neighborhood, looking in windows, checking everything out, it was a ghost town. Timmy's house, the one with a stone wall where we bounced tennis balls off of for endless hours as kids appeared as though they were on vacation. There wasn't a living soul around. Stu's house looked the same as it did so many years ago, his motorcycle was torn apart in the driveway, a greasy rag tied on the handlebar as a signal flag; "Out of my mind – back in five minutes," but Stu wasn't home. The backyard where I grew up was devoid of any evidence of children at play; no swing-set, no sandbox, no bicycles leaning against the fence. My childhood gang had grown up and moved on. I felt lost and abandoned. Words began to choke in my throat, which was something I tried not to ever let happen, but my vision was so real.

I remember telling the inmates how desperate and lonely I felt wandering around my old neighborhood like an alien. I relived that experience as if it was actually happening in real time; the soul-sick feeling in the pit of my stomach and a sense of lost-ness so acute I could have crawled instead of walked. The lyrics of *Desperado* couldn't have been more applicable to the story I told if I'd written them myself. I wasn't drunk or high that melancholy evening so long ago, I was broke, marooned, friendless, and ended up sleeping in the neighbor's garden shed with a bag of peat moss for a pillow. I could have thrown a stone through my old bedroom window. I tried not to, but began to cry in front of those fellows in their bright orange county issue jumpsuits with wide-eyes. I wept unashamedly as if I was alone in my own space where no one would see me, as I had done that distant night in a garden shed behind 617 Bennett Street at fifteen years old. After composing myself, I set about teaching the first lesson and wondered if anyone would come back the next day. I'd made a complete fool of myself.

The normal seminar schedule consisted of five two hour sessions over a weekend; Friday evening opener, morning, afternoon and evening workshops on Saturday and a wrap up for a chapel service with testimonies and certificate presentations on Sunday. I remember setting up the room for Saturday morning's session. The volunteers were subdued but encouraging about my "ministry" from the night before, which I felt sure made them wonder about me. I was also pretty sure that no one would come back after the previous night's crying jag. It didn't fit the MO of prison mentality, let alone a grown man crying in public.

The clock never lies in prison. It was pushing twenty minutes late of our scheduled time to start and it was just Cassie and me and the volunteers. I began thinking there wasn't one inmate who planned on returning and prepared myself for the inevitable; a corrections officer would soon show up and make the announcement that our meetings were canceled. And then, the irking buzzer sounded and the door lock clicked with a metallic snap. I was shocked. The inmates did come back, and brought their friends who brought their friends. Each session we needed more chairs and I thought we must have three-quarters of the population. The tiny room was crowded wall to wall and those young men hung on every word, singing along with the choruses and clapping hands. I was blown away.

I learned something that weekend. If you're gutsy enough to follow God's leading miracles can happen. If you're broken and honest about what Jesus has done in your life, people will connect with the gospel. Aren't most of us broken? Whistling in the dark? There's a good chance that some of those inmates were familiar with tears in their own lives, so I didn't feel like a freak after-all. When it comes to ministry, you give what Jesus has given you and let the chips fall where they may. You either make enemies or you make friends. God has continually given me favor and I'm utterly astounded. Many of those young men in the Clinton County jail responded to my plea that Jesus made sense for desperados and prayed the prayer of surrender.

I met Chuck Colson at a luncheon and we spoke at length. He didn't say that my ways were "unorthodox" as the pastor at Crossroads Church accused me of. Mr. Colson complimented me for my zeal and creativity. Gordy saw the chaplain's reports and inmates testimonies and pushed the envelope to keep me involved with Prison Fellowship. I relish Gordy's embrace and the wonderful experiences we shared with men and women behind prison walls.

Jay Gordon is a cat of a different breed.

I met Jay at the student union while shooting billiards. Several students who attended Lamb Fellowship would drag me along to do outreach on campus, one in particular named Thor, who was very zealous. I think he was the one to make our introduction. Jay was a gregarious young man from Beaver Falls south of Pittsburgh, with an athletic build, frizzy hair and a line of bullshit that was quite amusing. To call him brash or bombastic isn't a stretch of the imagination, but Jay was extremely intelligent and charismatic with a heart of gold. For some reason we hit it off. Jay and I were Frodo Baggins and Samwise Gamgee off on an adventure. He got his life back on track with Jesus and loved the fast lane.

Jay was an accomplished musician, piano being his forte, and soon played along with the worship team at church. I was on a rotating schedule as a worship leader along with several other guitar players and Jay made us all sound much better than we were. He and I had an intuitive, uncanny sense to choose and lead the songs that was surprising. We never had a prepared list and it was as though we could read each other's mind song after song. There were many blessed times getting caught up in the Spirit on the wings of melody and praise.

Our bond grew deeper. We'd meet every Tuesday morning at Dunkin Donut before work at five a.m. to shoot the bull. Jay had graduated from Bucknell and was an elementary guidance counselor at the time while taking grad classes. I was still banging nails and framing houses. I don't recall there ever being a time when I saw him the parking lot that I didn't roll down the window and blow the horn. Jay was a hugger, a wrap-you-up-squeeze-you-tight kind of hugger. Sometimes it made me uncomfortable in public, especially when we parted ways and he'd say in a voice that carried, "Love ya, bro." I'd look around and wonder what the good old boys were thinking.

We not only drank coffee but shared the cup from an eternal spring bubbling inside us. We'd preach and pontificate and prophesy to one another. We talked about the hard stuff, seeking grace for the up's and down's of everyday life, connecting in such a way that the ordinary became extraordinary and things we hoped for became a budding reality. We were men of God and edified each other accordingly, but we were men made of clay; weak and lustful and needing accountability, a sounding board to keep our feet on solid ground. Billy Joel sings an old song called *Honesty*, which is such a lonely word. Jay and I endeavored to be brutally honest with one another. We began to know what made each other tick and the hidden and deep issues inside my soul became easier to talk about. Hours would fly by as we discussed the good and meaningful things the Spirit was doing in our lives, as well as our bad choices and behavior. I was open to confess my unconfessed sins but guarded about the really touchy ones, as I think he was as well. All it would take was a look or a comment from either of us to get real. You can't bullshit a bull-shitter.

Jay was compassionate at wheedling me to take the next step of faith at my every misstep, often provoking and asking endless questions that could wear a fellow out, but he was insightful and gracious. He had a gift for listening, which was refreshing as most the Christians I knew would rather talk and offer advice first. Doesn't it make you wonder why God gave us two ears and one mouth? Jay heard the deeper cry of my spirit and spoke truth to it in many casual conversations, sharing insights that resonated in my life and gave me vision. I heard his spirit as well and picture it like we each had a tin can pressed to our ear attached by a taut string line that vibrated with the heart of the matter.

I recall Jay saying, "Dirk, you and me - we know too much." The comment certainly wasn't an academic assessment, I knew what he implied. We both loved the scriptures and would quote or point out a verse with intense feeling that was life-giving. His inference, as well as my understanding, was more about what we called revelation, the gems that were so dramatically real and vivid. "What's Jesus saying today?" was an often asked question to get the ball rolling during our times together. We partook of the organic, vine ripen freshness of God's raw grace, as compared to something manufactured or hot-house, plastic and tasteless. The thing about knowing too much suggested that we could never settle for anything less than receiving life from the Living Vine. Once you've tasted of the Spirit in a deep and satisfying way you'll never be the same. Along with the peace and joy comes a hard and clarifying word; "The fear of the Lord is the beginning of wisdom, and to him who has been given much - much is required." Jay and I were treading lightly on holy ground with our fingers crossed behind our backs.

Jay's a storyteller of the long-winded kind and sometimes tells stories about me that have been kind of embarrassing. I've never known anyone in my life that has such a knack for remembering details as well as he can. He'd brag on me when making introductions in a crowd and made me feel special among his peers. How ironic. Jay had a college degree and was taking grad classes; I was a high school dropout taking it as came. I suppose both of us were brilliant and a legend in our own minds. Whenever the weekend at Muncy Corrections came up (Jay was fond of reminiscing), he'd tell of another time I wept before a crowd of inmates.

Jay joined us when we did a seminar at the women's prison at Muncy SCI; one of the two women's State penitentiary's in Pennsylvania. The large chapel was full and buzzing with inmates. A dozen volunteers joined us for small group-time, the faithful gang that I knew and appreciated. Jay played a pivotal role, not just sharing his testimony, but playing piano for the worship aspect of our sessions. I think he especially enjoyed playing for the prison choir, and let me tell you, those sisters could sing and make Jay work up a sweat.

The story he tells, which for some reason I didn't remember until he made mention of it, is that I slung my guitar over my shoulder after finishing a song and had a funny look on my face as if not knowing where I was. That often happens when I get lost in worship. I raised my arms in slow-motion as if trying to embrace a stranger and began praying, or rather, sobbing as it turned out, like Jesus was personally pleading for those women's hearts to come home. It was an extraordinary unexpected moment when many women wept with me, opening wounds and shame and anger they'd locked behind prison doors literally and figuratively for years. I don't know how it happened but I kind of know why. Jesus is relentlessly pouring out his love to rescue a drowning soul; he's also looking for a willing vessel to use and express his heart.

It was like getting caught up in a tidal wave. Sometimes you just have to get out of God's way and let him do his thing. Do miracles still happen today? I believe they do. Such an explosive atmosphere charged with grace and mercy cannot happen at the hands of mankind.

The schedule went out the window that glorious morning, the planned lessons could wait. We waded through deep waters praying for scores of inmates, the team and I, laying on hands and hugging women from all walks of life wanting to touch the hem of Jesus' garment and be healed.

Gordy Barnes and his wife, Diann were there as well. They had an endearing fondness for the ladies and wouldn't miss the weekend seminars at Muncy Corrections every spring and fall. Diann sang special music with a sound track and always received a standing ovation. She had perfect pitch and a set of lungs every bit as grand as Sandy Patty or Adele and sang so beautifully that people's hearts were touched. Gordy stood beside the Chaplin in the back of the chapel, smiling I'm sure, his beard wet with tears of joy before coming up front to help us pray. He embraced me in a bear hug and whispered in my ear, "Dirk, Dirk, Dirk, you crazy fool."

∾

If you think of me as some kind of a weird, emotionally, unbalanced, weeping prophet, which really isn't a bad thing if that's the case, those days were filled with much laughter and adventures. Jay married a wonderful woman named Lauren, who was also a Bucknell graduate. She was brilliant in a quiet way and seemed to me the perfect counter-balance to Jay's gregariousness and bravado. I enjoyed Lauren's wit and how she laughed at my jokes, her eyes squinting and the way her nose crinkled in such a delightful manner. Cassie and Lauren got along and we were the fearsome foursome; going camping and whitewater rafting and wandering the boardwalk at Ocean City, Maryland where the world's best crab dinner is to be found. There was always music. Jay and I tag-teamed ministering to youth groups and conducted mini-worship seminars around the valley, which is fodder for more stories than time allows. We were on a first-name basis at Dunkin Donuts and regulars at OIP's for pizza. We shared relevant spiritual books with one another the likes of Henri Nouwen and Frederick Buechner, along with classic novels by Gene Stratton-Porter and Graham Greene. It was a bar-b-que at his place or mine, a walk-about on his farm with Malachi, his big, klutzy Newfoundland dog that drooled on my leg, or practicing music and writing songs. I helped him build a treehouse on his property that hung precariously above the creek, but more about that later. Suffice to say; boys will be boys.

# 7

*I* feel compelled to pull back the curtain and disclose some of things I've come to believe along my journey. They say that it's what's inside a person that counts; the subterranean, integral part of our ongoing life story. I know this a bit of a deviation, but beliefs and core values are the engine that motivates and make us who we are, and if I'm trying to write a memoir it's probably expedient for me to do so. I've changed over the years concerning some of my beliefs and will probably continue to change. Experience can sometimes be the best teacher if our eyes and ears are open to learn. It's taken me many times to learn some of my lessons well. I not only think of Mrs. Ludwig in grade-school who was patient and kind, but also Jesus, who was called a teacher in the gospels. Please allow me license to meander.

≈

I've seen some crazy stuff since being a Christian, some of it very entertaining and edifying, other's so appalling it leaves me feeling like jumping off a tall building. One of the things that boggles my mind is how people who've been redeemed, from whatever depths of despair and need they sank, could so quickly forget the mire Christ rescued them from. I'm guilty of it myself at times. Those are the kinds of moments when I look down from the precipice and think about jumping. What makes us falter? What makes us doubt? I think it starts with a loss of being thankful for one, which is a result of paying more attention to me than the Lord. Getting beaten down by fellow believers is another crippling blow to fledgling faith.

Gratitude can grow dim from comfort and familiarity in cozy and safe insulated pews. A kind of lethargy clouds vision when becoming overly-familiar with churchy routine, and questions sneak in the side door that tap us on the shoulder asking the question; "does my faith really matter?" If you're in tune with Christ the answer is yes, your life lived by faith matters more than you think, even if the harmonies may be a bit off key. In spite of failings, and we all do, you are valuable, one of a kind and indispensable in God's plan. We don't receive affirmation often enough, and as you know, a pat on the back goes a very long way. If by chance we give away the morsel of hope we possess, it'd certainly help lift someone whose faith is floundering.

Unfortunately, there are those around us who think they're holier-than-thou (the perfect ones!), that level both barrels to gut shoot at sensitive nerves the Lord may not as yet touched, like it's their job to fix us, like they know better than God. If we aren't wounded enough by our own doubts and shortcomings, getting wounded by a pastor or a brother or sister in Christ adds insult to injury and can suck the life out of us. What could be worse than having self-doubt and being pinned down by judgement from someone else, stuck fast like a butterfly on a matte board? And yet we struggle to rise up, brush off the dust, and venture on as best as we can.

I believe it takes a lifetime of walking one step at a time and hand-in-hand with the Master to begin achieving his likeness, and as a Christian isn't that the goal? It's not about pleasing man but pleasing God. God has infinite patience, more than any man or woman no matter how saintly they profess to be. He is mercifully forbearing and always forgiving our failings and foolishness. We all screw up in small or gigantic ways. I'll assume that you weren't a drug dealer or a serial killer. Maybe the worst thing you did was defiantly refuse to eat your green beans or said a bad word under your breath or told a white lie. Maybe you've lusted for someone during a church service, getting lost in fantasy and not hearing a word of the sermon. Has the F word ever been on the tip of your tongue when it was the most appropriate expression in a moment of total exasperation? Don't beat yourself up for being human. What we need is to be kinder to ourselves, even when we don't get such grace from our peers.

Peers? Let's think about that a bit. Leadership and those setting the example in churches or whatever ministry, may indeed have a calling from God, but sometimes the level of compassion falls short, lacking a connection to relevant human needs. I've witnessed this, and looking back have been guilty myself, wishing I would have been a more caring human being. It's a serious problem when law supersedes grace, and that bothers me, especially when people get wounded by those they trust in positions of leadership. Ridged dogmas can or will circumvent basic kindness and serving another who possesses nothing resembling hope. When it is in our hand to give aid and agenda and profit comes before empathy, we are no different than the Sadducees and Pharisees in Jesus' day. The ability to hear the human cry can so easily get buried under the maxims of Black-and-White; sin being the bottom-line, or non-conformity to doctrine, which is the battle cry of hardcore Evangelicals and self-proclaimed prophets. It's a slippery slope, this peer pressure that lurks in the church, the innuendos to join with the ranks and re-define things like judging morality and exclusivity and playing God.

As a new convert I was naïve and gullible, reaching with hungry hands for whatever was on the table. I cashed in my bell-bottoms and bib over-all's and cut my hair, tossed my rock and roll albums and reinvented myself with leisure suits and white loafers per the prerequisites spoken or unspoken. It was kind of like Dirk became Pat Boone as a guest on the 700 Club. With a King James Bible and a pocket-size blueprint that made my Christian life neat and tidy and so-called user-friendly, I bolted from the gates with new found zeal. Four points to this – six steps to that. Easy-peasey. I bought it all; the image and mindset, the lingo, hook, line and sinker. The church was the potter that molded my values and ideals, which is a very different notion than the prophet Jeremiah had in mind (I'm sure), when he prophesied about the potter and the clay. I was heralded for being what I now call a Christian bully, pushing the message of sin-sin-sin.

We were convinced that you had to conform to the hierarchical system of whatever denomination we were part of, aligning ourselves to be a "true" Christian accordingly and in total agreement to be in fellowship with said group who declares they are right. There are as many religions and doctrines as there are species of birds, and one group thinks they have the monopoly on truth? It's the same with political parties or personal ideologies. I learned to keep in stride as a young believer, sitting under the sermons at my particular church, and deduced that it was important to accept everything in order to *be like us*. I was inexperienced and insecure in my faith and bought the status quo mentalities without many questions, when I did question it seemed too late to make any difference. I must add that my church experience wasn't with the Moonies but mainline Evangelical.

I've come to believe there are more shades of grey in this thing called *The Kingdom of God* than any of us dares to admit. Whenever I sit among stacks of church files in the Lost and Found Department, I reflect on the many ideas that I once embraced; some good, yet others detrimental. Trial and error is revealing. However many years it takes, we're eventually painted into a corner with nowhere to go, the end-game of searching and making mistakes, when the wonderful balm of mercy comes to heal our impetuousness, our thoughtless judgements, even our cruelty to others in misguided zeal. Someone said: "Once saved –

always saved." I think we are being saved every painstaking step we take on this dusty planet. Without the hand of Christ to hold onto, make no mistake my Pharisee-minded friends who adhere to staunch black and whites, you're left fighting needless battles on your own strength. God is not impressed. I'd suggest being a little more open minded about the grey areas and practice the Golden Rule; give mercy to others as you would want mercy given to you. Meaning, of course, making allowances for one another's personal autonomy.

～

I had an ant farm growing up, one of the amazing things my dad bought for me when I was a budding scientist at ten years old. I would sit spellbound for hours studying the glass-walled observatory, watching the colony build roads and a veritable village, kind of like the world we live in with twisted paths and dead ends, seeking survival in an environment of constraints. The ants had their act together, they all got along. As a unified body they were building a sense of community or a country unto themselves in like-mindedness.

By simple observation, I think we have a far different approach to life than the ants. Instead of being a colony in harmony seeking common good, today's social norms in America are fractured and subjective, causing us to live individual, compartmentalized lives, more often than not based on color, politics, religion or demographics. As I reflect on the beliefs so many embrace that our country was founded on, it's not hard to see how far we've fallen from Eden. Would you agree that pride was original sin? I'm not a huge fan of the Puritans (talk about dogma or freedom of religion), and I'm not sure if we were ever a "Christian" nation. Sorry if that make me sound unpatriotic. I do hold to the wisdom in the preamble of the Declaration of Independence. *We hold these truths to be self-evident, that all men are created equal, that they are endowed by their Creator, with certain unalienable Rights, that among these are Life, Liberty, and the pursuit of Happiness.* The basis of belief in God is woven into the ideals that framed the colonies, if you discount religious dogma, burning heretics at the stake and slave owners. It sounds resplendent when we sing *God Bless America*, but I'm a realist. Are we the only nation on the planet that has blessing and privilege bestowed from the Almighty? And why are some more equal than others?

I have to ask a question, what is today's fabric that makes up this grand tapestry called the American Dream? Try these shoes on for size whether you're a Christian or not and see if they don't fit. How about bigotry and anti-Semitism, epidemic homophobia, misogynous leaders in high places, elitism, Wall Street with the top one percent holding economies under their thumb, the blight of keeping up with the Kardashians, rampant hypocrisy and self-centeredness. The poor are still poor, for which there is no excuse, and there's enough stockpiled weaponry to annihilate the entire world and be glorified as the last man standing in keeping our Constitutional 2nd Amendment Right intact, totally sanctioned by one of the biggest lobbyists called the NRA. I don't think my heart can take another school shooting.

It's time to take a deep breath and try to relax; I'm getting worked up. Oh, and don't forget to vote. I've certainly overworked the word hope, but I can only hope for better days, if not in my lifetime at least for future generations.

We presently have a Commander in Chief who signs checks to porn stars and autographs Bibles for the Evangelical Right with the stroke of the same pen, who never goes to church because money and golfing is his god, and boldly lies a hundred times a week. I boggles my mind that the likes of the Falwell's of Liberty University and Franklin Graham endorse him, rallying conservatives who conveniently set the President's morals and character aside. Red States voted in a reality star and that's what we got. He addresses the world reading the teleprompter like a 5th grader; no offense to a 5th grader. We have racial division, religious division, walls and no fly zones. Hatred roars in town squares and on college campuses, in break rooms at the work place, with neighbors and among families. We watch the nightly news between networks arguing about "fake news," a new term to discredit journalism and science and spin the political advantage from one party against the other. Rebel flags come out of nowhere as do Neo-Nazis and white supremacist. Sides are chosen, protesters scream from both sides with teeth bared to devour one another. The new anthem is: Make America Great Again, which seems to have blown up in our faces. To me, it's just a charade more concerned about numbers and ratings than meeting real humanitarian needs and dire issues. Whatever happened to presidential compassion for the world community and having a good rapport with our allies? For all the hoopla and talk, every time we turn on the TV something new flies in our faces, but not a whole lot has changed for the good. Promises were made, but not kept. It's not without reason that we don't trust politicians.

Is my criticism just of another misguided, over-reactionary liberal's observation of the current condition of our secular nation? I'm afraid not. I wish it was different, honest I do. Like a long-timer said to me when I went off from the county jail to court; "...facts is facts. Stick to 'em and don't let no one screw with ya." If I'm not remiss, there are more issues than I can begin to comprehend in the present quagmire of our country. It's no wonder young writers are publishing dystopian and apocalyptic best-sellers that are flying off the shelves. Why not annihilate the planet and start over? Everything seems so toxic. Where in the hell is there any hope?

However, and sadder still, it doesn't end there. Church pews are filled with anarchists spit-shined in their Sunday best, prevalent in every denomination that meets under the cross of a church building in every village, town and city from sea to shining sea. If we're such a Christian nation, why is there such prejudice and hostility?

It's said that Christians aren't perfect – they're just forgiven. What a nice bumper-sticker to solicit forgiveness when you turn down a wrong-way street or a comforting platitude on a Hallmark card, but what a crock! What a sorry excuse. Yes, we all fall short of the grace of God, even in secret. We make mistakes and say ugly and hurtful things to those we love in the heat of a moment. And aren't we sometimes the lawyer or the clergyman who crossed the street to by-pass and ignore the poor and homeless among us, as in Jesus' parable of the Good Samaritan? Correct on the first line of the bumper sticker: we aren't perfect, but what troubles me is why we aren't honest about it and change directions, find a new point on the compass and make a radical shift. Someone once said; "Maturity is growing from being fed to being a feeder; leading instead of being led." My fellow Christian, there has to be more than redundant failing and making excuses and quoting 1st John 1:9. Wouldn't it be better to find some way not to need forgiveness so often and grow and be part of a solution? Maybe we are just dumb sheep. God help us.

Another thing that perplexes me are the multimillion dollar cathedrals and gilded towers built around some mega-ministry with private jets (I'm tempted to name a few), amassing a staggering fortune that could feed and clothe the poor around the globe until kingdom comes. We just sit in our pews and nod our little heads and follow along. Personally, I find the message of these renowned televangelist's nothing more than milk-toast pep talks with the charm of a fortuneteller, coercing money and a loyal following. Tucked in-between the slick preaching and emotional stories is a subtle message of self-servicing. I know that sounds harsh and I'm sorry, but Jesus said to judge them by their fruit.

How many of us have thought or said, "It's not my job. If those heathens would simply repent then I'd... what? Foreigners should go back to where they came from, especially those with brown skin. AIDS is obviously the curse gay people deserve. Poor people should quit begging and get a job." Is it really all so cut and dry? Or could it be because of our so-called moral principles and politics that we believe what we believe and don't give an inch? And why is that attitude in the church? It makes me wonder why there aren't more verses in the Bible than there are to caution us about pride and its consequences. We slug along in routines and a belief system with blinders on according to personal bias, tunneling our vision almost robotically without thinking, looking out for number one. It's appalling.

In the real world we have good days – we have bad days. We suck or we're the King of the Hill. Paying forward is a novel experience in the drive-through at Starbucks when the price of a Grande could feed a family for a month in certain impoverished countries (shithole countries as we've heard lately from the President), but, hey, it feels nice to pay forward. We'll post how wonderful we are on Facebook and keep count of the "likes."

It's the little things that pop up in the trenches colored with shades of grey, those everyday encounters that are most revealing to me. I'm guilty of flipping the middle finger at some idiot who doesn't know how to drive, or at least shoot laser beams from my eyes to fry them to ashes. I've grumbled under my breath at the Hispanic influx in the trades that has caused the merchandise and signs in Home Depot to become bilingual. I tend to get impatient with slow people in the checkout line at Walmart and the grocery. I probably waste a tank of gas a year circling around to find the perfect, convenient spot, my blood-pressure going through the roof because some people don't know how the hell to park. Honestly, I'm embarrassed to be part of this: *all about me - consumer scene* and it makes me want to puke. What in the world do we do with Jesus' words? "In as much as you have done it to the least of these you have done it unto Me."

There, I got that off my chest. Right or wrong I feel empowered. I'm ready to fix a casserole for the charity meal on Saturday night at the Methodist Church or visit the nursing home with flowers and bags of Mini Peppermint Patty's. But where I fail more often than not is when someone stares me in the face at some haphazard moment and I'm too wrapped up in my own issues to see or hear their need, when it's inconvenient. Why am I always in a hurry? Simply put, I say to myself and to you as well, let's all try and do better. Better would be good.

A disclaimer is in order so you don't think I'm all negative and just pointing fingers. There's hope out there, honest to goodness, and it's genuine. I have good friends who are involved in reaching out to families that experienced the tragedy of suicide, Jackie Keck and Lori Geltel, but Kristen Rehak is who I want to brag on. She's bubbly and intuitive and extremely friendly, well respected and connected in Williston, North Dakota where I now live. She lost a sister in the prime of her youth who took her own life. "Out of the Darkness" is an amazing support group that ministers to the complicated and often swept under the carpet private questions of those acquainted with keeping secrets for years, surviving family members holding it together by a shoelace. The support group builds bridges across chasms of pain and sadness with sturdy walkways and safety nets and walk hand-in-hand to assist those dealing with misunderstanding, children having bad dreams, layers of family guilt and shame, offering hope in a heart-felt, personal way to facilitate healing. I mention Kristen because I know her and I've seen her character. She's faithful and genuinely cares, totally the Energizer Bunny. There's not a hint of doing it for notoriety. If tears are treasure, she is rich beyond measure. Kristen joins arms with countless thousands upon thousands of unsung heroes across the land that stand in solidarity with those living under suffocating piles of grief and pain.

I'm profoundly moved by caring pastors, both men and women that I've met, who nurture and have the right blend of humor and wisdom to care for the flock so that no one goes away emptyhanded. They hand-out winter clothing and bags of groceries, not just the standard Band-Aid; "You're in our prayers." Pastor Ross, the Methodist minister in Williston isn't only a friend, but exemplifies that serving is our calling. Volunteers from his church serve a free hot meal on Saturday evenings and holidays to the disenfranchised in town. Joni Eareckson Tada comes to mind, whose life has been confined to a motorized wheelchair (a quadriplegic), as the result of a diving accident when she was young. She has been a beacon of hope to the disabled community for years, touching millions of people with her books and message. And I whine about the damned bar-code not scanning my ice cream in the express lane?

I'm still thinking about the ant farm. There's an alternative dimension in American culture as busy as ants and gives me hope, even though the sense of community is almost something of the past. Today we text and make an appointment after scrutinizing our busy schedule. Who builds large welcoming front porches anymore to accept visitors, other than investing hundreds of dollars to decorate it for the seasons for curb appeal? But there are those in the patchwork of this country, urban and rural, whose lifestyle and heart of compassion is committed to serve 24-7. Maybe they don't have a literal front porch with a two-seater wooden swing, it's more likely they don't, but the welcome mat has your name on it, whatever your color or creed. "Come in, pull up a chair. Would you like a cup of tea?" Thank God for the remarkable remnant that holds us together.

I started this chapter by implying that what we believe is important, that the core of our refined ideals make up the moral fabric of who we are. It's kind of a daydream to think we stand alone and what goes on around us doesn't bleed into our mentality, principles that influenced us since Kindergarten. Let's be honest and rethink what and why we believe such things on a personal level. That's hard to do, as I well realize, for pride rears its ugly head in objection. But could there be more than parroting someone else's words? I think we need to dig deeper than discovering Fool's Gold and unearth the real treasure, find our own wording not based on some expert. If I can be convinced by their message I can just as easily be convinced by another to go a different way. We need to find our own bearings worth making a stand. I'm really trying hard to sift through issues that are important to me and discern what to set aside as nonessentials and find a compassionate approach to accept another's differences and seek common ground. It's a trial, but I think God would want us to try.

I mentioned that I'd seen a lot of crazy stuff these past forty plus years as a Christian and didn't I get off on a tangent? The account of my personal spiritual experience is just as colorful and topsy-turvy, so please bear with me.

And the ants are still happily singing *zippity-do-da-day*.

# 8

*Every* move of God brings with it a mixed bag of reactions, always has – always will. The term: *the move of God* may strike you as strange, but God is not sitting on his laurels chilling out to harp music. The concept denotes that God is doing something in real time besides keeping the universe in balance and on schedule. He's still doing his good pleasure creating a kingdom, not just in heaven but on the earth, and he wants to include his children to join along and be partakers.

I'm not a literalist to believe that the creation story in Genesis was an actual twenty-four day as we know it. I happen to believe that with God a day is likened to a thousand years metaphorically, and he's is still creating. I'm hesitant to call it evolution, but aren't we evolving, adapting and changing as the centuries quickly pass by? I have a sneaking suspicion that God is still up to something, but it's scary to see the potential (or consequences), that mankind may terminate the planet ahead of schedule by irresponsible stewardship before God has to step in.

Amuse yourself and read world and church history as the proverbial Siamese Twins. Both are entertaining, but the carnage may keep you up at night. Many are the stories of tyrants and madmen conquering lands in the name of a religion. But there were also men and women who received a revelation that played an integral part in the grand scheme, a brush stroke on the masterpiece intended to add another layer of color on the divine canvas. It's unfortunate that the message of visionaries and martyrs turned into walls (churches), erected around persons or doctrines and set in stone. This is what I call dogma; majoring on one part, mistakenly taking the timely and fundamental piece of God's current word meant to be a means and not the end to such extremes that has caused divisiveness and even genocide. In my opinion, God is patiently laying stone upon stone to build *His* Church, not man's meager facsimile. He is longsuffering and invested to accomplish his glorious agenda in our present hour. He's counting on our generation to get it done. What an honor is near and at hand; that we can join the ranks of good works done before us and continue building the emerging Kingdom of God. I'm pretty sure that means reaching across the boundaries and joining hands with believers of another name.

As I mentioned, the visible manifestation of God moving in the earth causes a reaction. One rejoices at the message and follows - others gnash their teeth and reject it. The thirsty soul thirsts for more, those who are satisfied with the way things are dig in their heels. Sometimes they throw spears. Personally, I've gotten spiritual whiplash when confronted and vacillated between new thoughts on faith that have challenged me. Those urgings are often uncomfortable with no exit door in sight, calling me to make a change, a paradigm shift in my belief and ideology. I don't like my ever-steady rowboat to be rocked. It's never been easy for me since taking that first huge step outside a laundromat to follow Jesus' footprints. Little did I know then how much change would be a part of the game-plan. I'll offer a piece of advice. When God shows up and gives you the impression that taking a new direction is important, don't to hesitate to hit your knees and pray hard, trust your guts. It's not a bad idea to be open to input from the good people around you and find confirmation. Being a progressive Christian is the adventure of a lifetime. As in a movie about a hero with a captivating plot, don't be afraid to put yourself in the lead role. An ardent seeker will face the danger and challenges, blazing the trail in the hope of finding buried treasure. Don't fret about timidity or inadequacies, God is adapt at changing us, honing and buffing our rough edges, and will continue to do so until this mortal flesh puts on immortality and the Kingdom is revealed in all its glory. We'll get there eventually. But let me bring this down to earth.

When Cassie and I returned from the Jesus Festival in '76 and ran into a brick wall at Crossroads Church, a pathway opened to us in exciting and new ways. Before us was the choice to follow the Spirit or stay where we were, we chose to follow the Spirit. We saw many strange and wonderful things in our travels over the years that you'd never see on a postcard. I observed firsthand that the current move of God in my generation brought out the best and the worst in people, the genuine and the bogus, asinine but hilarious shenanigans some folks did in their naivety and impulsiveness. There was a little bit of craziness going on in the aisle. Even the genuine out-workings of God looked bizarrely strange at times, but I don't mind craziness when it comes to the Lord. His ways are not our ways.

To every true manifestation of the Holy Spirit there's a backdoor open to counter-parts, not necessarily evil, which is a given possibility, but in as much as overly zealous and maybe slightly unbalanced believers (I say that tongue and cheek), acting as if on stage. Perspective and background are inherent within all of us when faced with something different and unusual. My tendency is to get nervous. This is only my observations and experiences and not a thesis on doctrine. I'll try hard not judge or be sarcastic; I merely want to show and tell some of the funny things and the "head-turners" like colorful illustrations in children's storybooks. You'll have to use your imagination and put on your thinking cap.

~

I've visited many church services over the years, most of them in an actual "church" building with their label on a marque or cornerstone, as well as others meeting in school auditoriums or a downtown warehouse. Cassie and I attended conferences in hotels and convention centers, sat in tent meetings with hard packed dirt under our feet, city churches, country churches, even a few living rooms and community parks. The verse goes; "...and wherever two or more are gathered in my name, so I will be in their midst." Thanks, Jesus. We're counting on you.

One of the more bizarre experiences I've had with certain brands of believers is one with the premise that when the Holy Ghost comes upon you, you speak in tongues. There is biblical support for the true gift of tongues, but you'll have to Goggle that for yourself. On an interesting side note, check out a search of Azusa Street where Pentecostalism in America began in 1906, it is fascinating. Cassie was a real tongue-talker and even sang in her new flowery language. I stuck my toe in the water, hesitant and cautious to say the least.

I've heard babblings rise in countless congregation on the waves of instrumental worship music that sounded lovely. There was also squawking, Middle Eastern intonations, wahoo-woo-woo gibberish and Pig-Latin. At a service I happened to visit, a man was yowling, "Shaw-Shaw-Shaw." I remember turning around to see if he was calling to a man named Shaw standing in the back and thought he was off his rocker. I heard utterances in a string of tongues that sounded as though someone was reading out loud to the class and another would follow with an interpretation in English, sometimes following the cadence to a T. Two gifts in one, like peanut butter and chocolate. Of course, there's always the other guy. Imagine a so-called Apostle laying hands on people to receive the Holy Ghost, coaching the seeker to repeat after him. "See my bowtie – tie my bowtie. Tie my bowtie – see my bowtie." If you repeated it real fast and ran the words together it kind of sounds like an oriental phrase, right? I've heard some real tongue-twisters in my time but that made me scratch my head. If the Holy Ghost wants someone to talk in tongues, I don't think it happens by being scripted at the hands of a short man wearing a bowtie working you like a puppet. I tried the tongue thing but I'm not really sure if was real or not. I didn't major on it. If I couldn't articulate my own words during prayer or worship, I figured that God knew my thoughts and kept to the English language.

We attended a Christian event in New Jersey at the Meadowland Stadium where I heard so many different dialects in tongues that it made me wonder if I was at the United Nations. Thousands of believers from all around the country gathered to worship together; Episcopalians, Presbyterian, Church of Christ, Catholics, virtually every denomination and non-denominational people were represented. Labels were left at home or in the parking lot. The weather threatened to drench us. Severe storms were reported countywide and the stadium was dead center on the radar map. The sky was dark and ominous all morning but we were spared, not a drop of rain fell. One of the speakers, Father Michael Scanlon, called us to unify in worship and raise our hands to heaven and pray for a breakthrough. It was overwhelming to be in the midst and join my voice with the throng. I was standing halfway up in the stands with my hands raised along with everyone else. In a way it reminded me of doing the "wave" in a stadium of NY Giant fans. I began feeling warmth inside my body like a fever was brewing or I was overdressed. My face felt hot. I opened my eyes and I nearly fell to my knees in awe. The dark clouds that shrouded us all day opened over the stadium and sunlight poured down upon us as if God was saying, "You bring me pleasure." I know it sounds melodramatic, but it happened.

At a time in my Christian sojourn it was wrong to dance. It was one of the twenty odd requirements for membership at Crossroads Church. NO DANCING. Apparently dancing was lewd and led to fornicating. Going to movies was another no-no. But in many worship services I've since visited, dancing was something I sort of came to expect. Being among fellow worshippers it wasn't unusual that folks raised their hands and maybe swayed or rocked back and forth in rhythm, but is there a limit as to how far such rhythm is allowed?

It doesn't take a long investigative search in the scriptures to discover that dancing is natural and common in modes of worship. If this is something new or perhaps odd to you, again, do a search of "dancing" or "dance" in a bible concordance, pay special attention to the Psalms. Dancing seemed to be okay with God.

In my experience, it's really kind of comical, for whether you're in a pew or folding chairs there generally isn't a lot of real estate to boogie. What people did was a sort of bunny-hop, bouncing on one foot, then the other with a little kick, staying in their 2x2 square foot of space. To me, it appeared that folks over-compensated the lack of room with energy, like they had way too much caffeine. It was an acceptable way to dance, or maybe the expected way to dance, the Christian version of the Charleston. Fashionably dressed women and gentlemen in Brooks Brother suits, scruffy dudes in tie-dyed T shirts, kids and everyday folks like you and me would bust a move along with the fast songs. Sometimes people would join hands and lead a train of worshippers dancing around the perimeter of the church like at a wedding reception. I learned not to stand too close to an open aisle. They've been known to grab your hand and drag you along. If you're nervous to jump right in, try it at home. Put in a CD or tell Siri to play some praise music and dance around your living room or out back, be free and worship God in private however it moves you. Personally, I think God gets greater pleasure with our worship when it's done in secret anyway. I dance around my house with the music turned up when a song hits me. I'm rusty as hell but it's good to move and flex and give expression to the moment.

I think it's spiritually as well as physically healthy to let loose. For the record, I prefer to dance at weddings or an occasional club rather than at church where I have elbow room and no one is going to judge me for dancing like Young Frankenstein putting on the Ritz.

A word about worship services if you'll allow me. Worship is old as eternity, as in the angels worshipping the Creator day and night singing, "Holy-Holy-Holy." It seems to be something inherent in the chemistry of redeemed mankind as well. Centuries ago after an arduous forty year journey though the wasteland, the survivors of Egypt's captivity camped and sang and danced at the Jordon River, praising Yahweh for deliverance while standing at the brink of the Promise Land. The Psalms tell us that David sang in the night while tending sheep, bearing a spear or slingshot in one hand and a lute or harp in the other. He wrote and sang beautiful lyrics which are in part what we still practice today. I can picture King David dancing around the sheepfold, smacking them on the butt and cajoling them to skip along.

Worship has drastically changed (evolved), since ancient times. From drumming on a hollow log to flutes made of hollowed reeds, composers blended instruments in magnificent symphonies and writers penned lyrics that became the majestic hymns we know today. They were revolutionary, with great verses the likes of *Crown Him with many Crowns* or *All Hail the Power*, but today they're neatly stacked in the back of pews and seem… outdated? We had mimeographed songbooks back in the days of Lamb Fellowship and got by because we sang the songs enough to become familiar and loved them. They connected us to God. Across the Christian spectrum the overhead projectors got bigger and in time became elaborate with graphic art and surround-sound like going to IMAX. Worship became a production, a performance, practiced and scripted. I'm not particularly a fan of it, I feel like it's impersonal. I happen to enjoy Christian contemporary music, but I'd rather play it when driving in the truck or while cleaning the house. Maybe I'm just getting old. I miss the simplicity. It seemed more real back then, worshipping from our hearts and not getting caught up in a stage show.

A deeper concern of mine is the message in what is now called worship music. My take on it is that much of the content seems very self-centered. "Heal me, lift me, forgive me, help me... I need grace... and Lord, you gracious." It's not hard to hear an orientation of I-I-I and me-me-me. Maybe Joann had the right idea calling the Savoir *I Am*. I am the life. I am the way. I am love. I am God, the approachable being of holiness. Okay; we are needy and we certainly need grace, but repetition (which many of the lyrics include), of anything drummed over and over tends to foster mentalities. If "Needy Ned and Nelly" are continually pandered to with a weak and feels good message with a retinue of fellow believers embracing emotional needs, how can they grow in faith? I'm confused. Isn't the idea to: "Rise up oh men of God and be done with lesser things," like an old hymn says? Isn't the purpose of cooperate worship to celebrate the Lord's glory? I love the idea of entering his gates with praise, exalting his Name with thanksgiving for what he has done. But have we evolved to such a place that our identity more conforms to secular entertainment or therapy (where's the mosh pit or Kleenex box?), and not the reverent hush of entering into the Holy of Holies and the joyful climax of being in God's presence? When we encounter the Living God, focusing on him alone, we may be healed and feel good, but regardless, our call is to praise God in all things whether we feel good or not. Is he not worthy? I'm no expert to criticize anyone's preference, but worship works better for me when I lift up my eyes to the Throne and get them off myself.

~

God is known to make cameo appearances and check in to see how his Church is doing. He seems to trust people to be his voice and his hands which seems to me like pretty risky business. One of the ways God visits with us is through prophetic ministry, not so much a "Prophet" per se, although I believe there are prophets in the world today, but through anyone willing to speak in his name in the first person. It's another spiritual gift listed in 1 Corinthians that you may be familiar with or not, but I'm sure you've heard the section read at weddings where Paul says, "If I speak in the tongues of men and angels and have not love, I am only a resounding gong... Love is patient, love is kind, love never fails." Prophecy falls in the same criteria in the proceeding verses. To speak in God's name the motivation *has* to issue forth from love and flow through the conduit of a humble servant. Even if it's a hard word, a word of correction or rebuke (prophecy is a two-edged sword), the word of God comes to us with mercy and grace. Go back and read between the lines in the Old Testament and see if the prophets didn't indeed weep as they pronounced judgement. We're encouraged to seek the gift of prophecy, for it strengthens, comforts and builds up faith in the community of believers.

The counter-part resembles the daily horoscope. Facebook prophets are a dime a dozen and come in many colors and flavors with the word for the day, promising peace via an inspirational YouTube video with a surreal backset and we naively click on "like" and "follow." We're drawn with expectation but disappointed fifteen minutes later when a credit card is needed for the miracle. Websites are easily accessed, ask Goggle any question concerning spirituality and the list of answers from A to Z pop up by the zillions. Charlatans and scammers and predators keep a keen eye for weakness to cash in. Are we so desperate to check out rogue sites for financial and marital advice or find serious answers to life's questions on Social Media? I've almost come to the point of drawing a line through Social Media altogether; it tends to raise my blood pressure.

Meanwhile, back in the church where the soil of prophecy is sown and tilled, there are those who are genuine. A check and balance in scriptures called discerning of spirits helps to keep things honest, something we'd do well to grow in. I'd get a terrible headache trying to explain it, but I have an ear to hear what God is saying. I hope I haven't been delusional or naively mistaken to think that God is still speaking and that I've heard at least a fragment of what was on his mind. There's a verse that encourages us to hear if we have an ear to hear, which implies that God is indeed saying something we'd do well by paying attention to. I also hope I haven't become too cynical about the inane things some people have prophesied in the Lord's name and entirely discredit the real deal, as I'm given to suspicion. Personally, I've been healed, blessed and guided by prophetic men and women that were intuitive to God's heart, those who spoke with integrity. I think I've been a blessing as well, even in an unconventional way.

I remember a time when a woman was standing in a prayer line at Agape Fellowship, probably hoping God would touch her to feel better about something. She was a beautiful woman, almost Sophia Loren-like, but she looked a wreck. She had dark circles under her eyes and physically trembled like she was left out in the cold. I had an overwhelming sense of compassion for the woman and eased out of my seat to join those who responded to come forward and stood behind her. I've mentioned that I sometimes see pictures in my minds-eye, and so it was as I prayed for her.

I envisioned her taking down laundry from a clothesline on a sunny summer day and saw an open meadow behind her. She was gathering up the sheets and held them to her face. I imagined she was breathing in the freshness of the linens, intoxicated by the fragrance. She had a dreamy look as if remembering some distant memory. Then, I saw her as a little playful girl helping her mommy and making a game with the clothes pins. In the next frame, the child carried one side of a big wicker basket with her mother on the other handle as they headed to the house. It was such a sweet scene to behold. I felt a chill when a dark cloud rolled in and the scene dimmed into shadow. My heart literally sank. I'm not sure how, but I knew in that moment this woman had lost her mother in some kind of unexpected death. What do you do with something like that? If I began sharing my vision (prophetic word), and was wrong, my words would more than confuse her, they may do damage. I envisioned those behind me; "Take that false prophet outside and choose ye good stones."

Whenever the thrumming intensifies and I become more certain that what I'm seeing or hearing is right and true and this moment has been prearranged, my approach is to stick my toe in the water before jumping right in. The way that so many "prophets" operate is to declare, "Thus saith the Lord," but I have always been more conversational. I went to the woman before anyone else had the chance, greeted her with a smile, and asked what she wanted Jesus to do for her. She had a mild breakdown and couldn't readily speak. Perhaps it was something she heard in the sermon or maybe the wording of my question that took her off guard. I told her to take her time and let her cry a while. When it seemed appropriate, I began speaking about what I'd seen, the meadow and sheets billowing on a clothesline on a summer day. Her reaction revealed something deep inside was touched and she implored me with a curious look to continue. I balked at taking the big leap, but felt I had no choice. I told her that I was truly sorry if I was mistaken and asked her if her mother had passed away when she was a child. The woman's eyes grew huge in shock or wonder and began filling with tears. "How did I know?" she asked. I said it was because Jesus showed me a picture of her childhood and I asked her if the clothesline or any of it made sense.

She told me that she'd grown up in the country out on Northway Road and they had horses, adding that her mother died of a rare blood disease. She was seven at the time, when on a hot August afternoon her mother collapsed in the backyard while carrying laundry and was taken to the hospital but never came back home. The woman told me she was a mother with a six year old daughter named Pammy and expressed having anxiety issues, never wanting to leave her daughter alone, ever. She worried that she may have some genetic blood disease unbeknown to her.

I reassured the woman that God was also a mother, our Mother in heaven, hallowed be her name. Mother-God understood her grief and wanted to heal the deep places, although she'd never actually forget the sorrow or escape the memory of her mother's death. God wanted to be her shoulder to cry on, her comfort and solace. PS, I added, Pammy was never out of God's sight.

I wish I would have gotten her name and an address, for the experience was one neither of us will forget. The woman hugged me goodbye, thanking me, and said she felt a fresh breeze heal her soul as I prayed for her. I learned to trust my instincts. You don't have to be called a "Prophet" to declare, *thus saith the Lord.* Perhaps prophecy is more about reaching out a guiding hand in the name of the Lord, revelatory and full of promise. I urge you, please, for Jesus sake, be careful about putting the label on a business card. You don't have to grandstand and declare *thus saith the Lord*, you just have to be available and willing to appear a bit foolish.

~

I had one of my annual hissy-fits on a Saturday at the grocery store. Cassie and I had been arguing all morning about something and I was royally pissed that I recall. She went in to do the shopping while I stayed in the car, stewing with the radio on. A Steve Winwood song came on and it made me turn the volume up. *"When you see a chance, take it..."* So I did. On impulse, I abandoned Cassie in the store pushing her grocery cart around, no doubt replaying our less than wonderful discussion, and took off for my old hometown. I stopped at a liquor store on the way. I suppose it was better than murdering my wife.

What is so painful and poignant about that episode was the look on her face when I returned home well after midnight, staggering drunk, humble and apologetic. She had to call a friend to come get her at the grocery store and take her home, which was embarrassing, and because of our standing within our circle of friends, I inadvertently caused her to lie. Cassie made up some kind of excuse to save me from ridicule.

The scene at J&R's Tavern on Broad Street wasn't really all that I'd hoped it to be, although I'm not sure what drew me there in the first place. I got pretty tuned up, not having to buy a drink as the long-lost homeboy returned from a foreign country so to speak. I drank countless drinks of Bacardi and Coke and could carry on intelligent conversations with fellow drunken geniuses after we smoked a blunt in the parking lot. Sometime throughout the night, I witnessed the Lord to an old acquaintance who was sitting on a barstool beside me. My reputation of being a Jesus-Freak preceded me and made getting reacquainted rather interesting. Shoopy (Billy Shoup), was a classmate going through the first stage of prostate cancer. No matter how inebriated I was, I must have thought he needed Jesus, and can only hope and pray something was communicated between us that made any sense. Many years later, I saw on Facebook that Shoopy made the "Deceased" list of classmates who've passed since graduation day in '73. My abrupt disconnect with fellow high school classmates is something I regret. I'd forgotten some of the faces, but many names on the list registered and surprised me. It made me wonder why I wasn't included. I hope Shoopy found his peace with God.

The next evening, Cassie and I went to "City Church" in downtown Williamsport for special services. The congregation of two hundred or so was an interesting marinade of young people and seniors, families, professionals and street people, great musicians, and yes, they liked to dance in the aisles. They were a fun bunch and normally I would have felt at home with them, but my tail was between my legs. Pastor Dan was a friend of mine, as was Wyatt, the worship leader. It was Gordy's home church and there was no escaping him or Diann. Because of my drunken episode the night before and hiding a guilty conscience, I tried in vain to avoid them. I had to attend the service to keep peace with Cassie; there was no arguing or making lite of it. I had never seen her so mad before. After sleeping it off for nearly the whole day, we went to the meeting against my better wishes.

The sign outside "City Church" blinked in yellow lights: *Come and receive your miracle.* A guest speaker was noted but I forget the man's name. He was from Colombia and billed as an apostle: *Healing Ministry.* It was sure to be a full house and I hoped to sit in the back, which didn't happen. Wyatt's wife, Gail was a dear friend and grabbed Cassie by the elbow and guided us close to the front where she saved seats.

The service was long, as in sit through excruciating butt pain and hold your bladder. Perhaps folks from third world countries are accustomed, but this guy was pushing my limit of patience. He ended his preaching and began pointing and calling out this one and that to come forward for prayer. He seemed to read people in a generic sense, naming diseases and maladies, proposing healing and miracles. He had a way about doing it that made me inwardly chuckle. The Apostle had a pronounced lisp when he got excited. Anyway, I was pointed to and bid to come to the front along with dozens of others. Of course, I didn't need to, but I went. Nobody knew other than Cassie that I was well over the legal limit the night before and drove home from the bar with one eye closed to stay between the lines. I hoped the Apostle wasn't the wiser.

As it happened, I was far down the prayer line with my hands in my pockets, nervously wondering why I was called out. I was healthy as an ox, other than being slightly hungover and parched, wondering if there was a drinking fountain somewhere in the lobby I could sneak off to. It wasn't healing of some grave physical need that prompted him to point me out, but we had a moment when our eyes caught. Sweat trickled down my back as I watched him come down the line in my direction. Everyone the man laid hands on toppled backwards, being gently assisted to the floor by "catchers" so they didn't knock their brains loose. Not one person remained upright as he prophesied and proclaimed their healing; they went down like dominoes. It's a phenomenon called being "slain in the Spirit," kind of like being blown over by gale force winds or round-housed by Mike Tyson. I don't want to be critical, but everyone? Doesn't that make you wonder? It did me. Every so often he'd ask for the person's name before praying for them and I made up my mind to answer should he ask me I'd say; "Puddin Tane. Ask me again and I'll tell you same." Okay, so I did prejudge him.

When he stood before me we sort of sized each other up in the briefest of seconds, eye ball to eye ball. He was a short man with a rotund body stuffed into a suit too small, slicked back greasy black hair over a moon face and that crazy Spanish lisp, dabbing at the corners of his mouth with a handkerchief. He planted a hand on my forehead with enough force to knock me back. So, that's the magicians trick. Push them over in the Name of the Lord. He began; "Thus saith the Lord." It sounded like the old cartoon character, Snagglepuss and I felt spittle on my face along with an insistent pressure to yield and fall backwards. "Look unto the hills from whence cometh thy help," he sucked in a wet throaty breath and continued. "And, boy, do you need help!" Folks in the congregation snickered or called; "Yes Lord. Amen." He went on, "The Lord is Thy rock, stand ye upon it... and don't look back."

That was it, he had nothing more to add or embellish upon as he did with the others. I felt sure he wanted to make sport of me and was irritated because he couldn't push me down. It seemed to me that he judged his success by how many people laid flat on the floor. But, you know what? It wasn't a joke. God called me out through that crazy Colombian apostle with a lisp. The cutting word was; *"don't look back."* It echoed on full volume in my thick witted brain still recovering from a hangover. I believe he saw my need. I surely needed help. The Apostle moved on down the line. I didn't fall down under the suggestive power he allegedly wielded, but it freaked me out that God took such a personal interest in me regardless of my blunder in the last twenty four hours.

I walked down the center aisle and wiggled my way along the pew like in a movie theater to sit beside Cassie. She gave me a wide-eyed comic look and held a hand over her mouth to contain giggling like she'd just heard the funniest joke ever told.

Let's hopscotch to another experience that I've had. You still have your thinking cap on, right?

There's this thing called the deliverance ministry that I epitomize like poking at a rattlesnake or taunting a crocodile with a short stick. I avoid it. I don't understand it nor do I care to. All I know is that the devil doesn't like me and I sure as hell don't like him. Frankly, I think the devil gets more credit than he deserves when it's usually us who are the guilty party. Reluctantly, I succumb to the doctrine and possibility there is such a thing as demon possession. The notion that some Christians have about being assigned a person imp, a lowlife demon to pester and tempt them seems foolish to me. "The devil made me do it." Really? Give me a flyswatter if that's the case.

I read the *Exorcist* in county jail years ago under one beam of flood light that penetrated my cell, long before the movie versions and all the hoopla. It gave me nightmares. There are rows upon rows of fictional books at Barnes and Noble cashing in on the demoniac genre that are popular and sell like hotcakes among whatever readers enjoys them. I'm not one. *Demon Spawn*, *Rosemary's Baby*, *Carrie* and so on with tantalizing covers is the section I by-pass.

I've mentioned somewhere along the line my innate qualms with the dark-side, things devilish with potential powers worse than a nightmare or a bad acid trip. I'm a very visual kind of guy and probably guilty of having an overly-imaginative mind. I find myself standing before the door of the Lost and Found Department, which seems surreal and haunting all of a sudden, and I'm drawn inside. The scenes of a reoccurring dream I had in grade school makes shivers go up my spine.

My brother and I shared a small bedroom on the first floor, each of us had a single bed and dresser where mom made sure our undies and shirts were folded, a desk and a window view. I think I was around six or seven years old at the time, gauging by the faded date labeled on a box of bad dreams tucked on the back shelf. It was just a kid's nightmare, but I'll never forget how terrified I felt.

It was wintertime and my window was clouded over in starry frozen moisture that I could scratch my name on. I was in a deep sleep, dreaming like I often do in Technicolor. In my dream, I heard sirens far off in the distance and it troubled me, not knowing for certain if it was real or not. The noise came closer as in block by block, a whooping, whiny, ringing unlike any police car or ambulance I knew of, growing louder. I envisioned the Blitz in London during the Second World War with alarms blaring a dire warning like I saw on TV. My heart raced, and then the sirens suddenly stopped. Although it was a dream, I recall rising from bed and standing at my bedroom window, huffing a blast of warm air and scratching a peephole. I was terrified by what I saw. An army of skeletons was marching down Bennett Street in rank, shadowy figures under the street lights, stomping with hard footsteps on the frozen pavement. The leader wore a helmet with pointy horns and swung a sickle. He raised a trumpet between snarling and taunting that I felt were directed at me and withheld blowing a note, looking me dead in the eyes. I was under his gaze like being under a spell, trapped and frozen in place. I wanted to run for the backdoor, but that meant taking the shortcut through Susy's bedroom, a quiet place I tried to avoid. There was no way I was going to escape through the living room or charge through the kitchen screen door. I debated about jumping out of my brother's window and make a break for the neighbor's arborvitae bushes next to the sandbox, but I was too frightened to move a muscle, holding my breath and trying to be invisible. When I saw a bony hand on the windowsill I awoke with a shout stuck in my throat. Sparky rolled over to look at me, but deep sleep had him down for the count. I wanted to warn him that the bad man was coming, but didn't or couldn't. I felt ashamed that my brother might be taken hostage if I did nothing to help him. I came to, alert and shivering as if chilled to the bone, standing in my PJ's in the middle of the bedroom.

As a grown man (and I realize it's childish), I still don't have the nerve to check under the bed when that kind of terror constricts my chest in the middle of the night. Getting out of bed to check a closet is out of the question. I always pray it will just go away or try to ignore it, rarely confronting such debilitating fear. Sirens still raise the hair on the back of my neck every so often. Since that night as a kid, I've hated the devil.

The coffeehouse days came to the end of its season after three and a half wonderful years. It was bitter-sweet to be closing the doors of *House Upon the Rock*, but it was time to move on. A friend named Tommy, who is fun and out-going, not to mention overly animated, came bursting in our backdoor one evening in a panic. He said that he'd offered a ride to a young woman who was drunk and was strapped in a seatbelt in his car, adding that she was possessed. Tommy said they'd driven around town for hours and listened to her go on and on in mindless gibberish, ranting or crying, sometimes incoherent. A lot of: *why-why-whys*. Coming to an impasse, he rounded up a handful of friends from Lamb Fellowship to help minister to her and clarify things. They didn't know where else to take her after there was no noticeable change after interceding and waging spiritual warfare. The sun was due to set and getting this woman to a safe place was expedient. The coffeehouse seemed their best option. Great. This wasn't my forte.

"Take her to Dale's house," I told Tommy, not entirely pleased to hear his report. "He's the devil-chaser, not me." Immediately I was on edge.

We had company and Cassie was soon putting supper on the table. Ron and Joy were homeschoolers, meek and mild with three kids. It was spaghetti and meatballs and we'd play UNO or Scrabble later. I humored Tommy and went to check things out. It didn't matter that the coffeehouse was no longer open, we had to care and reach out to anyone who came upon us, but if this person was truly possessed, I wasn't sure if it'd be a smart idea to bring her upstairs. What if after we fed her she started vomiting marinara sauce all over the place spinning her head in circles?

Ginger was her name, and she was slurred of speech and restrained in a seatbelt, slumped over and tangled up in the straps of a shoulder bag that may have been a mother's baby bag. I wondered if she was withdrawing from drugs. She looked panicky and on high alert. Ginger resembled Battleship Rita, stout and thick, a redhead, and appeared to be strong enough to compete in the women's boxing league. What arrested me were her wild green eyes. I introduced myself and tried to sound calm and reassuring, climbing into the backseat.

I answer to Dirk when my name is called, sometimes shortened to DK. When Tommy jolted me from my preoccupation by repeating my name louder, I leaned forward and gave him my full attention. I was miles away in my mind, spooked and wondering why I was there. He'd been filling me in on the previous hours spent with Ginger, about the struggle, the bizarre and crazy things he witnessed. He said that Kevin Messer, a fellow believer from Lamb who knew some Latin, heard Ginger curse and mock God in that ancient language.

"Dirk, I just wanted to give her a ride and it kind of exploded, what else could we do? This is like something out of a movie."

"We?" I said. "Shit, Tommy, you're the one who picked her up. She speaks Latin?"

I didn't see the situation remotely resembling a movie; real life is not a make-believe script to roll-play. We had a very troubled woman on our hands who was obviously ready to implode. Ginger shifted gears from being quiet and became aggressive, boisterous, cursing, off on a rant. She was angry, stressed out and under an avalanche of chaos. Was she crying out for help or desperate for attention? Was Ginger possessed? I sat in the backseat unsure what to think. Tommy drove us to the railroad bridge.

As soon as Tommy put the gearshift into park, Ginger thrashed and flailed out of the seatbelt and ran for the river. We interceded and rescued her from what we thought was apparent catastrophe. Tommy tackled her, both of them ending up on their butts at the river's edge. Ginger started hollering at the top of her lungs, groveling, cursing and spitting at Tommy, totally out of control. "Let me go! I gotta get out of here!" Her alleged demon was bold but began weakening. Ginger seemed to shrink into herself, somewhat confused.

When the evening began, I'd questioned whether she was demon possessed or a drama queen over-reacting, but I didn't know exactly what to make of what I was witnessing. She was off the rails and kind of freaked me out. Tommy had been with her from the beginning and was convinced she was demon possessed. I didn't see what he had seen. He cranked up the volume and did the; *Satan, I cast you out routine.* Ginger gave him a look and said in a rather flat voice, "Are you fucking kidding me?"

After I calmed everyone down, Tommy and I helped Ginger up the grassy bank back to the car. She had an infant daughter being taken care of by a babysitter and had to get back to her aunt's house. Ginger wasn't possessed, at least in that moment, but she had definitely been tormented by something. She became approachable and civil, just as normal as my sister. Cassie's evaluation after spending some time with Ginger was that she was suffering from postpartum and hit the skids with all that insane fight or flight reaction. Getting drunk only exacerbated the madness already troubling her mind. We picked her infant daughter up at the babysitters and Tommy took us back to my place. For some reason, Ginger didn't want to stay at her auntie's. We still had a room and bedding and I made the offer for a meal and a good night sleep.

Ginger was compliant, sobered and much more settled, even amiable and said, "Why not? Thanks, I'll give it a try." She carried her baby in a bundle up the long back stairs. Her jeans were dirty and grass-stained, she had dried tracks of tears on her face; Ginger was frazzled, exhausted and hungry. We traipsed in the door looking a bit sheepish. Cassie gave me a sideways glance and smiled, rising to greet Ginger. Ron and Joy, and especially their kids, didn't know what to make of it at first. The last they knew I was running off with Tommy to see about a demon possessed woman and here she was looking the worse for wear, invited to sit down at the dining table. Joy spoke to the children in an unruffled voice as best as she could manage, calming them from the sudden calamity and fears and reassured them that Jesus heals the brokenhearted. "It's what Dirk and Cassie do," she said. "If you only love those who love you, what credit is that?"

The rest of the evening was lively and almost magical. Ron and Joy's kids took to Ginger's baby with tender aplomb, making funny faces and getting little coo's and charming baby smiles in return. We all sat down and had warmed up spaghetti and meatballs and lemon meringue pie. Ginger played a few rounds of UNO after the baby was asleep. We put her in Lewie's old room, close to the bathroom. Ginger ended up staying with us until we moved. Her demons were left behind, tossed aside like a nightmare floating down the Susquehanna River under the railroad bridge. It was love and acceptance from the folks at church that was Ginger's deliverance, and a lot of counseling. I'll let the professionals deal with real demonic cases.

# 9

*Cassie* and I had many close "couple" friends. They were young and still on a honeymoon or married for 20 years or about to get married, an occasional serious boyfriend and girlfriend relationship. Jay and Lauren Gordon, Randy and Louellen Welsch, Matt and Beth Madden, Bob and Jill Thomas, Rusty and Janet Thompson, Molly and Elvin Stoltzfus, all of whom sparkle and make me smile along with so many others who've graced my life. You wouldn't know or appreciate them as I do. Each one would deserve chapters to begin telling their stories. They saw something inside me worth loving and getting close to, of which I am grateful for. None us were perfect, perhaps I was the less perfect one in the bunch. These where my friends, the ones who stuck by me as I have them, believing in one another.

Here is my predicament, which has been a damnable curse as long as I can remember. "Be the best - give 100%" my father would preach. It's a noble goal to shoot for. I heard the same line from many other peers who sometimes were a bit pushy. I don't know why I do it, but I'm my own worse judge. My friends didn't put this trip on my head, it's the way my mind works. I made mention of the Pharisees in Jesus' day with an axe to grind about judgement. If there's a detention hall in heaven it's probably where you'd find me. They judged by the letter of the law, scrutinizing every utterance and innuendo. Maybe I've already done the job for them. I see myself as both the perpetrator breaking the law and pleading for mercy, as well as the judge with a gavel raised to condemn and pronounce the sentence. Conviction enters, questions arise, and my lack of purity (100%), plagues me. My friends got a sneak peek at my actual batting average and were most gracious. Why can't I be a little more kind to myself? I'm so quick to offer grace to anyone else. Perhaps I should have embraced Buddhism; their belief system seems kinder than Evangelicals.

I've worried myself sick with a zillion questions. It stymies me sometimes to calculate the simple things; the square footage of 7'x12' for flooring or what an adverb is, countless times asking myself where in the hell I put the truck keys. I truly worry about how many brain cells I fried in the crazy LSD days. Profound questions blind-side me, bringing a hefty serving of humble pie and conviction without warning labels. "Here, take one of these along with your daily multiple vitamins." Correction has always been a bitter pill for me to swallow. If there is a town somewhere on the planet called *Perfection*, I could not have my mail sent there. Imagine someone asking you where you lived. "Oh, thanks for asking, I live in Perfection." Ha! Right.

I want to be honest in this narrative and I know it sounds like I never do anything right, but I've been right occasionally, hopefully more often than wrong. Still, there are times when heart issues float to the top, as in during my meditation-time whenever I'm quiet enough in my soul to hear the still, small voice, or when a word captivates me from scripture or lyrics of a song, and suddenly, guilt is in the skillet sizzling like bacon in hot grease. I shrivel and curl up and spit and call out a simple plea; "Where are you Lord?" I think that I've always struggled with questions about my faith. Faith has a tendency to take one beyond the familiar and comfortable to another place if acted upon, which sometimes seems elusive and kind of hard to adjust to. The everyday lunch table can become a holy sanctuary, a hike in the woods suddenly transcendent. Even local theater can be potentially dangerous when Shakespeare arrests me.

I have a friend who's had lead roles and can quote long passages from memory of various plays he's been in. Mack is theatrical both on and off stage, entertaining me on the road going to work whenever I need his help or just hanging out. There's never a dull moment. Take for example this quote from King Lear. *"Poor naked wretches, wheresoe'er you are?"* Ponder that a moment. Poor? Naked? Wretched? I fall in one or all of those categories at times when interfacing with my own life, often convicted yet again by not measuring up to 100%. For me, it's been friends who have not only shared timely answers but have been the answer. When my prayers fell short and didn't avail much, or God didn't do something when I thought he should or didn't do anything at all, it has been the caring hearts and hands of friends who have propped and held me up. And along came Howard and Terry Peace who were another strong link in the ongoing chain of priceless friends.

Howard and Terry were transplants from NYC to Lewisburg and grafted in with us quickly, growing like a fruitful vine, blessing me and so many others. They discovered Lamb Fellowship, now renamed New Covenant Church, and found their niche.

After a foundation was laid and we'd out grown Rooke Chapel, we purchased a brick structure that had once been a Presbyterian Church and set down roots in the community as an "official" church, no longer that questionable fringe group at the college. We yanked out the pews and sold them at a discount to some church in the valley, reconfigured the sanctuary with folding chairs and constructed a raised platform for speakers and the worship team. The only adornment was a large hand-hewn cross that hung on the gable end. The basement was previously used for children's church and social activities and was very accommodating. We began meeting on Sunday mornings like the rest of the respectable churches in town, but not to worry. No one wore leisure suits or ties or skirts and head coverings. You could come as you are; jeans, cargo shorts, flip flops, a go-cup of Dunkin Donut coffee in hand.

Howard was a little older than me, a scholarly and prophetic man, soft spoken and quick with witty one-liners. He was a gifted musician and played guitar. When Howard was in college he played with a band and wrote songs. The pictures he shared of those days made him look a bit like Jim Croce. Howard would teach or exhort us at times and always drew me in with intrigue to pay attention to his insight. At the time, he was in some kind of bank securities before "Identity Fraud" was a buzz word. Howard and his wife, Terry (Da New Yawker), had a son in grade school that enjoyed playing games. I called him *Evan Picone the Parcheesi Champion*. He's now happily married with a newborn son that gives me great pleasure. We spent countless hours lounging on the living room carpet or folding chairs on the deck, carefree and energizing times sharing stories and spiritual experiences. Howard got wind of a worship conference in Johnson City, Tennessee and thought we should go.

The event was held at a large church called *Shekinah Ministries*, which translated from Hebrew means the dwelling place or divine presence of God and denotes radiant glory. It was an international conference and a venue I'd never experienced before. Thank you, Howard for dragging me along. Shekinah glory poured upon me.

The pastor and emcee of the conference was a very articulate and strong woman, mature not only in years but in the Spirit. During one of the evening worship services she tactfully broke in on a rousing song and encouraged those who were present from countries around the globe to retrieve their nation's flag (along the wall behind the stage were a hundred colorful flags), and parade around the interior of the sanctuary as Joshua had around the walls of Jericho. It was a triumphant celebration. I took notice of a rather tall, black man who proudly carried his flag and something clicked in my spirit. My eyes followed him.

After the service, many of us went to have refreshments in the fellowship hall to mix and mingle. The gentleman I was keen on came and joined us at our table. He was tall, as I've mentioned, head and shoulders taller than me, well dressed and lanky and as dark as India ink. He was from Trinidad and introduced himself as Anderson Williams. I had no idea where Trinidad was on the map, for all I knew it was an African country, which was odd because geography was one of my favorite subjects in school. I spent hours as a kid studying maps and world atlases; give the big plastic globe a good spin and poke a finger to stop it to indicate where I wanted to visit or live. I daydreamed and vicariously traveled the world. I still do, thanks to PBS and the Travel Channel. Andy, as I came to know him, told us all about his homeland.

Trinidad and Tobago are the southernmost Caribbean islands with government. You can see Venezuela just seven miles from the tip of Icarus Point. I've been there. It's picturesque with sea swells and coconut palms, a small fishing village, but I was told not to linger as Icarus is a dangerous place. Drugs flowed in and out across the shark infested strait from the mainland. Trinidad is a rather large island comparatively speaking to dots on the map like St. Lucia or Aruba. Andy extended an invitation to come and visit, adding that he could set up an itinerary and keep me busy preaching and doing outreach if I was so inclined. The notion drew me like a magnet with a budding sense of urgency. Howard had been tapping his fingers on the tabletop like playing the ivories on a piano while Andy and I talked.

"Dirk," he said, "this is why you're here. Meeting this gentleman is a divine connection. You must go to Trinidad."

It was confirmation and I looked to Cassie to discern her reaction. She'd also been quiet during our conversation and smiled with a nod as to say yes; "You must go, I'm in total agreement."

∾

I was contracting and running my tail ragged during the building season. Work would generally slow down around the Christmas holidays into January; March was typically a dead month and we'd travel to visit family and friends. I'd lay off my crew and try to keep my lead man busy helping me with remodels until spring broke and we got back in full swing. Cassie and I decided to go to Trinidad, not just for a week to maybe check things out, but for the entire month of March. I'd never been outside the good ole USA except to Canada a few times (Niagara Falls and Toronto), and wasn't prepared for what awaited me in Trinidad.

When I disembarked from an air conditioned 737 on the tarmac at Piarco International Airport it was the shock of a lifetime. Not only the stifling heat and humidity, or the sea of dark faces jamming and elbowing their way through customs, or the scores of taxi drivers and vendors yowling in foreign sounding languages, it was the overwhelming sense that I was completely in over my head. Panic rose in my chest. I was lugging two suit cases, a backpack and a guitar and sweated my ass off. I can still see Cassie's look of terror as she struggled to keep her luggage in tow.

We cleared customs with one minor setback. I swear they only hire intimidating thugs and dress them in Gestapo uniforms to put you through the paces. Passport in hand, answer the questions and usually they just stamp your entry, waving you through. I didn't fit the profile of a cocaine smuggler and was surprised when Mr. Customs-man asked me to open my suitcases. With little to no concern how well I'd folded and packed everything so orderly and secure, he rummaged around the contents, balling this thing up, shoving that aside, and dug out a plastic bag with a dozen little squeezable bears of honey that I'd packed as gifts. Apparently honey wasn't allowed and got confiscated. I found out later there was nothing illegal at all, he wanted them for himself. It seemed like a minor thing but it shocked me. As a dumb Dutchman from farming country I had a lot to learn.

Andy arranged for a driver to meet us, and when I heard my name called over the pandemonium it was instant relief. Ziad introduced himself and began helping us with our luggage. He was an East Indian Christian and very hard to understand. When I made to get into his van, Ziad asked me if I was planning to drive. The steering wheel was on the opposite side as was the side of the rode we travelled. The short-lived and cherished moment at hearing my name called, bringing a sigh of relief, evaporated quicker than the fat rain drops on hot macadam.

Everyone drove at break-neck speed. The horn was obviously the most important feature of a vehicle with many intended translations and volume. Ziad weaved and veered and stopped abruptly, blasting the horn in Morse code, and we'd get whiplash when he took off again. All the while, Ziad was trying to have a conversation with Cassie and me, but neither of us understood a word he said. We cringed, sweated (no AC), and gripped each other or whatever was within reach to keep from being thrown from our seats. Did I mention the fumes? There were those, too, really bad fumes. The only air inside Ziad's van came in our open windows. Along with it came a cacophony of noise and smells that were at first repulsive but pulled me in with eager interest. Welcome to Trinidad.

Ziad announced that we were in Tunapuna and turned off the main road. We pulled into a circular driveway with a dried up fountain in the courtyard of a large mansion with a big front porch. Ziad tooted the horn and we were soon greeted by a middle-aged woman as round as she was tall with arms reaching to hug us. A crazed bush of salt and pepper hair as if enlivened by static electricity circled her dark welcoming face with the most charming and contagious laughter this side of the Pearly Gates. Louise McIntyre was incredibly gracious and accommodating and I could tell just a wee bit eccentric. She smothered us with affection and made us feel right at home. We were installed in a large bedroom, shown the way around the house as if we were royalty and given a lovely meal, which was a treat after travelling all day. I appreciated her hospitality that first evening, as did Cassie. Louise made our transition to such a different culture easier and pleasant. This was to be our home for the month and many future trips to Trinidad.

Ziad bid us good-evening and said that Andy would be by in the morning. The plan was to meet the senior pastor at the Centre (he didn't call it church), and brief us on our itinerary. Okay, so we hit the ground running. But I soon came to realize that the matter of time meant something different for "Trinnies" than we were accustomed to. If Trinidad was represented in the World Trade Fair the exhibit would be a clock without hands. 6 a.m. for me meant getting up at 5 to shower and have coffee. For Cassie add another hour. After breakfast we waited and waited on the front porch. Neither of us got much sleep that first night, I could have stayed in bed two more hours.

The sun broke and shone warmly with the promise of an exciting day, and still we waited. I wandered around the property checking out the flowers and fruit trees. Colorful birds flittered in the high branches; a two foot iguana moseyed out a gap in the back wall. I was enchanted, this being my first time in the tropics and plucked a mango. Much to my delight, a troop of children dressed in school uniforms trickled into the courtyard two by two or in small groups. Some carried instruments, others shoulder bags. They were shy and friendly and giggled. Of course, you know who made a fool of himself and embarrassed Cassie, but the children were amused at my antics.

Louise ran a music school in her house. She taught classical piano, string instruments, voice lessons and my favorite; steel pans. We were serenaded by calypso and a plethora of divine music that was absolutely wonderful and more than made up for barking dogs, roosters crowing at odd hours and the general racket that went on all night in the neighborhood.

Andy eventually came to pick us up and we were introduced

to his friend, Glenn Forde, who resembled Charles Barkley. Yea, I know; Trinidadians named Andy Williams and Glenn Forde. Crazy. Cassie and I climbed in the backseat and they took us to the Centre in Tunapuna, a town swallowed up in the vast growing capital city of Port of Spain. Ironically, we could have walked to the Centre, which Cassie and I did many times.

The Senior Pastor of Faith Revival Ministries (the Centre), was a man named Bertril Baird. I've met precious few men in my lifetime as intense as him. A look from the man's eyes made you wonder if you were saved or check to make sure your shoes were tied. To call Bertril intimidating is pulling the lever back a notch or two. He was serious about the Kingdom of God and there was no frivolity whatsoever in his character. Bertril's testimony, now obituary, states that he was born and raised in Tobago, the sister-island to Trinidad taking only a half hour flight by a puddle jumper from Piarco.

Tobago isn't developed so much for tourism, although there are a few resorts and a golf course. What's enchanting is the natural essence and true island vibes. Tobago's been dubbed as Robinson Caruso's Island. On my first visit, I awoke excitedly and walked along the beach at sunrise, feeling like I was the only living soul for miles and miles, listening to the surf and my thoughts, enamored by being in such a distant paradise, glad that it was Friday with the promise of evening entertainment. I trust you'll get the intended pun about Friday. One can rent a scooter and circumvent the coastline on a leisurely tour or take an hour trip to Scarborough, the capital city, barring you didn't run into a herd of goats or a stray bull blocking the road. The beaches are breathtaking, not to mention topless. Local main staples included flying fish, cou-cou and amazing conch soup.

Bertril Baird took the commandments of God literally and knocked on every door in Tobago as a young man witnessing the gospel of Christ. His mission? "I would not wish to have one man's blood on my account for leaving him in darkness." He came to

Trinidad and founded this thriving ministry with no less heart and spirit. As I came to know many at the Centre, they mirrored Bertril's mentality. Did I mention that they were serious?

Andy was an associate pastor at the Centre and conferred with Bertril about my being there to serve. They must have thought I was Billy Graham or something by the schedule. I was handed a detailed daily print-out that left little time for leisure, not that loafing was remotely my intention. I embarked on this trip knowing it wasn't a vacation plan with all-inclusive fruity drinks and a chaise lounge chair on the beach, but holy smokes! Bertril laid hands on my head and prophesied a commission to go forth and bear abundant fruit. I knew he didn't mean garnering guava or papayas. He liked me, I think, and I actually saw him smile a time or two.

"Gird your sword upon your side, O mighty one," he said. I'm paraphrasing, but that was the gist of his proclamation. I will never forget the piercing look in his eyes and wondered how in the world he thought I was mighty. "The Lord has called you to Trinidad for such a time as this. We have sown in prayer and righteousness; the fields are ripe unto harvest. Go and do the works of the Lord."

It was a bit overwhelming. I wanted to be like him and follow his example and I sure hoped that I wouldn't let him down. With a solemn nod and a dazed look on my face I said yes and amen. These guys believed in me, or they were throwing me to the sharks. Either way, my mettle was about to be tested.

Andy had his own schedule to keep. He was well known in the country and spoke at services in a variety of venues that demanded his attention. He could be out of the country for days or weeks at a time, or addressing a thousand people at a political prayer breakfast in Port of Spain or conducting a teaching series in places like La Hoya or San Fernando. I saw little of Andy. Crazy Ziad was my tour guide and chauffer and I was forever indebted to his care. We went Ziad's bank and exchanged green backs and

Travelers Checks into colorful monopoly bills. The exchange was seven TT to one US dollar, so a large pizza would cost something like $100. It was amusing to do the mathematical equation for everything from a bottle of pop to a postcard.

The first few days on the ground were spent doing outreach at Talparo near Asa Wright Natural Preserve. Asa Wright is a bird sanctuary in the rainforest where you walked on narrow suspended bridges in the treetops with resting places along the path. It was prime viewing for hundreds of different tropical birds; some would eat seed or a banana from your hand. I was especially entertained by the hummingbirds that whirled around me in a feeding frenzy among the flora, sometimes lighting in my hair.

I don't recall the pastor's name of the church in Talparo. He had a large family, all beautiful young girls who were shy and had fine singing voices. His church was small, maybe forty locals who faithfully met in a wood structure with a galvanized roof. Ziad promised to return by ten that evening to pick us up, but what's time in Trinidad?

I spent the day walking around the village and surrounding area to get a feel for things. These were poor people with gardens and hand wash tubs, maybe a scrawny cow tethered in a field, dogs so thin you could count every rib. I marveled at the board houses and chattels painted in pastel colors surrounded by flowers, bougainvillea and fruit trees, snug little homes with wooden shutters. The children would cease from playing and weren't a bit shy to check out the white stranger wandering their neighborhood. I loved their faces, wide-eyed and giddy yet timid, bursting with amusement and curiosity. It took me back to my days doing bus ministry and realized that on future visits I should have a puppet and hard candy in my pocket.

I was informed to call greetings from a distance before approaching to knock on someone's door like we do in America. So I called, bidding a friendly hello, hoping for a welcoming open door and visited with folks where an invitation was offered. Morning and afternoon passed, sweat ran down my back like I'd run a 5K pushing toward the ribbon. Everything at every turn was new; this strange culture so energizing and challenging, so deliriously enthralling. I engaged people at the market, not a bit hesitant to shake hands while making introductions, inviting them to services we had planned. A big momma, whose toothless smile lit up her dark face, had piles of fruit on her table and wouldn't take my money when I gathered some silk figs and a few oranges. Almost everyone I spoke with said they would come to hear me preach. I hoped they weren't just being polite.

I got a kick out of the fellows playing dominoes. Besides the national pastime of cricket and football (what we call soccer), domino games are everywhere a baobab tree grew or whatever vast umbrella of foliage provided protection from the scorching sun. You could hear a domino game in progress before seeing one. The proper manner of slapping down your domino on the table sounded like a gunshot, generally followed by laughter or cursing.

Our service on first night was well attended but mostly just the regulars who brought a guest. I preached about the two men on the Emmaus Road who had an encounter with the resurrected Jesus. The verse about how their hearts burned within them as Jesus spoke was my pivotal point. The message was well received. On the second night the crowd doubled in size and people stood outside looking in the windows. The third night we decided to hold the service behind the church in an open field. The pastor managed to find folding chairs and ran extension cords to jerry-rig lighting and a sound system. It was well past eight o'clock when we began the service and the crowd grew.

I stood on a piece of carpet behind the church pulpit they'd carried outside; a simple mahogany lectern. A bare light bulb that must have been a thousand watts hung over my head from a branch, attracting a swarm of evening bugs that batted against my face. It was time to do my thing, which was a few praise songs with the old Gibson guitar, a warm-up routine about where I was from and my testimony, and launch into the sermon. I sweat like a pig and my shirt was soaked to the skin while ladies sat in the front seats in long sleeve dresses and hats. At one point in the message, I reached for the microphone to wander from behind the pulpit and felt a tingling sensation. I mused that it might be the Holy Spirit, but when the mic touched my lip I got such a jolt from faulty wiring that it nearly knocked me down. It was a "drop the mic" moment. The ladies in the front row went wild and jumped to their feet. "He got da Holy Ghost! De boy's got da Holy Ghost!"

After pouring out my heart and soul sharing the gospel, hoarse from projecting my voice (the mic lie on the rug where I dropped it, an untouchable thing), I invited anyone who wanted to meet Jesus to come forward for prayer and a good many responded. I wondered if some of them thought that when I laid hands on them, they, too, would get zapped by the Holy Ghost. I encouraged those I prayed for to meet with the pastor inside the church for follow up. I recall a few young men of college age were eager to step up and help the pastor. Of course, many slipped away after coming out for an evening of entertainment. The village didn't have a cinema, I was the show. I recognized many faces from spending days in their village and round about the area. Planting is as critical as reaping the harvest. Maybe my brief stop at Talparo was meant to cultivate the soil and sow seed for the next crusader of Christ.

The following days were a blur of teaching and preaching, Ziad running us here and there, pushing his van like Charlton Heston racing his chariot in Ben Hur. He was always in a hurry. We travelled around the central regions ministering at churches, house churches and newly planted up-start churches. We coordinated with locals and set up meetings in the open air. One evening we conducted a service under a carport in the hills at a village named San Juan beside a creek where people bathed and carried water in buckets back home. It wasn't that they were so primitive as not to have pipe water, they were thrifty. Andy had sent a good word ahead and I was always warmly received. Making the acquaintances of godly men and women; pastors, lay ministers and the countless friendly people who embraced me made my sweat and toil all make sense. We shared a common mission and they made me feel like I was an asset to fulfilling their God-given vision. It was humbling.

I ate and drank whatever was set before me, elevating my faith to new levels on saying grace before meals. "Please, God, don't let this kill me." Every time I turned around a fruit drink so incredibly sweet was handed to me. Their main staple was generally chicken and rice and pigeon peas. I tasted a whole new palate of spices unknown to my bland, oh-so-familiar Pennsylvanian cuisine. Curry and hot sauces, cumin and sweet peppers, fried fish, ox tail soup, plantain, doubles, roti's, and pone which was made of cassava and grated coconut that had the consistency of finger Jell-O; such a wonderful blend of West Indian food!

Ziad took me to Manzanilla on the east coast, a two hour drive from home away from home in Tunapuna. Another driver was arranged to meet me and take me to the south coast for an extended weekend of meetings in Guayaguayare. I waved farewell to Ziad and walked a few hundred yards to breathe in the sea. Coconut palms towered above me, permanently bent like rocking chairs by the lashing sea winds. Dozens of random coconuts lie brown and hairy and split on the coarse sand, debris collected at tideline that created a ridge and pickings for the scavenging birds. It was a welcome moment of solitude, pushing the pause button on a hectic schedule to recollect my thoughts on that desolate beach. A green lizard seemed interested with my company and scurried round my feet, but I couldn't coax it to nibble on my granola bar.

I wore a Swatch, remember them? I compulsively referred to

it. One hour, two hours and where was my ride? Being so remote there wasn't much traffic and I debated about walking, maybe stick out my thumb to hitchhike if ever a car came by. I located a mound after pacing up and down the road and decided to station myself there to keep a lookout in case whoever was coming for me might eventually show up. I couldn't possibly be missed. I was a white guy with a shoulder bag and a guitar case who definitely looked out of place standing in the hot sun. Within minutes my ankles and legs began getting a creepy crawly tingling feeling. I was wearing a pair of loose fitting L.L. Bean Chino slacks and began batting at my legs and did the shaky-shake thing not sure what to make of it, when suddenly I started feeling needles or stings or bites. It got insane. I pulled my trousers up and my legs were covered with fire ants from the knees down and making inroads into my socks. The mound I thought was so smart to stand on was their castle and I had seriously pissed them off.

I jumped off the mound onto the broken macadam, thrashing madly. The stinging sensation was working its way up the elevator. "No! Not there!" I stripped off my shirt and pants and began flailing them against a palm tree, frantically swiping at my sorry legs as the ants found purchase, biting and swarming up my torso in a fierce frenzy. It was total mayhem. Wouldn't you know it, my ride showed up, with his wife, and there I was in my Fruit of the Loom's behaving like a demon possessed lunatic.

Guayaguayare was my destination for a solo mission of four days in the bush at my own request. Andy humored me, I'm sure, and arranged the ride, a guide (who never showed up), and a house. The rest, I told Andy, I'd figure out when I got there. He shook my hand and said, "Go for it." I imagined having an experience like in National Geographic magazines or the apostle Paul in the Mediterranean, mapping out my own way. I wanted a true missionary experience off the grid. Silly me.

It was dark by the time my hosts drove us into the small coastal village. They were nice folks, seniors, not very talkative. The gentleman drove so slowly I wondered if we'd ever get to Guayaguayare. They were Anglicans, he and his wife, which is probably the most predominant denomination in Trinidad. Mother-England's strong hand of rule and influence that shaped the country until their independence was still very prevalent. The gentleman said that Apostle Anderson had called and made the arrangements and reassured me that they'd look after me, which was of some comfort. At least I knew two people in Guayaguayara I could call on if there was a need.

We passed through what was called town and I found myself tracking the headlights on grassy back roads as if it led to nowhere. At last we arrived at my prearranged accommodation for the next four days and I bid them good-evening and another rambling apology at coming upon me nearly naked. I lugged my gear up tricky steps to the door of a house on stilts that slightly swayed underfoot like Jay's treehouse.

The "house" was an open one room cottage on poles that was accessed by a ladder-like series of steep steps. No phone, no TV, bare bones. There was a kitchen with basic wares, a gas stove top and a fridge that didn't particularly work well. My hosts had stocked food supplies for me, beans and rice, bananas and a sack of sugar. Interesting. Obviously I was on my own. A barrel on the roof (solar power), fed a plastic pipe that ran to the kitchen sink and a bathroom with a rust corroded shower stall. The spigots ran slow with scalding hot water at first, turning cold after a few minutes. I was getting accustomed to cockroaches the size of my thumb and the little neon lizards hanging around were friends who ate bugs, but when I saw a millipede about a foot long slithering along the baseboard I freaked out. Their bite can make you very sick, so it was get him before he got me. I eventually cornered the slippery rascal in the shower stall with a steady stream of urine. Serves him right, pissing him into a corner, and administered the coup de grace with a mop handle. After a quick rinse to wash off of the day's journey and soothing ant bites with some aloe the kindhearted Missus offered for relief, I stretched out on a hard mattress with one eye open.

I've made mention that I don't relish the demonic stuff, right? Somewhere in the middle of the night, the shutters wide open to get all the air I could with no bars or protection other than being six feet off the ground, I rolled over feeling a strange premonition that someone was watching me. I turned and saw a face at the window opening that seemed to be glaring. It looked like a fiend, threating and menacing, a phantom with what I thought were red eyes. I wasn't sure if was an actual demon or someone wearing a mask, or if it was the sleepless night playing tricks on me. I wish I could tell you that I confronted whatever it was in the Name of Jesus, but I can't. I froze; terrified, holding my breath like a seven year old and wished to God I had listened to Cassie and travelled with someone. I don't want to belabor the point, but I've come to firmly believe in the "Buddy System." The face vanished and eventually I must have passed out from fright or exhaustion. I didn't wake until well after noon the next day.

After taking a cold shower, I walked to the bay within view of my abode and located a shop that had basic groceries. I bought bottled water, some homemade currant rolls and a jar of instant coffee.

Guayaguayare was a small fishing village in 1982 with a dirty wharf, a bar and a repair/tackle shop. The time that I happened to be there it was virtually a ghost town. Skiffs and fishing boats were out for the day. The cove may now offer a resort and rent surfboards as the sea is rough. I decided to explore and do a bit of recon.

There were very few people out and about on the road and I started approaching homes, quickly coming to appreciate the caution of not walking into someone's property but calling greetings instead. I wandered upon a cluster of houses with ragged colorful Hindu flags in their front yards, inhabitants I assumed were friendly folk like Gandhi. I saw little temples set up on porches with offerings to Vishnu, Brahma or whatever, bowls of water and tidbits of food, knives, feathers and bones arranged around candles. There were always mangy watch dogs to be wary of, lifting a tired eye to scrutinize me.

At one particular house, a woman old enough to have served Lord Nelson welcomed and entertained me. We partook of tea and fish-head soup and something made with breadfruit. She was a Spiritual Baptist by the way she dressed (Ziad informed me about them), and had it not been how hospitable she was I probably would have been spooked. The Spiritual Baptists are a combination of African lore and Catholicism, not unlike folks you could encounter in deep Cajun Louisiana, one group among the many mind boggling religions in the West Indies. Main-stream Christian and non-denominational churches, a Hindu temple and Muslim mosque, Pentecostal, Anglican and a version of voodoo called Obeah made up the colorful fabric of Trinidad's people of faith. The old woman was chatty but hard to understand. After a nice lunch, she informed me that she had a grandson living in a shack behind her house and asked if I would speak to him.

It didn't take long until she dragged a young man into the gallery by the scuff of his collar and deposited him in a chair opposite from me. She stood over us like a larger-than-life Mother Superior in a black full-length dress and a turban of white scarves towering from her head, surveying us with raven-like eyes. Without a word she turned to go inside and left us alone. The fellow's posture was tense; his jaundice eyes kept darting back to where he came from. I wished that his granny would have allowed me to go to him so I could have seen how he lived.

His pallor was ashy and grey for a West Indian man. He lacked teeth and looked emaciated and I was sure he was suffering from AIDS or drug abuse. He couldn't have been twenty years old, looking as though he'd likely die before his next birthday. My heart went out to him but I didn't know what to say. In clear conscience I couldn't offer him "Canned Gospel." We sat for a long time in silence, both of us nervously tapping our toes; he never gave me eye contact. I prayed for God's help before speaking, and as happens often, a memory came to me like having a vision.

Of all things, I saw my mother's face the evening I arrived home from the Richmond Jail fiasco. It was daunting, this memory that has plagued me all my life. I was paralyzed in the moment; sitting across from the skeletal figure of this young man who studied his bare feet, and I felt what may have been my mother's heart of sadness when she looked into my eyes, the eyes of her runaway prodigal son. She'd wanted to ask why, but neither Mom nor I knew the why of it back then. I felt that it could have been the face of Jesus looking into my soul, brokenhearted at my waywardness. The first word spoken between this young West Indian man and me to break our awkward silence was, "Why?" I more choked it than pronounced it and reached to him.

Feelings rose from deep within me and I began to cry like a dam broke, a torrid of tears flowed like a spillway down my face. The bottled up guilt I'd so carefully stowed away in the Lost and Found Department of my memories, taped up in boxes and buried so many years ago, split apart at the seams. Part of the anguish I was feeling was for the desperate soul sitting across from me. After sharing my runaway story with him I said; "You know; people like us need Jesus."

I don't remember going into the whole spiel about the gospel, I was pretty sure he knew he was a sinner. It was a given that his granny constantly reminded him that hell awaited sinners. I couldn't help myself and asked him if wanted a mortician or a fresh start on life. I think what sunk into his head were my tears, not so much my words. I'd like to believe that he made the correlation about the pleas of my mother to me as those of Jesus pleading for him. Something seemed to register. He almost begged me to pray for him, and another awkward moment of silence followed. I was stunned at his response.

I led him in a simple prayer to accept everything Jesus had to offer; forgiveness, healing, grace, deliverance, salvation, the whole enchilada wrapped in a bow. When I opened my eyes, the expression on his face was drastically changed from when we'd first met. I can't say that his bloodshot, jaundiced eyes were clear, but they looked different as he gave me eye contact for the first time.

A few minutes passed and he abruptly stood to return to his shack out back without a word, rather in a hurry. I thought, well, that's that, he's going to snort or shoot or smoke something and this was all just a ruse to keep his granny from beating him. I wanted to gracefully bow out and thank the woman for lunch, but suddenly, the young man burst back into the gallery with a beat up bible duct taped at the spline. He planted himself in the chair across from me and asked, "Where do I start?" My jaw hit the floor.

How would you answer a question like that? I wanted to say rehab, detox, therapy, nutrition and diet, don't take another toke one day at a time. I reached for his bible and thumbed through the gospels happy to find Jesus' words in red letters. All I could offer was; "Read and reread the red letters." Pointing to a passage I added, "He is the way and the truth and the life... get to know Jesus better every minute of every day as best as you can and you will live."

～

I walked dirt roads and donkey trails around Guayaguayara for three days taking an occasional shortcut in the knee-high grass and visited with dozens of people. There was a coastal track that I followed back to my stilt-house, a familiar path so I wouldn't get lost, and stopped at a rum shop near the wharf one afternoon dying for an ice cold Coke. An awning stuck off from the side of a house that served as a patio bar with a Carib sign, the local beer. The patio roof was thatched with palm leaves that clattered in the hot breeze; a haze of pungent smoke rose from a grill smoking fish, indistinct music blared from a boom box from somewhere inside. Several men leaned on the bar and watched me meander my way toward them. I was parched and didn't think there was anything to be concerned about. This was a public establishment, what could possibly go wrong? I slung my backpack on a stool and said hello.

Rum comes in all varieties in the Caribbean, every island has its unique brand and label. Tourists not only imbibe at the resorts or beach bars, but flock to the duty-free stores from cruise ships to buy the nectar of the mighty sugar cane. One can purchase differing labels of pints up to a half gallon handle of clear or dark or spiced rum depending on your fancy and credit card limit. The fellows I greeted had glasses of clear rum in hand, no ice, and seemed to have been at it for some time. I stood at the bar being eyed up by four sets of blurry eyes and taunt faces, waiting to be served.

"If ya a be friend den have a drink wid us mon, udder-wise dere's nothin ta talk about." A scruffy man in a tattered T shirt slid his glass toward me. It was greasy with nasty fingerprints and lip smear, back wash I'm sure, and he wanted me to have a drink as if it was on the house. "We heard all 'bout ya, mon," he said. "My cousin paid ya a visit de first night you showed up. Norm ain't normal but curious as a monkey dat boy is. He been keepin an eye on ya."

The four of them laughed like it was a grand inside joke. So, Norm was the visitor who scared the daylights out of me that first night and not some demon as I'd feared.

"Alright," I said, mustering my nerve. "If I agree to drink this will you come hear me preach?" I may have offered something more on the line of being a recovering alcoholic or my testimony. I made mention that if Jesus could turn water into wine he could certainly turn rum into water and they laughed hysterically. I tossed down a healthy swallow of rum from the man's glass that hit my throat like petrol on fire. Maybe I should have prayed first.

I had some gospel tracts in my backpack and handed them to the fellows and we had a good time telling stories. I drank three bottles of Coke to wash away the after-taste of rum and enjoyed the bantering. I told them I'd let them know when and where I was preaching. They promised to be there.

The next day I heard my name called, which startled me. I was walking down the road to town when a teenage boy waved and came toward me.

"Are you de man got mashed-up by de fire ants?"

I detected a hint of humor and wondered if the whole village knew about my episode. The boy's name was Grant and had a basket of food his grandmother had sent along, the folks who picked me up at the infamous anthill. We sat in the shade and ate chicken pelau and drank fresh made sorrel. I asked him to help me arrange a place to hold a gospel service, adding that it didn't have to be fancy. Grant said that his grandfather had a large carport where they held outdoor fetes and entertained a good size crowd. It sounded perfect. He said he could make it happen and pass word around. The plan was to have a Saturday night meeting when the wharf offered rum, reveling and loose women.

I heard my dad's voice in my ear as I walked back to the stilt-house, "By God boy, you've got a wild hair up your ass." I suppose that's one way to look at it, whatever I was doing was certainly wild if not crazy. I wondered why I was doing this, this... what? What *was* I doing in Trinidad of all places? I saw glimpses that I was doing God's will, a mission that began at Shekinah Ministries in Tennessee with my friend Howard, and the idea of being on the right road brought me joy and a sense of meaning. Having a purpose resonated in my soul and put bounce in my step. Strangely enough, the extraordinary was happening at the hands of an ordinary uneducated carpenter. I felt like I was keeping good company with the simple fishermen and common disciples that Jesus chose in the gospels. I was encouraged to be among the good guys making a difference, even if it was just a small difference in the world.

∼

As Christians we are all called to serve the kingdom of God and I think it starts as simple as sharing our testimony. You may be very different than me, but each of us has a story and given a God ordained mission. We're endowed not only with fascinating life-stories, but with a talent, a vocation, some kind of special knack for doing a task in life that nobody can do like you. You are one of a kind and unique; there's not another like you nor will there ever be. Perhaps you're an artist or a musician, a teacher, a student, a mother, a welder bringing home the paycheck and you don't see that what you do in this world is a lofty career or a noble cause. This may surprise you, but life is more than just a paycheck. You can make an impression, sometimes a lasting impression by your example and words. If we reflect Christ-likeness being faithful even in the smallest of things we're a conduit for God's love to flow through. I think my calling or gifting as it may be is to reach out and gather the lost souls, relate with them wherever I can and hear their desperation, hopefully pointing the best way I know toward grace and healing. I can also swing a pretty mean hammer and build you whatever you want.

Is it a spiritual calling, this unsettling yearning that burns inside to see and do impossible things within or beyond our vocation? I think it is. If given to our own ways we'd probably be more inclined to be timid and selfish and pass on looking foolish or renege for fear of failure. I have asked this question hundreds of times with trepidation and trembling whether behind the pulpit or standing in sawdust with my nail bag on; "What do you want Jesus to do for you?" I'm humbled to stand in God's shadow and try to represent him, seeking to discern his intentions and dare to act on faith to meet someone's need, offering a little help, a Band-Aid, a cold drink of water. Jay said that we knew too much, and I'm beginning to realize the truth that there really is no escaping from accountability for what God has given me or how to speak of it. It's sobering yet joyful also, as Isaiah prophesied; *"How beautiful on the mountains are the feet of those who bring good news, who proclaim peace and bring good tidings."*

What about these spiritual gifts and callings, what in the world do we do with them? They're gifts for one, undeserved and irrevocable, bestowed upon us by God's good pleasure when we were in the womb. Have you not ever asked yourself why you are who you are and why you are here? What we do with this gift was eloquently defined by a retired pastor who said, *"Be who you be."* He was a sage of old-school wisdom and delightful humor, cruising around in a wheelchair at the nursing home when I was slapping paint and he was spot on. Yes, I wholeheartedly agree. Bottom-line, we can be no more and no less than *who we be*. As I see it, it's the hand we've been dealt and it's up to us how we play it.

෴

Saturday night came and the stately couple who brought me to Guayaguayara prayed as we set up folding chairs. Grant was there with his girlfriend and a friend of hers and lent a hand. A few dozen villagers arrived and sat quietly under the carport, mostly elderly folks and women with children. A man I had met who'd lost a leg to a shark while net fishing was sitting in the back with his son. A giggling group of teenage girls stood offish outside. I was a little disappointed with the small turn out and wish I could tell you that the heavens opened and poured down showers of blessing on a large gathering, that it was a memorable occasion with healing and miracles. God was present, which is no trivial matter; a sweetness of the Holy Spirit infused our worship, at least for me. The young man I'd prayed for wasn't in the crowd. His granny was, she sat in the front and wore a colorful cotton dress and a church-ladies hat, not the garbs of the Spiritual Baptist. I would make it a point to speak with her after the service to inquire about him and pay another visit.

I shared a message from Ezekiel in the Old Testament, if I remember right, the story about the valley of dry bones that received the breath of God and came to life. I could picture it in my cartoon mind as if in 3D. In the biblical account, the valley became a stir, energized by the wind of God. I envisioned a massive dust storm, funnels like a tornado sweeping across the landscape, God's breath tearing open graves. Stick-like men without form arose from the dust. Bones reassembled like a song I sang as a kid: "...the shin bone's connected to the knee bone, the knee bone's connected to the..." Tendons and skin grew and whole men and women rose up as an army. My point was that God creates something new and vibrantly alive from the dust of our lives, reconfiguring us to serve his purpose.

The man who offered me his glass at the rum shop was standing in the shadows. I smiled and nodded at him. If there was only one person who heard my message and chose to receive the breath of God, I prayed it was him. He slipped away before I could speak with him.

Cassie often traveled with me, but when I was away she wasn't idle. Several women from the Centre came to visit at Louise's, offering companionship and rides to various meetings. Cassie wasn't a teacher or a preacher, she shared her testimony. She also did a powerful dramatic monologue in the person of Mary Magdalene at the empty tomb of Jesus. The message wasn't just an Easter story but the crux of Christianity; Jesus rose from the dead. Cassie wore an authentic costume with simple props and shared the script from her heart as though it was her personal story. Her portrayal of Mary's encounter with the resurrected Lord was riveting.

As the story goes, Mary Magdalene mourned at the tomb Jesus was buried in, she was alone, wanting to take care of him, but he wasn't there. Her fear or shyness, as well as Judaic law, forbid her from entering the empty tomb. She came upon Jesus posing as a gardener and besought him with a broken voice for answers. "Please tell me where you have taken him and I will go and tend to his need." I've heard Cassie do this a hundred times and every time she comes to the part where Jesus reveals himself and calls her name, "Mary," I get a lump in my throat.

Cassie was a real prayer warrior as well. I know she held my hands up in prayer and faith while I was out stomping the bush. She also helped Louise around the house and probably got under the maid's feet in the kitchen, where Cassie learned to cook some West Indian dishes.

"Dirk," she said one evening as we sat on the porch, "you've grown. I'm so proud of you. I hear nothing but good reports. Sister Baird brags about you and says Bertril is paying attention in hopes of bringing you onboard fulltime."

It's nice to have your wife compliment you. I winced when she squeezed my inner thigh and batted a seductive eye; those damned fire ants wreaked havoc in the nether regions.

Cassie and I took a day off to sightsee with Ziad at the wheel. We'd become friends and I was beginning to get most of what he said but never really got his jokes. I laughed along when there seemed to be a punchline. Ziad was fun to be with. He drove us up the mountain road which snaked a narrow and treacherous series of switchbacks with no guard rails barely wide enough for two vehicles to Maracas Bay. The cove was picturesque with a white sandy stretch of beach surrounded by cliffs and an expanse of mild waves of aqua blue water. It was paradise compared to the bush county and poor villages I'd grown accustomed to. I got sorely sunburned from swimming in bath-warm water and wandering the coastline. There was a delightful gathering of tourists at the beach bar, mostly Germans or Canadians, where I ate a swordfish sandwich and greasy chips while interacting with fellow Casper the Ghosts turned a shade of painful red. I'd packed some toys and played Frisbee with young locals on the beach. From my crusty salty hair to my surf shorts drooping with wet sand, it was all fun and games without a care in the world. Cassie slathered up with sunblock and stayed under an umbrella with a book. The sun was brutal by mid-afternoon and we decided to call it a day after being baked like a potato.

Ziad spent the time sleeping in his van and took us back to Port of Spain to do some shopping. He treated us to Indian food at Apsara, a very expensive restaurant, where we shared a veritable smorgasbord of delicacies sopped up in flatbread and eaten with our fingers. He teasingly said that he had a surprise instore before returning us home to Tunapuna.

Ziad headed south of Port of Spain to the Caroni National Park, an extensive basin of freshwater and tidal inflow I'd seen going to Chaguanas to teach a two day seminar. I remember thinking it looking like a swamp that never ended. Ziad couldn't keep a surprise any better than a six year old and informed us (after I plied him with questions), that it was a great place for bird-watching. He knew that I was kind of a birdwatcher as I made mention of them, and reminded me of the afternoon at Asa Wright Preserve where I'd spent hours and took three rolls of film. Ziad was always a good sport.

He drove around on muddy roads until finding a lookout that appeared to be a dead end overlooking Caroni Park. It was surreal. The horizon melded between heaven and earth making it difficult to tell where the sky met the sea. Within twenty minutes, hundreds upon hundreds of Scarlett Ibis flew in to roost in the trees for the night. They are crane-like, some with four foot wing spans, appearing as ancient pterodactyls colored brilliant red. The evening sky was ablaze as they settled in the trees.

I marveled at how our sightseeing day had gone. From the road trip over the mountain to Maracas Bay, a sumptuous affair at Apsara for lunch and now another experience at Caroni that stirred my imagination. No LSD trip or painting, no photograph or the best description no matter how eloquent and wordy could articulate the spectacular view of Scarlett Ibis turning an evening sky fiery red with a blood orange sun setting over the sea. I gasped, utterly wordless, breathing a silent prayer in awe and thanksgiving. I was present at the right moment and blessed to see such wonder. Ziad's smile caught my eye and he winked conspiratorially; his plan and timing had worked to perfection.

We'd only shaken hands or patted one another on the shoulder for the last month. He wasn't a man given to expressing his feelings outwardly other than his laughter. I wrapped him up in an embrace as a boy overjoyed at the gift he'd just received and totally surprised Ziad. For a man of never-ending conversations and constant enthusiasm whenever we were together, he sputtered and stuttered, taken aback, and embraced me in return. I have to say that embracing Ziad was something I wanted to do the first night we met at Piarco airport thinking he was a savoir of sorts. He served us well. My experience in Trinidad wouldn't have been the same without him.

～

Andy had us stay close to the Centre the last several days of our trip, inviting me to sit in on teachings and involving me with men's groups. We went out for lunch and spent more time together. One afternoon, Andy had a prearranged and rather pressing visit at the prison that was impossible for him to keep, and as I had a background with prison ministry he asked me to take his place. It was a scheduled affair that had to be kept by the clock. Ziad was late, so I took the bus.

The main road ran 24-7 with heavy traffic in and out of Port of Spain. A short taxi van was called a Mini, a Maxi carried twenty to twenty five people. They were colorful and loud, blasting Dub or Soca or calypso. Whenever I hopped on a Maxi, my preference was the rowdier the better.

I waved one down, boarded, and sat next to a gentleman in a dark blue suit with epaulets on his shoulders that made him look very official and made idle talk. I handed him a gospel tract, giving him time to read it, and began witnessing the Lord to him. He studied me, raising his eyebrows a few times, and reached into his suitcoat, pulling out a government badge of some sort with his picture.

"Do you have papers?" he asked. My confused look gave me away. "Is your passport stamped as a church worker?" It wasn't. I was on a 30 day tourist visa. "If you're ministering in this capacity you need papers." I asked him if I was in trouble and he nodded somberly. Could I get arrested and go to jail? He nodded again. I threw up my hands and thought; *Go figure! Why is it that I always get in trouble?* I said to the gentleman something like, "Well... if I'm in trouble we might as well finish here. Do you know Jesus?" He chuckled and said, "I wanted to see if you were for real. Yes, I'm a Christian. I must say your boldness is refreshing." He gave me his card, a kind of *Get Out of Jail Free* card like in Monopoly and told me if ever I needed an advocate to call his personal phone.

Port of Spain Prison is an old concrete walled fortress in the heart of the city. I've been through the routine of clearing security in a maximum state or federal prison, but I never encountered soldiers with automatic weapons. After surrendering my passport and signing in, I was padded down and led to a series of metal stairs to the fourth floor. The heat and stench was stifling. The officer pulled a chair up and pointed down a narrow hallway where cells lined each side. He sat down, thumbed the safety strap off his service revolver and spoke the only words thus far; "5B." He motioned for me to go and checked his watch.

Andy gave me an overview about the young East Indian man I was there to visit. He had brutally murdered a man and his wife in San Fernando and was scheduled to be hanged before Carnival, our version of Mardi Gras which was only weeks away. The rampage had occurred several months before while he was drugged out of his gourd on crack cocaine and the result of a petty robbery gone horribly wrong. He was competent to stand trial and given the death sentence. They don't mess around in Trinidad with long drawn out appeals.

I passed the cells on both sides of death row observing the men out of the corner of my eye. They lie on cots, some sleeping or studying the ceiling in deep thoughts, others watching me at their barred doors like caged animals. No one was allowed to utter a word, yet despair and anger screamed at the top of their lungs. At the end of the hall I stood before "5B," the man's cell I was directed to, and was caught off guard to find him standing as if expecting me.

He stood a few steps from the bars in the small confines of a cell with his hands behind his back, stiff at attention with an expression on his face I couldn't get a read on. Was it stony, unremorseful arrogance, or was it the vacant stare of a man counting the last days until he was put to death, by all appearance denying emotional connections and consequences? We both held apprehension in check. It seemed as if neither of us could breathe and I wondered what he thought of me, a total stranger gazing into his face, each of us frozen in time. The young man looked to be in his mid-twenties, tall and very dark skinned in contrast to his grey prison clothes, with a striking head of jet black hair neatly combed to the side. He was clean shaven and handsome, he could have been a bank clerk in another life. His unblinking eyes probed mine with curiosity. I wondered if he was shackled from behind as he didn't move a muscle.

I had fifteen minutes with this condemned man so I cut to the chase. After introducing myself, I asked him in so many words if he was a Christian. I half expected him to say no, that he was Hindi. He said yes. I asked him if he was ready to die. Again, he said yes. I asked him if there was anything I could pray for. The young man said to pray for his family and the family of those whose lives he'd taken. I could not touch him but leaned forward.

It was honorable of him to request prayers for the families but I asked, "What about you?" He shook his head slowly as though processing conflicting thoughts before answering. "Maybe just some reassurance." I told him there was only one reliable source of reassurance worth banking on and reminded him of the repentant thief who hung beside Jesus at Golgotha. He smiled with understanding and resignation and allowed me to lead him in a prayer to confirm his commitment to Christ. I added words of comfort as best as I knew how. The guard made a sound to indicate that our time was up. Fifteen minutes flew past like standing at the curb and feeling the wake of a car speeding by. The young Indian man thanked me and I wished we could have at least shaken hands.

My knees were weak as I followed the guard back down the stairs. Never before or since have I met anyone who knew the day and the hour they would die.

~

Andy and Glenn Forde, aka Charles Barkley who took me to task one afternoon playing basketball, drove Cassie and me to the airport. We checked our luggage and sat at a table under an umbrella having refreshments. Andy said I should consider coming back and apply for an extended visa, adding that Pastor Baird was impressed with my ministry and there was a place for me to fit in. Hearing his approval was the best affirmation I could ever receive.

"You've made quite an impact," he said, "I'm sure a lot of people will never forget you." Andy's eyes got big as a grin broke his face; "The man who survived being nearly eaten alive by fire ants and kept on preaching. You're a legend."

"Does everyone in Trinidad know that story?" I had to laugh at myself.

"The tale gets bigger by the telling," Andy said. "The punchline is the ants never had de white meat before!"

⁓

There are those in the Christian community who can recall every soul they saved or think they've saved. I didn't realize you should keep count. I suppose Tom Brady knows how many touchdown passes he's thrown. I think I'll let God keep score, I haven't a clue.

As the plane banked over Trinidad, I gazed out the window above a beautiful island so diverse and colorful, a culture and people that had profoundly changed my life. Cassie and I made good friends in such a short time. Ziad and Louise, the children from her music classes, Bertril Baird and his wife, leaders at the Centre, pastors in Talparo, Todds Road and those in Guayaguayare, not to mention the scores of compassionate people who made my journey unforgettable. I thought before leaving home (presumptuously), that my trip to Trinidad was to offer the gospel to those poor natives, when in the end it was me who was the poorer. The people of Trinidad gave me more than I could possibly hope to give back in return. My soul was overflowing with emotions as the flight attendant did her spiel. Drinks would be served when we reached cruising altitude. There was an ache in the pit of my stomach to be leaving. I heard steel pan music in my head and imagined smelling curry.

# 10

*My* father had his first heart attack in his mid-fifties. Quadruple by-pass was in store as were two more dings on his heart in the next years. It was a wake-up call to retire from the bank where he was a landmark. Everyone in town knew Ken Heckman. They moved to Deland, Florida and built a lovely, scaled down plantation style home with a wraparound porch. Mom's flower gardens won her acclaim and ribbons in the garden club and were the envy of the neighborhood. Dad's brother, my Uncle Bill and Aunt Irene lived in the same neighborhood and they all loved to entertain "Snow Birds." Cassie and I visited my folks as often as possible, usually around race week at Daytona, which was only half an hour from Deland. Cassie's mother lived between Pompano Beach and Ft. Lauderdale at the time, and Cassie had a good friend in the Melbourne area, so we'd spend a few weeks soaking up the Florida sunshine and visiting with everyone. One particular visit comes to mind.

I'd been hoping to find a way to make amends with my father for all the crap I pulled back in the day; build a peace-bridge and try to restore the connection of what I'd broken in my careless rebellion. Most of all, I wanted to let him know that I loved him. There was no way I could do it in a letter although it was tempting. I wanted to tell him that he was a good father and apologize for the problems I caused at home. Those difficult years weren't his fault and I so wished to make an attempt to placate the awkwardness that we each still carried however hidden. The bad stuff was never discussed by silent mutual consent, but I couldn't just sweep it under the rug. I prayed and anguished, looking for the right opportunity when we could be alone together.

On an idyllic Florida afternoon I asked my dad if I could tag along to the country club and jokingly said I could be his caddy. My folks golfed regularly, and when they weren't playing it was on the TV; the PGA Tour or some tournament. My father was a big fan of Arnold Palmer. Although growing up around golfing I never picked up a club other than the Fred Flintstone plastic set when I was a kid. At best I was a competitor on the mini putt-putt course.

Dad and I walked the back nine and I was expressing to him how it might be therapeutic if I had a hobby as it seemed that all I did was work. Maybe golf or fly fishing or buy acrylics and an easel to paint still life. After a few holes, Dad said I should consider fly fishing. I sliced the ball, drove it in the rough, lost one altogether (a well-used Titleist but apparently as valuable as gold), and on a par four finally putted in well over par. Not my thing. But I wasn't whacking a golf ball around to particularly learn the game. I was waiting for the perfect, magical moment when I could give my little speech.

We stood in a bunker looking at my ball that was barely poking out and he handed me the sand wedge. The sun was behind some magnolia trees, above us a dazzling Florida sky, truly the Kodak moment between father and son that I was hoping for. My Dad stood with his hands in his pockets, being patient as I took a few practice swings. I worked up the nerve and turned to look at him saying something like how much he meant to me and how he always knew just the right thing to do, like picking the right golf club. I wanted to say so much more. I wanted to say that I loved him, but it kind of stuck in my throat.

We were never a Walton family as in; *"Goodnight John Boy. Goodnight Dad. Love ya. Love you, too."* I don't recall seeing a lot of affection expressed at home when I was growing up, although dad would give mom a peck on the cheek on the way out the door to work. I don't remember being hugged. We weren't huggers gushing, "Have a good day." Mom made sure our coats were zipped up, that our teeth were brushed, homework finished, and before shooing me out the door made sure that my sneakers were tied and I had lunch money. I don't think or question for a minute that I wasn't loved. Maybe it was the times, or that both of my parents came from German stock given to stoicism and principles that frowned on expressing outward emotions. Perhaps neither of them saw much affection growing up.

I stood in the bunker with sand in my Docker boat shoes, my well planned speech spinning in my brain like a hamster on a wheel, and blurted out as best as I could. "Dad, you're the best. Have I told you that I love you?"

I kind of expected a moment of recognition and the two of us embracing, the halleluiah chorus resounding in the breeze. Dad gave me a puzzled look; his eyes betrayed thoughts reeling in his mind that I couldn't discern.

"Aw now," he said, reaching to pat my shoulder. "Let's get this damned ball on the green."

And that was my Walton Mountain moment.

However, things changed after I got the damned ball on the green. We got just a little bit more relaxed being in each other's company, but we never played another round of golf.

I don't think my father knew what to make of me. Here I was, the golden boy who played Little League and basketball and had trophies, but quit sports in exchange for some warped alternate identity that caused shame on the family name. I was the oldest who was supposed to set an example but instead ran away, a bright kid who dropped out of high school and spent time in jail, rehab and all the many stages when I should have grown up but didn't. In the good times, and there were many, Dad was in the backyard after work with my brother and me, horse-playing or tossing a football back and forth. In the bad times I fought with him verbally as I became incorrigible and mouthy, on more than one occasion things got physical. My metamorphous to becoming a man was anything but smooth and steady. It was a journey of jerks forward and jarring setbacks; and then I go and get religion!

My father was never comfortable whenever I brought up the subject of religion and I regret not being more sensitive. I didn't take the time to inquire about what he believed and wish I would have, I was kind of preachy. Looking back, I can only imagine his objections. He paid the bills and kept a roof over our heads. He never went to jail or got drunk except maybe once. Dad was a moral man, a Marine, a Korean War veteran, solid as a rock in our hometown. Who was I; the renegade - derelict son that had brought embarrassment on the family to tell him that he needed Jesus? I saw his rage one evening when I became a little pushy to offer him a book and he literally turned his back on me and went into the kitchen. The book was titled *Born Again* by Chuck Colson. I'm sure that I meant well but it blew up in my face.

Mom had watched the Watergate hearings on TV between minding children and tending house, she knew about Chuck Colson, Haldeman and Ehrlichman. Her comment was, "Well, he's a Republican. I guess crime does pay." My folks listened politely to my stories about prison ministry, but Mom had little time or interest in prison reform. If that was something I felt I should do, by all means do it, she said with a wave of her hand as if shooing away a fly.

I don't recall there ever being a visit at the coffeehouse. I'm sure it would have freaked them out. I can only imagine their impressions of Lewie the Leprechaun and Dad asking, "Are you running a nightclub or a rooming-house?" I think they thought that what I was doing scandalous at best. We had a get-together at Uncle Bill's and I entertained everyone with stories about

Trinidad, careful not to mention things that would upset my mother. I shared some of my experiences, but mostly things about the culture and the food, and, of course, the fire ants. I thought they'd get a chuckle out of it. Mom has a way of making a frown with her eyebrows that conveys displeasure easily read. Dad asked me why I went halfway around the world when people needed "saved" right here in the USA. The discussion would become quiet; about all I could say was that I had to go wherever God led me, which went over like telling a joke and forgetting the punchline.

Cassie and I would typically make the 45 minute drive to my hometown to visit with them, but I always looked forward to their visits with us. We lived in Mifflinburg and saw my parents on their way back from visiting Kenny in Laurelton as it was along the way. They were comfortable visits in our charming brick Victorian home in a normal setting, sipping sweet tea on patio chairs without crazy people living upstairs. I'd take my father to one of my jobs sites and show him what I was building. I could tell that he couldn't have been more proud. My mother commented on the gardens that Gladys Coleman had planted; perennials and flowering bushes she could name, the south-side a lush border of colorful irises that made her cheeks blush with pleasure. Dad liked the Scarlett "D," an old hotel with good food just a four block stroll from our front porch on Chestnut Street. Wednesday night special was all the chicken and waffles you could eat; good old Pennsylvania Dutch cooking. The gravy was very close to Grandma Belle's. I called the owner Lester Sleaze because he was always a little too touchy-feely with my wife. Dad got a kick out of him. Besides running the restaurant and bar, Lester also roasted peanuts. An alluring aroma wafted in the air on the days he was in production mode that made me nostalgic like the carnival came to town. You bought them by weight in burlap sacks, but the "D" also sold 50 cent bags and Mom made sure to always have one ready for their drive back home. Dad could get sleepy at the drop of a hat and she'd shell and pop a peanut in his mouth. He jokingly said she was making him fat.

My mother is a moral woman who's agnostic at best. We've had few in-depth one-on-one discussions over the years about spiritual things; I can count them on one hand. I always felt inhibited and our talks were strained from the beginning, being as I was the one who started down that rabbit hole. When my mother is finished with a conversation she shuts it down rather abruptly saying, "Let's change the subject and talk about something happy." I respect her convictions and have come to the place where I simply listen and give her space. We've never argued, but our conversations have always reached an impasse. Her core moral ideals are rock solid, but as I see it, and maybe I'm wrong, her belief in God as a supreme being is ambiguous, bordering on skepticism, which is understandable. I can't imagine the pain and questions she must have endured (and still endures), after losing two children and having an autistic son. She's a very intelligent woman, almost intimidatingly so, opinionated and outspoken, but not trusting fate to a distant God who hasn't been fair. I've seen her strength and faith in something to hold the family together.

As the years pass we're all getting softer and starting to mellow like fine wine. I'm hugging now, although not a Gordy Barnes or Jay Gordon hug that squeezes your breath out. Mom is warm to it but dad's still more at ease with a manly handshake. It takes a long time to build bridges.

∽

My brother married a hometown girl and had two boys rather quickly. He and his wife, Cathy moved from Pennsylvania to Mt. Dora, Florida where he worked as a finish carpenter for a millionaire investor doing high-end remodels and made a good living. Sparky took his boys out fishing for grouper and sea bass or whatever, and coached them in sports that the boys excelled in. His life was even-keeled and happy until out of the blue, one day the Navy showed up with documentation that Sparky was AWOL. This was years after he wore a white uniform and stored it the back of his closet. He dutifully saluted and was taken in handcuffs to the brig in Jacksonville. It was such a sudden shock. Sparky had his trouble in the Navy but was positive he'd received a discharge of some sort; how else could he have lived as a free man, working and paying taxes for so many years? It took nearly a year in the brig until things were sorted out. Of all things, it was a paper glitch that put incredible hardship on Cathy and the boys, not to mention knocking Sparky's confidence in the dirt and giving him a chip on the shoulder. Thanks a lot Uncle Friggin' Sam.

Uncle Bill stepped up in a bigtime way and helped relieve some of their financial pressures and Sparky admires him to this day with the greatest respect. There was a debt he was never asked to repay. I didn't hear about the incident until after Sparky spent some time locked up and should have gone to visit him. Instead, I recorded a thirty minute cassette tape of Keith Green's music from the *No Compromise* album on a portable tape player, dubbing in snippets of the gospel message, basically preaching to him, and sent it off in the mail. Back then you could receive packages like that in prison. Sparky never made any mention of it. From where I now sit, my so-called inspiration was the wrong thing to have done. He didn't need being preached at. He needed his brother's support.

I can picture a guy from men's group who I didn't particularly like. He was spiritually belligerent and that's putting it nicely, a bully-boy who was probably picked on as a kid, and was edgy and critical and anti a lot of stuff, outspoken against Catholics and infant baptism for example. I'll give him a name because I can't seem to bring it to mind. Douche-Bag, how's that? You would have taken him for the son of a preacher when his face would pinch like he'd sucked on a lemon, leaning in to add his two cents. His comments were generally along the lines of correction, very judgmental, black and white, and what annoyed me was that he thought he was always right. He quoted Luke 14:26 when I described the situation and asked for prayer at the men's group for Sparky. *"If anyone comes to me and does not hate his father and mother, his wife and children, his brothers and sisters, yes, and even his own life – he cannot be my disciple."* You know what? I have a problem with how the verse is often used, as Douche-Bag so arrogantly put it. You may be a literalist but I'm not; it's a freaking parable. I'll have to ask Jesus about it when I see him, but I don't think he meant in any way to endorse alienating or scorning our family. I'm sorry, I just can't see Jesus being like that. I'm pretty sure Douche-Bag had the wrong idea. He can kiss my shiny hiney.

One of these days, and very soon since this memory has come back to me, I'm going to make the trip and buy my brother a beer to find out what the hell happened in his life at that time. I want to ask his forgiveness for being harsh and overly zealous. It's never too late to seek apologies and make the wrongs we've done to loved ones in our immaturity and impulsiveness right again. My new mantra is: "Blessed are the Peacemakers."

You've probably gathered that this section is about my family. To write and tell of it is bittersweet, but strong love has held us together in many changing seasons. Perhaps the real reason that I feel compelled to make mention of family is because I want to give them credit. May it be on record for eternity, I owe them a debt I can never repay.

I've never been close to my three younger sisters, which is a sad way to begin this. In the elementary years we all had lunch boxes and followed a trail like ducklings to the Lyter Building. Teacher after teacher encountered one of us in class eager to learn. My sisters filled our home with happy activities and seemed to live in a world of their own. They had each other and friends and did what girls do. I teased them as big brothers often do. When I was approaching Junior High and began staggering off script, we became strangers.

~

My baby sister, Jody is the caboose in a train of eight siblings. Presently she's remarried and living back in Williamsport, PA. Her husband is a good man and they're work-out gurus and health food fanatics on a strict Keto diet. I don't hold that against them. They're into a healthy routine. Jo's fifteen years younger than me, looks college age, and could easily run circles around me. She can probably bench press twice what I can. Jo works hard to keep fit, but you can't help but credit some of it on good genes, that and lots of money spent at the salon. She'll be the big 50 this year and is back in college taking nursing courses. I'm in awe of her will and drive to excel at everything she does in life. Even as a kid she was a busy little bee. Dad called her a pioneer girl.

We talk occasionally, well, actually we text; the real conversations generally happen at Christmas and crisis times when one or the other of us picks up the phone. Jo has had her hands full raising three good looking boys. The oldest is athletic and as a teenager resembled me to a T. Pat is one tough SOB. Her middle son is an aspiring artist and a talented photographer with long blonde hair halfway down his back that fits the role. Dan's on the quiet side and reclusive. Jo's youngest has made some bad choices, getting into trouble like his uncle Dirk. We call him Jake. I feel for the kid and wish I lived closer. You have to love your siblings, it's the unwritten rule, but I really like Jo regardless of family ties. I'd like to think we're friends, but we could do better at friendship, which starts with me taking that step.

Melissa is my oldest sister and kind of a hard book to get a read on, or maybe a closed book. Again, I don't really know my sisters. She was the one who tended to Kenny in the years when Kenny was tearing our house apart. It fell in her lap whether she wanted it or not and had to grow up quicker than normal. Mom was a wreck from losing Susy and her days were full with taking care of Kenny. Missy was a perfect little helper. At the time, as I've said, I was beginning to cause chaos as a rebellious juvenile and didn't hang out and get to know her.

Pissy-Missy (the nickname I teased her with), was disciplined and task oriented in every endeavor she took on. She went to college, or should I say three colleges in the span of her young years, and majored in English, History and liberal arts. I'm not sure exactly, but she's certified to teach in public schools. For fun she directs and choreographs her local theater group. She married a handsome Catholic young man and presently serves on the administration board at a huge parochial school in New Jersey. Missy is very talented and as smart as mom, scary smart, and the times we locked horns she chewed me up and spit me out. I always thought her to be critical, but it's Dad's genes that make her who she is. No nonsense and play by the rules is the code.

I'm easily intimidated and absolutely hate any kind of confrontation. My insecurities about the past cause me to be withdrawn whenever anything remotely from yesteryear comes up with my sisters. There have been times I've wrapped up in a blanket of insulation and tip-toed around getting close to make apologies or an explanation, of which my sisters are owed. Someone once said that a person wrapped up inside them self is a small package. Ouch! Hide and seek was a game we played as children. Maybe I should grow up and have the hard discussions with Missy. I'll ply her with white wine beforehand.

Missy and her husband, Tom lost their middle child, a gifted young man who was well connected in school and church. Matt was a charming, bright shining star. He was a drummer in a Christian contemporary band and a quiet leader among his peers. Matt was home from college for summer break and had a fatal car accident on the way to a part-time job interview. His loss rippled throughout the community. When I think about the effect that his death had on Missy and her family it's sobering. Matt's Christian testimony was strong with endless possibilities and promise. If I was God, there'd be some explaining in order. I respect and love Missy, hoping to one day share the cup of pain and healing and find answers. I believe she'd like to as well. Perhaps I'll call Missy tomorrow, but tomorrow never seems to come.

Silly-Jilly is my middle sister and has had a hard row to plow in her life. To begin with, I'm sure there was competition between the sisters growing up and I think she's had a difficult time with self-esteem. Jill is a fun and out-going person, overly talkative, a blonde haired, brown-eyed looker who resemblances what Susy might have looked like had she lived. Jill has a big heart and absolutely adores animals. It would have made sense if she'd gone to college and been a veterinarian or owned a pet shop. Unfortunately, getting average grades came hard for her.

Jill has worked most of her adult life in geriatric facilities at barely above minimum wage and has struggled to make ends meet. Her marriage hit the skids after putting up with abusive behavior from a habitual liar, an adulterous and manipulating husband. Asshole-Ronny turned their three young children against Jill by coercion and lies. Last winter, twenty odd years later and the result of a serious injury, her kids are finally taking steps to reconcile with her. In all her pain and struggles and disappointments, Jill has held firm to believing there's a silver lining in every storm. Mom has written check after check to help Jill out, and I get that. It seems like every family has one in the mix who gets dealt a shitty hand, but Jilly, God bless her, and in spite of all her adversities, is doing okay. My only advice as her big brother is that she needs to find a better boyfriend. Jill deserves a prince in shining armor.

I've heard the murmurings of how awkward things were for my sisters in school following a brother with such an illustrious reputation. "Oh, you're Dirk's sister," a teacher may add with raised eyebrows. I deserve a good slap on the kisser. I'm sorry for all the uncomfortable issues I've caused them, for the hassles and battles they shouldn't have had to fight. Wouldn't it be nice if we could all go back and start over? We're not totally estranged, my sisters and I, but we're in different time zones and that sucks.

The older I get the more I realize how important family is, and that's another subject I'm trying to figure out.

~

The definition of family in our present day culture has drastically morphed from the days of Ozzie and Harriet in the fifties. Those who grew up like I did watching "Father Knows Best" or "Leave it Beaver" probably grumble about the 21st century family. Today's cartoons and sit-coms are flagrant with disrespect and mock old-school family values. Presently, I'm trying to understand this short-attention-span generation that finds amusement in sarcasm. I may have become the liberal I used to despise when I was a constipated evangelical, but I find some humor in South Park. The script has changed, and although it's difficult, we're squeezed to adapt and fit in with the new millennium where personal convictions are challenged. If my being a liberal makes you choke on your Tootsie Roll I'm sorry. I've mentioned previously that I'm a dreamer with utopian ideals, and I'm not the only one.

Every town, city or neighborhood has a myriad of diversity when it comes to the family scenario. A lot has changed from fifty years ago. There are single moms working overtime or two jobs to afford daycare, divorced dads assembling a tricycle or a princess-palace in the backyard for the weekend visit with his grade-school kids. Among the single-parenting families striving to make ends meet, much more diversity is refashioning our communities. Integrated into the milieu is the gay couple, a family down the street from Saudi Arabia or one of those "terrorist countries" whose women wear a hijab, mixed race couples of any imaginable ethnic background, a tribe of Hispanics living under one roof. Good families, working, tax paying families. Must they, too, meet some perquisite according to our expectations or proclivities to be welcomed and included in the neighborhood? I bring this up because in the last four years hate mongering and divisiveness based on ethnicity and sexual orientation has visited every community and home that has a TV. Let's be smart about this; maybe they're of a different color (I'm speaking to us white Anglo-Saxons), those who have an accent, maybe they can't even speak English, or they go to a Mosque or a Synagogue, but are they not entitled to the same rights that we have?

Perhaps a family new to the neighborhood has bought the house across the street and their kids leave stuff on the lawn that annoys you, no sprinkler system, the grass burned-out and weedy, or the sidewalk and driveway marked up with chalk drawings when your property is pristine. Some of these families might not value the things you value and celebrate holidays that you don't. Is it time to install an ADT home alarm system and look into getting a concealed weapon permit? What's up with all the walls and snap judgements based on any of the above, and why all the accusatory finger pointing these days? John Lennon's song *Give Peace a Chance* comes to mind. Could it be that simple?

Let's leave the family scenarios outside the walls and consider the notion of family inside the walls of the average American family. In a serendipitous way, Hallmark movies attempt to portray realism in an unrealistic way that captivates an audience. They're so predictable and sappy. The only family movie I remember being true to life and touching me was *On Golden Pond* with Kathrine Hepburn, Henry and Jane Fonda. The plotlines may differ, but after all the turmoil and conflict there's a happy-ever-after ending. In the matrix of normal life it generally is happy, at least to some degree, but I have friends who've been injured by family dynamics and battle to find solace or meaning in their suffering and alienation that appears to have no happy-ending in sight.

I've been one of those noisy neighbors that politely make introductions wherever I've lived, trying hard to remember names. There are those living within a stone's throw of our door who've suffered from family trauma. We don't know who they are because they hide it so well. We'll chit-chat across the fence or in the parking at Safeway, asking, "how are you're doing?" without really taking the time to consider that a reply might be forthcoming. Perhaps the guy you see jogging every morning has lived alone for years as the result of painful events and made a geographical move, justifying it by a career or education. Others are abandoned or divorced and getting by under unfortunate circumstances for no apparent reason they can begin to understand, issues like infidelity and control, daydreaming about pulling off the perfect murder. I personally feel the pain and anguish of a friend whose husband was self-destructing with alcohol and had to run for her sanity, taking out a restraining order to safeguard her children. And there are those separated with extreme guilt from single-handedly destroying a relationship through unfaithfulness or getting busted with a porn addiction. I don't frequent bars anymore, but how well I remember the single's scene at happy-hour; the fake bravado to disguise loneliness and exaggerated enthusiasm, tossing back drinks with names like "Sex on the Beach" or "50 Shades of Grey" as a substitute companion. If that's your gig, you've probably already had enough free advice and well intentioned little talks about how to find solutions, blah-blah-blah.

My heart goes out to those living under constant pressure to conceal scars of abuse, be it emotional or physical, when estrangement was the only sane and safe place to seek asylum. It's too bad shit happens. Maybe a padlock was installed on the outside of your bedroom door to enforce parental law when you were a kid, as being grounded was taken to a senseless level like locking you in prison. Or perhaps it was something as harmless as hoping the Tooth Fairy left a quarter under your pillow, but instead you had a tooth knocked out by a drunken father. Deep wounds of sexual abuse, molestation, even out-right rape lie repressed under layers of fear. Compounding the pain is an iron fist that hangs over their head with fear of exposing the perpetrator, often with dangerous threats if they're revealed. I think about the daughters (or sons), who confided with their mother in the hope of understanding or retribution for sexual impropriety, but there are mothers who are trapped as well, whose hands are tied and just as fearful of exposing the truth because the monster lurks so near.

I feel bad for those who grew up being laughed at; lied about, back-stabbed, surviving under parental authority that majored in fault-finding, ridicule and judgement that stifled normal growth. Sometimes abuse is subtle, going through years of being unappreciated, ignored, not being invited to a special occasion. The innocence of adolescence comes and goes with many growing pains. How many years have some of the very people we interact with, or ourselves, carry the suffocating weight of being manipulated and feeling that somehow it was our fault? What about the wicked brother or sister that added misery to insult when they were the ones who should have been disciplined and got away with it by preferential treatment? I get angry at the end of a movie or a book when evil isn't served justice, but that's just another unrealistic happy-ending, isn't it?

My home-life wasn't hard or abusive compared to the hell others have experienced, or the hell you're still going through. My story may seem fairly plain and docile; apple pie and The Wonderful World of Disney, but don't we all go through our own seasons of hell? However unique the circumstances may be, either totally chaotic or occasional conflicts, my take on it is if for no other reason we're in relationships, imperfect as most of them are.

Every relationship, whether it's parental or between brother and sister, husband and wife, friends among friends or student and teacher; whatever, they're all of them tricky and risky business. Our personal experiences involved interacting with others and lent to fashioning our character. Some experiences could have been (or still are), enormously exhilarating and wildly fun, healthy, but as sometimes happens, the bottom falls out and everything gets turned upside down like crashing a board game in the heat of a moment. It doesn't matter if all the pieces are in the right place and you're winning and walking on sunshine. Without warning, sirens be-damned, disaster strikes and our world crashes around our feet. If you're like me, the tendency is to react by isolation and hiding the pain, mostly because it's been rare that anyone particularly cared enough to listen.

It might be a minor glitch that intruded our happy place or something serious that comes at the hands of family or close friends. Conflict happens to all of us, these twisted turns of fate, the roller-coaster ride of emotions that we have to deal with. I've found that life is full of paradoxes, a combination of joy and sadness and many unforeseen contradictory things. The puzzling side of the ledger that causes me to question is who's really at fault, and all too often I've blamed myself. The effort it takes to figure out the bad things and the why of it wrenches my neck like an owl looking around warily and suspicious, ready to attack or cower and hide under the safety of wings. Life isn't fair. We ask: "Why me?" I'm pretty sure that isn't the right question to ask. When the crap hits the fan it knocks our breath out and can lay us low for a full count flat on our backs, swooning and dazed. No wonder we wind up battling addictions and dealing with enough depression and humiliation to entertain turning the car wheel into an oncoming semi going sixty miles an hour down the highway.

Or, we could pray a really simple prayer and call out for help.

Without taking the risk to confront the problematic issues from horrible relationships and seek some kind of reconciliation to find healing we'll drown in our own demise. If the option is to resist and hold on white-knuckled, deliberately refusing to forgive, stubbornly drawing the line in the sand, there's a good chance we evolve into a kind of hermit crab carrying his or her home on our backs all alone. I'm a one of those, a hermit crab, dragging around years of slime along my trail, years of shoulda - woulda - coulda's. I think I chose the right word to find clarity and resolve; it involves risk, which in my mind is synonymous to faith.

What I hope to suggest is simply taking that first step, which is forgiving yourself. Reconnecting with family comes second, but if there's a way to promote healing, risk it and take the initiative. Fake it if you have to, or sneak in a word to test the waters. Try telling your mother, if she's still alive, that you love her no matter how critical and domineering she may have been. Send her a card if you can't say the words. A card may break the ice. Who doesn't like getting cards? Propose taking your outwardly hostile or emotionally distant father on a hike if he can walk. Drag him away from work or daytime TV or hitting Beefeater's and tonic before noon to a favorite lookout, maybe for lunch at a restaurant he likes. Get some fresh air, and for God's sake, tell him that you love him while you have the chance. What do you have to lose? The only two people who matter the most in the world is our mother and father. I'm sorry if that grieves you, but without roots, who in the world would we be? I find it interesting that one of the Ten Commandments says to honor our mother and father. There's no mention of whether they're good or bad.

I'm guessing that for some it's too painful to even consider healing the breach. Personally, I can't relate to a depth of suffering so horrific that it's like a descent into hell to go back home. But I can imagine anger festering and hate stewing for years on the back burner becoming familiar, comfortable, even the norm. Hate is a narcotic, a slow drip in the veins numbing pain and memories or inciting them. Contempt and accusations when expressed feels good when we get it off our chest at whatever volume we play it at, silently in our heads or at the top of our lungs. Payback offers temporary satisfaction, a swift climax, the deep cathartic sigh of relief, but it's an awkward reality that rarely lasts.

It's sad and rather unfortunate that more times than not

the person or persons we have issues with and wish were dead probably don't have a clue what they've done to us, or they don't care. In the end, after exerting all our energy, our stubborn, bitter hatred wears us down like crashing from a sugar high accomplishing little more than turning us into the shuffling Mummy wrapped in bonds. Forgiveness withheld and the offense against us replayed over and over will eventually make us as ugly and ignorant as the one who hurt or hates us. Do we become like them? Justified in our foxholes tossing hand grenades?

This isn't a deep revelation and I'm sure you already know this. By surrendering and trying to let go of the really crappy stuff one step at a time and forgiving the unforgivable, healing can begin because you've opened a gate to allow forgiveness to flow into you. Forgive and you will be forgiven is a promise Jesus made, who always has our best interests in mind. We're primarily responsible for our own lives even if someone else chooses to ignore us or reacts differently. It's on them. Yes, it's risky business, but this much I know; even making the effort to forgive takes a little weight off your shoulders.

I'm trying to make sense of my life, of family and friends, the pain and the joy, and little by little the journey is bearing some fruit of healing, albeit hard won. A dear writer friend prompted me to write my memoir, which seemed ridiculous at the time. Jackie Keck was writing her memoir, which I'll tell you about later. She kept a journal and said how helpful it was to put the pen to the page. "Written words have power and magic," she said sounding like a gypsy. "Once they're on paper they're like a prayer. You can fold and make an airplane out of it and fly it away to any old place you please. Let it catch the wind and fly to God's mailbox." That old gal was onto something.

∽

I asked God for guidance to find inner healing and was lead to the Lost and Found Department. As always, a room of surprising secrets awaited me. I can't tell you the number of the room as at a motel, or the exact room in a house with many rooms and point you to the right door. It reminds me of the wardrobe in the Narnia stories that is a gateway to a faraway land. I'm not sure if I find it or it finds me. I've a sneaking suspicion this is where God's mailbox is.

The hidden room, my haven of late, has wandering narrow aisles like a basement library or a storeroom with bins and shelves and towering racks of memories labeled alphabetically in chronological order. They're color coded like indicators on a traffic light with stickers of green and yellow and red. You know how it works. Go – wait – stop. Timing is everything. If you find yourself at the Lost and Found Department and are curious enough to enter you'll have the option to begin sorting, waiting, or not sort at all. But the time will eventually come when the shitty stuff tucked away will fall in your lap. Don't be alarmed. It's not all bad.

Awaiting to be discovered or rediscovered are books and artwork from Kindergarten and onward, a variety of shoes you've worn over the years and the places they've taken you, different haircuts and styles in so many changing seasons, a favorite toy from a long ago birthday or Christmas, a photograph album or scrapbook, phone numbers of old friends and some who maybe weren't really friends, scribbled on the back of match packs or a business card that brings back faces and names and places. Somewhere in the milieu is a collection of record albums full of songs that still sing in your soul that you remember on the first few notes with such powerful association to the past. Memories and events come at you from all directions bursting like Fourth of July fireworks, some painful or too beautiful for words. The Lost and Found Department is a veritable warehouse of bits and pieces of our lives buried under years of forgetfulness (sometimes deliberately forgotten), painful images pushed to the side and moments of blissful and cherished images emerging in the distant fog, all of it within reach. We're drawn with inquisitiveness as a child to a kaleidoscope or at times rubber-necking morbidly as if wanting to see blood and gore from driving by a car accident. "Go ahead," a voice whispers, "take a peek, I double-dog-dare you."

I speak of memories, those long ago experiences when we were grade school kids like Murray at the blackboard, of being embarrassed or wrongly scolded or even being rightly rewarded. The challenge of tramping off to college on your own, feeling homesick or glad to finally be free from parental control, or falling in love or getting jilted and heartbroken by a lover. And buried deeper still are the really horrible memories we don't touch for fear that if we did our heart would turn to stone. It will take effort and courage to go against feelings, rummaging through dank pages of pain and looking for what was lost, digging deep to find some essence of absolution and make peace with the past, or revel in the surprising discovery of happy times we've forgotten and rebound in renewed joy. When you find it, and you will, healing is a pearl of great value. There's an old Phil Keaggy song with a line that goes; *"Like waking up from the longest dream, how real it seemed... until Your love broke through."* I think it's like that. We don't have to understand healing to be healed any more than understanding God's blessing to be blessed.

I offer this encouragement; embrace the moment of impact when revelation meets the now staring you in the face. Healing can't be bought but it can be found, though not to contradict myself, it can sometimes be rather costly. What is necessary for healing boils down to a choice of personal surrender, or laying down our lives as the gospel puts it. We relinquish the grip of our agendas and expectations and let go of the wheel, or as the saying goes in AA, Let Go - Let God. The question is how desperate are we, and are we willing to explore the labyrinth and pay the price even at our own sacrifice to be healed?

# 11

*Central* Pennsylvania is a beautiful place to live or visit, as I'm sure you would say about wherever you're from. It was my home for 49 years. I've jokingly made the comment that God practiced in Virginia and New York and got it right in the heart of Appalachia country. We call our neck of the woods; *Pleasant Valley.*

Rolling mountains of hardwoods turn vibrant with color in the fall that entertains the inner child with wonder. Rivers and lakes and streams with rainbow trout and bass (a fisherman's paradise), charts an intricate tapestry on the landscape. Cold water gurgles from springs fresh enough to drink from that we carried home in jugs before there was such a thing as bottled water. The area where I live is surrounded by sprawling farms rich with agriculture, corn, soybeans, acres of tomatoes, strawberries and even tobacco grows from fencerow to fencerow as far as the eye can see. Amish buggies trot along on the country roads that you have to give right-a-way to. My bank in Mifflinburg, a town founded in 1792, has a loafing shed and hitching posts for the horses. You had to watch where you stepped in the parking lot. Quaker meeting houses, massive Victorians and flagstone Federal-style homes two hundred years old that were on the Underground Railroad in the Civil War are still lived in or turned into museums or gift shops. Picturesque barns and covered bridges worthy of a Kodak moment and country stores with homemade goods where you can buy whoopie pies and scrapple gives you the sense of going back in time. I could go on and on and this is just Union County.

The old fashioned tradition to load up the kids and take a Sunday afternoon drive is a wonderful way to spend the day. Among my favorite daytrips was starting at Country Cupboard for breakfast before a drive to State College on Route 192. A stop at Halfway Dam for a pit-call and a walkabout was relief in uncountable ways. The road trips never disappointed me, small villages with an old hotel having draft beer and family-style food, a gift shop with local artisans were worth stopping to check out. Going in other directions, Ricketts Glen, the Pennsylvania Grand Canyon near Wellsboro, or hiking up High Knob are great places to find your Zen. A small campground nearby that backs up to the Chillicothe Creek called Shangri-La was another goldmine.

After returning from Trinidad I went through a phase I call "plateauing." If you've been a Christian for some years (or maybe it's just life), you'll understand and relate. There's a lay-over between Candyland and Mordor, kind of a roadside rest, but I want to address this in light of our spiritual experience. The unpredictable cadence of ups and downs and leveling off happens to a person of faith. My choice in using the word plateau as a metaphor implies there's a place for a season to layover between mountain top experiences when God is near and dear and the dark valley of questions and estrangement; safe terrain to regroup. It'd be exhausting to battle without a breather. Thank God he knows how much our fortitude can handle. These are times to wait out the maelstrom of seasonal storms, a time of normalcy, repose and healing, of life getting even-keeled. I'm certainly not saying that I enjoy chaos, but for me, those times tend to conjure boredom, restlessness and lethargy, the wearisome same old routine. If I was intuitive and realized the Lord was allowing me the opportunity to recharge my spiritual battery it was a great time to read and pray more. During one particular long dry spell when I was spinning my wheels and needed a change of scenery from work and weekends spent in prison seminars, the drab grey walls and razor wire, I took Cassie on a shopping trip to Sportsman's Warehouse. It was early summer in the mid 1990's and we bought a crap-load of camping gear. Cassie wasn't a Girl Scout and it was fun to show her the ropes.

Whenever a free weekend turned up, Cassie and I explored the State Parks in Pennsylvania; a map indicates there are over a hundred to choose from. We'd find the perfect spot in the trees or along the lake; location – location – location, and set up camp. We'd make love and christen each new site, checking an X on the State Park map as a notable occasion that I kept it in the glove compartment of my truck. I'd scout the area and gather firewood, tend the fire, take a nap or row around Lake Jean or Bald Eagle Reservoir or wherever we happened to be in a canoe, mindlessly fishing and relaxing, generally being a slug. We'd hike and played games at the picnic table. Cassie did most of the cooking, and when she wasn't putting together a sumptuous meal, she'd spend hours doing her own thing. I never once worried about her being out on her own. I was and still am an avid reader. Perhaps that summer it was C.S Lewis' space trilogy or *Watership Down*. I read everything Robert Ludlum published (one of my dad's favorite authors), and discovered the *Bourne* series that I found to be much better than the movies. I'd get lost for an entire afternoon with a book while lounging in a hammock.

We'd often have company, as campers are famous for being friendly, and make S'mores and share stories. I'd play guitar and lead everyone who joined us with campfire songs in the evenings and peppered in Sunday school choruses for the kids. My claim to fame was singing every verse of *King of the Road*.

Shangri-La Campground was only half an hour from home but felt like a faraway paradise. It was just across the river, and along the way was a drive-in restaurant called The Fence where the best fish sandwich basket could be had. Shade trees bordered a muddy creek that provided plenty of catfish caught on a worm. There were flush toilets and hot showers, a camp store with ice and Nutty Buddies and the essentials for campers. In a mowed field was a play park with swings, basketball hoops and horseshoe pits. The grounds were secluded and you felt like civilization was on the opposite side of the world. Shangri-La was a fitting name indeed. On one particular weekend, quite expectantly, I had an experience in my soul like a Monarch butterfly birthing from its cocoon.

I stirred awake as sunlight warmed the tent and eased out of our doubled up sleeping bag. Cassie liked to cuddle. I've always been an early bird and snuck out after struggling with the stubborn zipper and stir the embers to life in the fire pit. After rinsing out the old percolator for coffee, it was "Dirk-time." We'd played Canasta well past midnight and Cassie was still sleeping. I lugged my fold-up canvas chair, balancing a go-cup of coffee in hand along with my bible and notebook in a backpack, and wandered to the creek for some quiet time. I needed something "God breathed" and fresh, a word to jump start getting off the plateau and out of my complacency. One can live almost indefinitely on a plateau if not mindful of stagnation.

I turn to the Psalms as one might do rising in the middle of the night with a parched throat longing for a drink of water. David, the Shepherd King, was a man after God's heart and my idol, although maybe I shouldn't have put it that way. We're not supposed to have idols. I'm captivated by the fact that although he wasn't perfect he was the anointed one, an underdog who fought and slayed a giant, but more so that he was a musician and left us a record of his life in lyrics. David was a man made of flesh, not a mythical character of legend like the Norse god Ragnarok. David was a great warrior and served Israel as an honorable king, as compared to his predecessor Saul, but he was weak and lusty and fickle, getting into trouble with a woman named Bathsheba. He's someone I can relate to. I also relate to Peter in the gospels with his head-strong boasting but denying the Lord in a moment of weakness. I sat beside the creek daydreaming as caffeine began pumping into my blood. If my recollection is right, I was pondering the verse in Psalm 139: *"O Lord, you have searched me and you know me."*

David often made mention that the Lord knew him, which probably didn't take a great deal of effort on God's part. If God knew him, he knew me. Like it or not we're under God's scrutiny 24-7. It's not hard to find that notion a comfort and be reassured by God's compassionate attention, but it also troubles me. I know I never measure up 100% and that's a sticky issue, however, God unquestionably knows my heart and is looking out for my good. I'm fully aware that such a phrase can be used as a cop-out or an excuse to justify sin. "I'm sorry for what I did," rolls off the tongue whether we are truly sorry or not, adding a modifier, "but God knows my heart." He does know us, our motives and intentions, those things below the bottom-line that we may not even know about ourselves.

I felt a strong unction to make a confession of faith. I needed to claim my birthright as a son of God, not claim the thirty or hundred fold scam that name-it and claim-it televangelists preach. Confession is a good thing. Honest confession cleanses, clarifies, redirects. I pulled out my notebook and wrote down my thoughts, surprised that it vaguely took on the form of poetry or a song. I went back to the campsite to check the fire and retrieved the old Gibson from my truck. What developed was a tune in three cords and a minor in G, a simple song, but destined to mark my life and the lives of hundreds who would sing along. It was such a blessing, this gift from God, lifting me from my plateau and putting fresh wind in my sails beside the Chillicothe Creek at Shangri-La.

## The Tent Song

*Oh Lord, I confess you alone are my lover*
*In the cloud by day Thou dost cover me*
*In the cloud by day Thou dost cover me.*
*So I'll roll up my tent and pack away my bed*
*For the glory of the Lord is moving on ahead.*

*In the night Thou dost lead my path by*
*your fire*
*Oh Lord, when you move I'll not tire*
*Oh Lord, when you move I'll not tire.*
*So I'll roll up my tent and pack away my bed*
*For the glory of the Lord is moving on ahead."*

I remember being startled when Cassie touched the back of my neck. She awoke upon hearing me singing and had snuck up, standing quietly behind me with not just sleep in her eyes but tears.

"That's a beautiful song," she said. "I'll get the tape player. You can't forget this one."

I've often thought about adding a verse or two thinking it was incomplete and too simplistic, but it is what it is. The story of God leading the Children of Israel through the wilderness by a cloud by day and a pillar of fire by night merits study and meditation. Subjects like protection and illumination, waiting for guidance, Sabbath rest and a sense of mission are a few of my favorite things besides strawberry shortcake.

If ever I boast, I boast in the Lord. I wouldn't be alive if it wasn't for God's mercy. I've done some things right in my life, the good stuff, surprisingly. Some of it may be rewarded when I sit with Jesus face to face and share a cup of new wine. Some has already given me a great reward of satisfaction and fulfillment this side of heaven's gate. For a guy who should've been named Gilligan that's not too bad. You remember Gilligan, the guy marooned on an island with the crew of the *SS Minnow*? In every episode he'd flub up, but at the end, his mishaps and misadventures and bizarre antics turned out harmless and hilariously funny or he saved the day. Yeah, I think Gilligan would have been an appropriate name for me.

I can picture myself as the kid who offers his mother flowers torn off at the stem from the neighbor's garden, smiling a silly half-cocked grin, proud as a peacock. "Oh honey, what have you done now?" Mother would say, going to fetch a vase. I'd like to think I've done some good deeds and made my Father in heaven happy as well. I hope and believe in the good news that God views us as his blessed children all the time, mishaps included. I'm sure there are a few others besides me who are relieved to be included in his family. So we mess up – big deal. We're still God's kids.

Here's a strange picture that just came to my mind, an abracadabra moment. Please forgive my tendency to daydream. You might think it's a slight of hand magic trick when God pulls the happy rabbit out of his hat and not the ornery, obstinate, dirty one with a twisted ear and a missing nose, but it's really quite simple. It's the only rabbit in his hat, kind of like us. In spite of our crabby annoying bitchiness and self-centered wants (me-me-me), our sulking pettiness and innate narcissism, we're washed clean and spotless, all our frayed edges stitched up better than new, emerging to a new day as a bright-eyed pure rabbit. I hope it's not sacrilege to picture God giddy with happiness when we twitch our nose in curiosity and nuzzle against his chest.

# 12

*A* couple from Bristol, England came to visit our fellowship and conducted a week long teaching series on the early church based on the Books of Acts in the New Testament. The message focused on the importance of community being central and lived out in a practical sense, of relating with intimacy, sharing all things in common. The ideals of modeling the body of Christ upon such simplicity and being so connected resonated in our little church. Overall, I'm pretty confident that we were tracking in the same vein, but we were young and naïve. A kick in the butt served us well. I wanted to believe in the unbelievable dream recorded in Acts chapter two, paying closer attention to the section describing the fellowship of believers as Luke recorded it rather than making an issue over tongues in the beginning section. The prototype of the early church sure was different than most of the Christianity I'd been familiar with.

We embraced the teaching and decided to walk closer with each other and hang out more often. Cassie and I bought our second home in Lewisburg to be closer to our church family. One of the places some us routinely gathered was at a family restaurant called *Amity House* in our shopping center. We had our own table of twelve in the back corner. I indulged in enough banana splits to sink a ship; or rather, they sank in my waistline. As a small microcosm of the Body of Christ, we grew that summer, spending quality time together and bore the fruit of deeper caring and love, being much more involved in one another's lives. But intimacy also reveals hidden flaws. Not everything glimmers and shines in the kingdom. Regardless of setbacks, you can hang your hat on a promise: *All things work together for good for those who love the Lord.* It just might take a while.

I received a troubling phone call one evening from a dear sister in the Lord. She was engaged to a young man who had a handsome face if he smiled, which he rarely did. His face often looked more like a wax figure that slightly sagged from being under a heat lamp. He was a very gifted pianist and could play Beethoven's 5th or 9th or any symphony with his eyes closed. He was a genius but also manic-depressive. In a group situation he was generally quiet, surprising us sometimes by being unusually animated. He was just a little mad but I took no issue with him, I had many so-called "crazy" friends. With medication he was social and charming and intelligent. I can't mention names, but she loved him, planning a wedding later that summer. The fellow lived in his own place across town. She gave me an earful on the phone that he was having a bit of an episode and would I go see him. I had no idea what she meant by having an episode or what I was getting myself into.

The front door was open when I arrived as if he was expecting visitors. The living room glowed and I heard music from somewhere inside and assumed he was playing the piano. I called upon entering and followed the sound of classical music to the dining room to find him pacing the floor; six or eight jerky steps, then turn on his heels and back again, over and over. He didn't hear me or know anyone was in his house. In the corner was a record player turned up nearly at full volume, maybe Tchaikovsky. I gently lifted the needle and the room suddenly became unnervingly quiet. I stood in the archway and called his name, receiving a perturbed look bordering on scorn. I knew that he knew me but it was as though he stared right through me, a stranger of no consequence. He glowered at me, looking really pissed off that I had the audacity to turn off his music.

I know virtually nothing about mental illness and he kind of scared me. I asked him in the friendliest, calmest voice I could manage if he would come into the living room and sit on the couch with me. I suggested prayer. For a man of slight build and stooped shoulders he seemed to enlarge and became threatening. "It's me," I pleaded, "your friend Dirk." His eyes raged. I feared that he would do violence to me or to himself. Unfortunately this was way before cell phones and I left him on the couch, finding a wall phone in the kitchen to make some calls. His fiancé was my first call. After explaining the scene she said to call for an ambulance, apparently he'd stopped taking his meds. I didn't want to do that. I didn't wish for him to wind up in the psych ward, which seemed like a pretty good bet. Instead, I called a friend.

Jay and Lauren came right away and we spent the better part of the night trying to reason and talk sense and comfort him. His fiancé arrived but remained in the shadows, always observant and off to the side. We shared a few cups of tea in quiet tension and sporadic rounds of verbal abuse that was mostly directed at me, the likes I'd not been subjected to for a very long time. After exhausting every possible approach and attempt to minister peace and sanity, we loaded him into the backseat of Jay's car and took him to Geisinger Medical Center. From there it was up to the professionals.

We were relieved on one hand, the long night was grueling, but it was sad as well to leave our friend behind. I wanted Jesus to make everything right. I prayed for a miracle, but in the end nothing turned out the way I expected. Instead of a miracle, the fellow was committed to the hospital. I recall standing in the parking lot when the ordeal was over gulping in cool air as the sun came up, craving a cigarette.

So, what's the moral of the story? Maybe it's as simple as

being available to help someone in need even though you're not equipped, but trust that God is.

The couple did in fact marry later that year. He stuck to his medication and worked for the college playing piano for services, weddings and special church events. His wife was an RN in the pediatric unit at the hospital. They were good for one another and in the coming years had two beautiful babies. We remained good friends. I wonder if he remembers anything from that bizarre night. Maybe some things are better left forgotten.

I was doing a remodel for some friends in the church when another curveball knocked me for a loop. Again, I'll give them an alias to maintain their anonymity. Steve was going out of town on a business trip, and before leaving we had gone over the details concerning the work and had a plan. Tammy, his wife was the outspoken one, changing things and making it quite clear what she wanted. No problem. I generally dealt with the wife on home improvements more than the husband anyway. The husband usually comes on board with a check at the end. There was an air of hostility in their banter that made me uncomfortable and didn't want to get in the middle of things. I hadn't seen this side of their relationship; they were so sweet in church.

I've been in married couple's homes doing remodel projects for years and have had many pleasant experiences working in partnership with those who agreed on design and colors and things like tile and trim. If I'm working there for an extended period of time we almost become family. The projects always go smoother that way, and the celebration upon completion and seeing a couple's mutual excitement at their dream come true is rewarding. Unavoidably, there's the job from hell. Cat lovers are my least favorite clients, not because I dislike cats but that I'm allergic to them. One of my pet peeves, even before unloading tools and materials, is when I find myself walking on eggshells and trying to avoid couples changing things from our last planning meeting, belittling and nitpicking at each other as though it was the glue that held them together. I'm ready to run for the hills. It's like getting caught in the crossfire of bitchiness, one-up-manship, "I wouldn't do it that way," and old gripes thrown in the mix to get the last word. I'm standing in their space to remodel and alter things like I have what... a magic wand? It's tempting to ask the cats for their opinion. When it gets to be a bit too much, I politely excuse myself, going out to the truck for anything to get away. I'd sit on the tailgate and replay the drama. *If my wife talked to me like that I'd draw the line.* Draw the line? Really? Cassie could be a perfectionist and nitpicky to the sixteenth inch but typically I'd walk away. Eventually we'd find a compromise, as do most of my clients. It's rather unfortunate that imperfect men marry perfect women.

Steve was away for the week while I tore apart their laundry and bathroom, reconfiguring it into an open concept. Tammy had a pot of coffee on every morning and we'd visit and go over things related to the work. By the middle of the week she was confiding personal things; martial problems, disillusionment, sexual frustration was implied, and how lonely she felt. I listened and showed an interest, but it slowly began dawning on me that she might be taking my sympathy in the wrong way.

Counselors can get into trouble and often do. The vocation to facilitate healing involves listening and discerning deep, hidden needs. A good counselor is not only classroom educated but intuitive, sensitive, able to hear what's below the surface. A client becomes trusting and dependent, opening the most vulnerable secrets and pain in their life. The sharing of personal guilt and hurt and loneliness becomes lucid, transparent, exposed with confession, and hope hangs like promising fruit within reach. Questions and answers are volleyed back and forth to find light at the end of the tunnel. In the matrix of thrumming emotional and mental juices flowing in such a personal manner, it's easy to succumb to an affair of sorts (even for spirit-filled people), however innocent in guise and totally harmless, yet volatile and potentially dangerous. Sympathetic words become the life-preserver for someone drowning and it's only natural that they reach out. Touching is the clincher, for a touch has latent powers. Tammy reached for my hand.

Toward the end of the week she came in to check out how everything was going. She may have overheard my grumbling. I have a habit of talking aloud to myself while working out a problem about some adjustment on construction. I was building a custom cabinet over the tub and shower surround and it needed trim I hadn't planned on. Tammy was wearing a clingy Nike workout get-up, bare-foot and no bra, and stood on the edge of the tub to see how the cabinets would work, although you could reach the doors from the floor. She wiggled suggestively at about eye level. Nice butt, I have to admit. It was going on lunchtime and I bowed out, asking her if she wanted anything from La Casa, a great sub shop in town, and was blockaded at the backdoor.

"Can you please just hug me and stay for a while? Don't run off."

Tammy was an attractive woman different in ways from Cassie, and isn't that what draws a man to look at someone other than his wife? She was taller, had shoulder length dark hair and a runner's body, 10-12 years younger. The hug was obligatory like I was hugging my sister, or so I tried. Yes, the bells rang in my head and stirred in my loins.

Call it divine intervention or a moment of clarity, but something gave me pause and a prayer rose from my soul. I don't remember exactly what I prayed, if it was for me or for her, but I held her by the shoulders and looked into her eyes. Was it by the Spirit of God or fear or intuition that made me hit the brakes? I'm not sure. The temptation to kiss her beat like a drum in my soul. I'm no saint, but I prayed for Steve and Tammy, I prayed they would discover something they hadn't found or find something they'd lost. I spoke to her as from seeing a vision, a snapshot photo of a giftwrapped package waiting for them to open together like on Christmas morning. Thank God that he intervened with an image to catch my attention. I prayed that Jesus would heal and bind them together as one and rediscover what drew them together in the first place. It was short and to the point. We didn't talk afterwards. She appeared broken. I turned and went to lunch, taking the rest of the afternoon off to let things cool down.

I confess that I've had my share of fantasies and *if only*, but I'm glad to have been saved the consequences of making a wrong choice, not just on my part, but the wellbeing of my friends. The complications would have been disastrous. Steve and Tammy are solid to this day with grown kids and probably still yammering at one another in a new home, hopefully getting along better on projects.

Maybe everything didn't glitter and shine, but we had the essentials engraved on our hearts. Love, patience and the willingness to walk together were the roots that bound us and made us a community. We tried to exemplify Jesus' life and allowed one another the room to grow as well as fail. Being small in numbers made it hard to hide or disguise real life issues of disagreements, slights and offenses, pride and sin. In an atmosphere that fostered acceptance we did our best to forgive, made meals for one another, visited the sick among us and prayed and cried on each other's shoulders. I can testify to the brothers circling around me and laying their hands on my wounded soul many times, weeping with me, encouraging me, challenging and steering me in a direction of healing. The couple from England who taught a series on authentic church dynamics ignited a flame under us that prioritized relationships within the body of Christ. I'm ruined as a result. Church, as I now see it, will never be the same.

# 13

*I'm* amused by sites that draw my attention while driving down the road and make my head turn. Ring-necked Pheasants and deer always make me slow down, as do old barns, one room school houses and farm equipment working the fields. Yes, I lived in a very rural community. Signs along the county roads are also head-turners, you see them everywhere; placards of so-called words of wisdom from Christian enthusiasts. Granted, I live in the heart of Amish and Mennonite country, but what's up with the negativity? It's like the framed needlework hiding Warden Norton's wall safe in "The Shawshank Redemption." *His judgement cometh and that right soon.* Signs are nailed to a post beside mailboxes, others are stuck here and there along fencerows or on a tree in front of farmhouses declaring that very thing, and quite frankly it bothers me. Judgement - Repent - the wages of sin is death, that sort of thing. I have to admire the country bumpkin who scales a rock face or a bridge with a can of white paint and a brush and scribbles *Jesus Saves* in places I wonder how in the world he managed to get to. What are people thinking? Do they honestly believe someone driving by takes notice and suddenly feels great remorse for their sins? I think most of them shake their heads like me at the ostentatious display of such a limited understanding of the word of God, wondering if there isn't any good news concerning the gospel.

It's easy to lambast the sinner, for the fact is we're all sinners and deserve a good lambasting. The alternative is investing the time and paying attention to people who have been victimized, grieve and hobble through life without a whole lot of hope. I use the word invest deliberately, because to reach out and be the hands of Jesus takes being approachable as well as an enormous amount of patience and spending time in the trenches.

As Christians we are called to go forth and make disciples. The first step is simply being willing and available; the next steps take you wherever God leads and that's where it gets interesting. If you're listening and obedient and want to help people it will take you down a path that squeezes both time and resources. But most of us are selfish or timid, and isn't it easier to hide behind a verse painted on a wooden sign? Ambivalence is one thing, for many of us are too insecure in our own skin to reach out, but to hold an axe over someone's head with threats like "turn or burn" and take the high seat of judge and jury isn't only a perversion of the spirit of the gospel, in my opinion it turns more people away and does more harm than good. Maybe I'm just hypersensitive concerning judgement, but wouldn't it be better to meet the needs rather than tear down a person? How about building bridges of love, turn our living rooms into hospitals of mercy, shine a little the light in the darkness? Hope and peace and joy are perhaps among the rarest commodities in our land and what most people are looking for. I haven't seen a display in the grocery store: buy two – get one free with the coupon.

How are we to be God's hands in the world if we only shake the safe hands of those in our church? I wonder how many Christians have close non-Christian friends, or is that going outside the box and taboo as well? I can hear Douche-Bag railing on me in men's group; "Come out from among them. You're compromising." I shared the testimony about my encounter at a rum shop in Trinidad when I prayed not to die if I took the offered drink, hoping for an opportunity to share the gospel, and Douche-Bag wanted to judge me? Screw him and everyone like him is what I want to say. If I had the courage, I'd grab a bucket of paint and a brush and climb up beside the *Jesus Saves* message on the cliff and add: *and is a friend of sinners.*

～

Operation Rescue was a nationwide Pro-life organization started by Randall Terry somewhere in the 90's. There were flyers on a table in the entryway at church about an upcoming event. They were sponsoring a rally in our state capital and a friend and I decided to go. I've mentioned Thor; he was the college kid who inadvertently led me to my best friend Jay in the early days of New Covenant Church. Thor isn't anything Viking-like besides his name, although his roots are obviously Norse being a Samuelson. He stands six foot-five, a bean pole, soft spoken and gentlemanly by nature. He's the only guy I know who stops at stop signs and uses hand signals when riding his bike. I can't picture him with a war shield and an axe hanging on his back while peddling his Schwinn. We drove to Harrisburg with the sole mission of supporting a peaceful anti-abortion protest.

I had mixed thoughts about the issue and shared my feelings with Thor. We both felt some trepidation about what we were doing, however for different reasons. Thor was decidedly pro-life. I was decidedly undecided. I believe in Pro-life (I actually voted once for Reagan on that one agenda when a hundred others irked me), but my conscience also believes in a woman's right to choose. It's not as ambiguous as you think. I have convictions that both are rights every individual can freely chose, and even in the tension of opposite points of view we should be able to coexist and hold our planet together without tearing it apart over one issue. I unequivocally believe in autonomy and personal choice and hope that my heart is equally open and loving on all sides of the issue. Whoever said that there are two sides to every story had wisdom.

We gathered on Front Street, a main thoroughfare along the river in Harrisburg, over a hundred strong in front of a well-known abortion clinic. Thor and I stood on the sidewalk as observers, just one more number to add to the protesters ranks on the evening news. I didn't hold a placard or join in with the chanting, I watched and prayed. There were couples who turned away either reconsidering having an abortion or fearful of the TV cameras. I felt bad for the women who pressed through the crowd to keep their appointments. They were assaulted with a barrage of abusive language as if getting pelted by rotten tomatoes or rocks. Murderer! Baby Killer! You'll rot in hell! The accusations gave me concern as to who the real victims were. Such loathing and vehemence cut the morning air, most of it coming from the male protesters. Isn't that odd? The women were less vocal.

Don't ask me how the event took such sudden turn, yet again my mind slips and the details escape me. This was my first time at a protest. Maybe it was being inexperienced or my naivety, but Thor and I got caught up in a small group who decided to outflank security and entered the clinic lobby. Someone produced a length of tow chain. We huddled close, the dozen or so of us, looping the chain tightly around our feet or hands and padlocked ourselves to a commercial heat unit. Just in case you thought I was wishy-washy, let me ask, have you spent a night in jail for protesting abortion, whatever side you're on? Do you have a criminal record of trespassing and conspiracy? Did you shell out court costs and fines? Thor and I did. The city jailers were even so kind as to make me unlace the thin leather ribbing from my Docker boat shoes. Guess they thought I was psychotic and might hang myself. I don't bring this up to make comparisons about how adamant you are for being Pro-Life or Pro-Choice, nor do I imply that I was the better Christian man, but it makes me scratch my head at how I'll be judged for the stand I take.

The abortion issue is volatile and full of passion, how well I know. My empathy swings both ways. There's another group that rarely gets any mention of: the fathers. I'm now 65 and my days of being fruitful and multiplying have faded. I never had children. Cassie had a complete hysterectomy at twenty-something that probably saved her life. The one chance I had, and this is getting way ahead of my story, was with a woman when I was separated who became pregnant and decided on having an abortion because we were just getting started in a relationship. She suffered from complications and it's questionable if she'll be able to have a child again. We both lost. You have no idea how much I've grieved. But at the end of the day, I respect a woman's right to choose what she wants to do with her body and her vision of life.

As simplistic as it may sound (some will call my reasoning moronic), I believe in my heart of hearts there's a special place in heaven for the babies and they'll live for eternity in the care of a wonderful father. My consolation is in knowing that many of them are in a better place and have been spared the terrible scars that could (or would), have happened in uncountable cases. Rape and incest are not the sole exceptions. I can think of a few more; alcoholism, drug addiction, malfunctioning fathers ill-equipped to provide and be a loving father, jobless and demanding servitude, not to mention those with a criminal record of abusive and violent behavior. Consider the mother who has an evil side worse than Gollum strolling through Walmart in her pajamas, clouting and yelling foul-mouthed insults at her kid in the cart for just being a curious kid. It makes one wonder what she does in the privacy of her home. Maybe she didn't want to be a mom in the first place; perhaps she shouldn't have been. The result of unprotected sex became a scornful weight too difficult to be responsible for, encroaching a career-plan or welfare and food stamps allotment and having to stay sober, and unfortunately the poor child takes the brunt of outrage and resentments. The scenario of a friendly stork delivering a bundle of joy is a farce for such a "mother." If there is a Romper Room in heaven, I hope that every child gets rewarded a toy or Hersey Bar, as well as love.

It makes me sad that we don't live in a perfect world, but I sure don't want legislation requiring by law what anyone should to do with their private lives. Where would such directives take us if morality is based on the government? China does it, and who among us would want to live under the shadow of tyranny? I don't think it's about Conservatives vs. Liberals. Perhaps the greater challenge (instead of protesting), involves helping a woman on the road of turmoil to find saving grace and figuring it out between herself and God. People like you and me are either grace-dispensers or soul-wounders. Our outspoken principles create openness and second chances or closed doors that foster isolation and contempt. You choose which one seems most like the heart of God. When it comes to choice, I choose mercy.

As long as I'm skating on thin ice and second guessing myself to proceed, I have a dear friend to tell you about. My experience since knowing Mark introduces another controversial topic that has been redefined in my life.

Mark, a made-up name after the famous and flamboyant Mark Twain, has been a long-time friend of mine. He checks in periodically on Messenger with pics of holiday gatherings with his friends at an elaborate table. He always adds a gem of humor or a genius one liner. I envy his success as a therapist and how connected he is in his community. Mark always looks healthy and tanned, devilishly grinning like he has a trick under his sleeve. He and his partner own a beautiful home in Delaware and a condo in Florida. Mark has his doctorate and worked hard to get where he is. Life has treated him well in spite of struggles and humble beginnings.

I'm a dyed in the wool heterosexual, but I wholeheartedly embrace my gay friend. Mark and I never had an agenda to try and change each other's mind. I don't recall ever having heated arguments or trying to coerce him to repent of his sexuality.

We were friends and talked about Jesus. He struggled to hide his identity when he was young and visiting with us at Lamb Fellowship when I first met him. Mark lived behind Cassie and me at the time and we spent a lot of time together. He wasn't much of a cook and openly shared his life with us while double-dipping nachos and guacamole. Mark was given to brutal honesty if he trusted you. He loved Jesus, unquestionably, and had deep insights. His sensitivity to the love of God was probably his equilibrium because society in those days frowned on homosexuals.

He was confronted by the leadership at Lamb Fellowship and given an ultimatum, basically repent or be banished, a hard line to draw. Mark took it in stride, sometimes flippantly and cavalier with a brave shrug and a smirk, or get unusually quiet, overcompensating rejection and his inner turmoil in mood swings and would disappear for a while. I looked for his car in the driveway every morning before going to work and checked in on him. They were agonizing days for Mark, floundering with identity, questioning why he was born the way he was, uncertain why God would deal him such a challenge. I'm not going to say that he had a darker side, that's his business, but I'm sure it was a struggle for him to fit in with the overall church scene. I felt bad for Mark when he left the fellowship. Cassie and I missed the times he would just drop in and eventually lost touch with him.

I always had respect for Mark. He worshipped with us and was well liked, flitting like a butterfly and very involved socially. He was a part of our tapestry, another color or flavor that added zest. I can still hear his laughter. Whenever he shared anything about Jesus he'd light up, his hands moving faster than his words like an excited Italian. When Mark was no longer among us a sad void took the place where he should have been. I felt torn between choosing sides that never should have been an option. Aren't we called to love one another? Or does that mean only the ones we agree with? You can say one thing and quite another by actions.

Here again is one of those controversial issues that spike blood pressure in conservative churches and voters in red states. Like the issue of abortion, the LGBTQ community is under the gun. There seems to be no middle ground on either side of the fence, no truce, no willingness to re-evaluate. Many mainline church denominations have adapted to the new millennium and accept the homosexual community, daring to bare the labels of those for or against. Thank God a gay person can attend church somewhere and be comfortable.

This is a very ambitious subject for me to tackle and one I'm neither educated nor eloquent to address on any front, especially in a theological way. Let me go out on limb rather precariously and suggest that the Bible is a guide book subject to personal revelation, albeit God-breathed. We're offered a map to chart our course with things like devotion, verses resplendent with poetry, proverbs to glean wisdom, parables that teach love, guidance concerning finance, marriage, insight into history and culture. Every angle of relational issues is addressed. We have a glimpse of the universe God created in amazing splendor for our enjoyment, landscapes and celestial galaxies.

Jesus painted pictures with words and if entertained they make us think, or at least ponder his profound ideals. He probably grew weary from debating with the Sadducees about rules and law. If the actual law applies and merits condemnation, then gluttony and cowardice and adultery and lying must be included. But we don't hear that part of the message from a two ton hippo hiding falsehood, complicity and compromise covering their own sin behind the mighty pulpit while spewing judgement on gay people. A tiny voice whispers in my ear to be kind and put it a different way, but it's hard. It's so tempting to say to such a person, "Go on a diet and see a doctor about your blood-pressure. Get your sphincter checked, you asshole."

I'm completely inadequate to speak from a gay person's point of view, but can only imagine they must feel that their lifestyle is the second unpardonable sin according to conservatives. I have no intentions of confronting or converting anyone's opinion one way or the other. If the Bible is a God-breathed inspirational guide book, we each of us have to honestly discern and follow our own path. What I hope to convey is the living testimony about a friend who has encouraged my faith and still does. However, the question begs attention; can a person be gay and be a Christian?

As I'm writing this account I have to be honest, more questions than answers arise. When I was a teenager I thought I knew everything. Of course, there were things that I knew and didn't question; the foundational morals that my folks and peers taught me back in the 60's. Before the bumper sticker was famous, thoughts popped up in my mind like the big bopper to "Question Authority." I was raised in a blue collar town hearing slurs; nigger, kike, wop, gook, spic, fish-eater, dike, queer or faggot. And when I thought that I was free of crude slurs by going to church, I was surprised at the innuendos dressed up in acceptable language to make prejudice palatable. One could put down a different kind of person, ethnic or otherwise and go to church on Sunday without any qualms. That stinks, but it was pretty much the norm and still is. How someone can sing a loving hymn about the family of God one day and joke about lynching a nigger or cutting off a queer's genitalia the next day is beyond me. I've walked out of the room at overhearing less. I'll be as succinct as I know how and call it what I believe it is: dysfunctional society in bed with formal religion. As I see it, societal morality reeks of being prejudice and hypocritical and status quo religion certainly isn't spirituality.

∾

A song comes to mind as I take a break to get out of this chair and stretch. It's a nice day outside, although spring is still a ways off. Taking a walk and getting fresh air helps me think clearer. I'm also curious to see what's been buried under the snow for five months of another North Dakota winter. I hear a cut from the archives of a favorite LP in my mind as I wander about the yard; *I am the Walrus* by The Beatles for some crazy reason. Music has a way of changing directions in my mind and finding a more centered place. I remember lyrics and licks and know what's coming next on hundreds of albums. The refrain of; *"I am he as you are he and we are all together..."* put a bounce in my step while picking up a shopping bag of litter from around the property, singing *"coo-coo-ca-chew."*

I was reminded by a scripture that says we were chosen before the foundation of the world and engraved on the palm of God's hand. We are therefore one with God, a permanent tattoo, if you would; flesh of his flesh and bone of his bone. The only way I know how to begin understanding such a beautiful picture is by embracing the idea that we are not human beings having a cosmic spiritual experience, but rather we're spiritual beings in the midst of a human experience. This perception was a game-changer. If the real "me" is spirit, renewed and made truly alive by the touch of God, then should we not live accordingly from that core? Why try to alter God's design according to man's laws or expectations? That does not mean to imply sidestepping the need to ask for forgiveness when God taps us on the shoulder. Mark may have seen this truth long before me, the freedom to be our created selves in divine union with God without apology, compunction or secrecy. Why not be yourself and be happy with it? Whatever our identity may be and however it has emerged, the crux of the matter is that we are who we are and want to be wanted and to love and be loved, which beats in the essence of our soul. If that miracle becomes a reality in Jesus, the beautiful union between life-giver and life-receiver, then blossom whoever you are in whatever lifestyle you choose and still honor God, blossom freely in your uniqueness for the whole world to see.

It takes courage to be different. Mark was an example of bravery and showed me there is a place for those who are spiritually homeless. Ironically, I, too, have felt like a man without a country. He hears the still, small voice in his heart and has found his home in Jesus. Gone are the accusations, the dogma and a sense of fear-based faith. Mark stands in solidarity with likeminded believers in a caring church family. Reciprocity and support and the liberty to be real and not phony must be salvation for him at long last. The war is not over by any means, but he wins battles and skirmishes and stands with Jesus as his compatriot as I do in my world.

The stigma hasn't evolved a whole lot and still raises blood pressure to dangerous levels. Hate mongering is the new norm. "If you don't like it – leave." But where does that leave people who choose an alternative lifestyle? Where do we send them? To hell? Wait until you discover a family member is gay and see if it doesn't soften your perspective.

Mark and I have recently reconnected and I have it in mind to visit his church if and when we meet up. I look forward to it. A Gay Church? Why not? We love and worship the same God.

# 14

*The* late 90's was a whirlwind of prison ministry and short-term missionary trips around the Caribbean. My business was doing well with decent help and afforded the finances for time away. Our church was gracious in their endorsement and financial assistance. Cassie and I went back to Trinidad several times. We always stayed with Louise in Tunapuna, which had become home away from home.

Andy arranged our schedule with churches the Centre networked with and were sent out to minister as if shot from a cannon. Of notable mention is one evening when we held a meeting in Arima in central Trinidad. "Living Hope" was a small congregation of mostly poor people who gave of what they had with rich hearts. The thing about Trinnies that always amazed me was that they never apologized or complained or made excuses for their lot in life like we Americans tend to do. The island mentality that I encountered, lent itself to accepting and adapting to life's circumstances with a smile on their face. If a pastor handed me money I'd give it to Andy to use appropriately for their needs, like helping out for a new roof or a PA system. My pet peeve was noticing the lack of good books in homes and churches in the villages I visited and put a bug in Andy's ear to invest in Christian reading materials. I never turned down the opportunity to partake of meals and often spent entire afternoons with families who made me feel like I was at home. Upon leaving, I'd be blessed with gift bags of fresh fruit or garden produce and always a warm hug. Louise was pleased with the armload I'd plop on her counter, clucking jokes while sorting through my bounty. "It appears the meeting went well." Dear Louise, ever one to return the favor with a fruit drink or salad and listen to my stories. I loved the tropical palate of whatever you could hand pick in season, mangoes being my favorite.

Ziad took me outside of Arima to new territory that looked and felt the same as most of the towns I visited. Markets and shop owners whose merchandise spilled onto the sidewalk, street vendors selling food as well as scruffy vagrants begging pocket change. It'd become familiar. Off the main road, residential homes of stucco and block and board houses stacked side-by-side bustled with activity. I did my usual meandering round-about and invited folks to special services at "Living Hope." The schedule was outreach and teaching a three day series.

On my second evening in Arima, I was leading the worship service given full leeway. I embarked on a rousing version of a song called *The Banquet Table* hoping I wouldn't break a string on the old Gibson. The congregation joyfully participated after finally getting the words and rhythm as we sang it over and over. The message I planned on preaching was about the Lord's Table, not necessarily the idea of a heavenly setting or Communion with bread and wine, but a place of nourishment and supping together in intimate fellowship here and now with the Lord. Jesus seemed very fond of sharing mealtime with his friends throughout scriptures. I can imagine olive oil or the fat of lamb dripping from his fingers as he passed the bowls, sharing stories and breaking the bread of life.

I wasn't doing the Christian Charleston, but I was vigorously bouncing around on the platform. Joyful musical moments can unhinge me and I tend to pull out the stops. You ought to hear me singing in the shower when inspired. Anyway, I couldn't have looked any more ridiculous than Mick Jagger jumping around on stage at my age.

There was a drummer who erratically kept a beat, a young guy banging a tambourine nonsensically, and behind me was a musician who looked like a shrunken man. He wore a gaudy purple silk shirt buttoned to his neck, the fabric hung off his boney shoulders like a scarecrow, and he was playing a very out of tune electric guitar trying to figure out the rhythm. Several women of East Indian origin were the choir behind us and sang along in high pitched screeching voices like a bird being strangled. *"He brought me to the banquet table and his banner over me is love."* This is not embellishment, it really was that crazy. As I said, I was whooping it up. Before I finished the song, as bizarre as the evening was going, the floor suddenly gave way under me. I landed lopsided but on my feet, standing waist deep in a hole of splintered boards. It took me back to a basketball tournament in Renovo when I broke through the ice in the company of my old friend Murray. I shook it off with laughter although feeling quite embarrassed, and quickly recollected myself to crawl back on level ground to resume playing the song. Follow the bouncing ball! Thank God there wasn't a full basement or I may have broken my neck.

You should have heard the response. It was as if heaven opened the flood gates of joy and released resounding celebration, the banquet table forever etched on their minds. I'm sure the entire village heard the racket and must have made them wonder what in the world was happening at the church. Is comedy a spiritual gift? Could parody be somewhat prophetic? It should be. The service went better than I expected. What an odd way for God to give me favor among strangers. I'm sure that I gave the folks in Arima something to talk about for a long time. "You shoulda seen de minister! Dat man mashed up de stage and kept playin' his song!" I offered to return and do the repairs but they laughed it off. "No worries mon."

~

Another mission opportunity that Cassie and I ventured on was to the island of Grenada. Its coastline is scenic, the interior a patchwork of rainforest, villages, cane fields and somewhat mountainous. Commerce is predominately supported by tourism from the cruise ships that come into port at St. George's, the capital city. We stayed with an older woman named Teresa in the hill region and affectionately called her Mother Teresa. Having learned not to assume that a basic fan might be provided, Cassie managed to pack a modest sized oscillating fan in one of her suitcases. The first night in Grenada was like all the nights we spent in Grenada; hot, muggy and mosquito infested. I lit a mosquito coil and assembled the fan, forcefully plugged it in an outlet hoping the breeze would keep our pestering, biting friends away and offer us some relief. The fan whirled at high RPM's like it would take off and fly around the room for all of thirty seconds and died with an awful smell, the motor fried, the cord nearly melted. Grenada's circuitry wasn't 110 like our homes are wired for back home. So much for a fan.

It rained intermittently every day for a week, heavy at times and causing some flooding which hindered our schedule. Part of our itinerary was joining with a ministry called YWAM (Youth With A Mission), doing open air services in a large savannah not far from the capital. Cassie and I saw some country in our free time and explored under an umbrella. We toured a nutmeg factory (a major export), at Gouyave, visited a rum distillery, shops and markets and a nature preserve with colorful birds and chattering monkeys. We also visited a historic landmark of interest. In 1983, President Reagan sent Marines to thwart the Marxist regime in Grenada. It's called the "Intervention" and lasted little more than a week. We saw a wall pockmarked by bullets and shelling with the 82nd Airborne's emblem faded but still visible. The Grenadians have a fond appreciation for Uncle Sam. It was chilling to imagine the fighting and made me think of counter-revolutionaries the likes of Che Guevara and guerrilla warfare that I'd read about. I salute the Marine's tactical maneuvers and bravery to rescue a country from oppression. Thank God for democracy.

One of the easiest roads connecting the capital and the opposite side of Grenada, besides the coastal route, passed in front of Teresa's house. The road was a narrow two lane that weaved up the central region across the mountain and through the rainforest. Teresa lived just shy of the summit on the east side near the village of St. Cyr. Every half hour a van would chug its way up in a cloud of fumes going one way or the other. I had a scheduled service to conduct in Grenville, a sizable town on the east coast.

It was mid-morning as I walked to a bus stop in stifling humidity but at least it wasn't raining, steam rose vaporous from the road. I looked out for mounds with fire ants, not wanting to make that mistake ever again. I also looked forward to seeing some new country, antsy to get the chance to preach, no pun intended. At last a van arrived that proved to be an arduous trip. I worried that we might have to get out and push, the van gasping and grinding gears, I could have walked faster going up the grade. After cresting the summit on the downhill side, the driver rode the brakes. You could smell their slow rubbery death. The van took on not only villagers but a tethered goat, people with sacks of fish or chickens in a cage, and an old man with his snarling lap dog that looked more like a rat than a dog. The smell inside the van from animals and BO and fumes was nauseating. I could have sprayed a can of Febreze up my nose and it wouldn't have made any difference. My freshly bathed body and pressed shirt and slacks were a stinky, sweaty mess when we reached Grenville. I felt a sense of relief at making the trip alone and made mental notes ripe and juicy for the telling. I couldn't make this stuff up if I tried. Cassie wouldn't have found anything humorous about traveling the St. George's-Grenville Highway as I did.

The service in Grenville was held on the second floor of a

secondary school. It was an industrial looking building in need of repair, big open windows with bars, everything inside and out was painted pale blue. I was met by the pastor and taken to the auditorium where an audience of a hundred or so patiently sat in hard chairs under ceiling fans that did little to cool the room, awaiting my arrival. I was late by a long shot, which I couldn't help, and was frazzled from trying to hurry, but hurrying isn't an island mentality. Anxiety about being on time is an American obsession. The auditorium was crowded with middle school to Jr. High age children who looked like patients waiting for the dentist. Several women kept order, overseeing the assembly, teachers no doubt. Obviously the agenda was to reach the younger crowd and enliven them. I had no idea how long they'd waited.

One must be quick on one's feet when God rearranges expectations, but isn't spontaneity a blessing from God? It makes us set aside preconceived notions and trust him. I tuned up the old Gibson and played Sunday school choruses on their wave length to get the ball rolling. Instead of preaching, I shared amusing children stories, adlibbing the *Velveteen Rabbit* and pantomimed the parable of the lost coin in the gospels like Charlie Chaplin that made everyone laugh. I get a kick out of how frequently the notion of things being lost and found comes up in Jesus' narrative. After all my crazy antics, I shared the gospel in a nutshell and invited anyone who wanted to accept Jesus to come forward. No one moved. I waited. My heart sank and I was all but ready to wrap things up and say a closing prayer. And then there was a stirring that echoed in the silence of the auditorium as a couple of young girls walked toward me nervously glancing back at their friends. Soon, I heard chairs sliding on the concrete floor as others came to the front. Little by little a crowd of shy kids gathered to receive Christ. I marveled how the Holy Spirit was chipping away some of the timidity and peer pressure and moved upon them to respond to the gospel. That's a very brave thing to do when you're a teenager. The pastor and his wife and

I prayed for each of those kids. I was asked if I would come back to their school and preach to whole classrooms and special meetings in the auditorium. Apparently my foolish presentation impressed them.

If it rained, which it did often, Cassie was now prepared (or forewarned), about the van trip and joined me in Grenville. We ministered in the school from first bell to dismal, classroom after classroom, floor by floor, each time unique and entertaining. The schedule was turned on its head. Our next few weeks were very different than what my expectations were in coming to Grenada, but God opened a door that opened many more doors for us. I rediscovered the importance of ministering to kids, not only because it's fun, but because it's a high calling to be taken seriously. Just like in prison ministry when I thought that reaching the ones in county jail could save them serious trouble down the road, so, too with teenagers in school uniforms. If you're a youth minister I applaud you, and please don't grow weary in your labors. Cassie and I did a lot of school ministry afterwards, even when we were back in Trinidad. Can you imagine public schools in America allowing the gospel to be preached at assembly?

Dear Mother Teresa grew vegetables in a gully behind her house, and one morning her father stopped in to tend to the garden. He was a jovial old man pushing eighty who resembled Uncle Remus in a pair of faded overalls and a woven banana leaf hat. A machete hung from a rope belt and he greeted me in a friendly, gravelly voice. The garden didn't resemble your typical garden laid out in neat rows with plants terraced, organized and weeded; it looked like there wasn't a garden at all. The gully was thick with flora, high brush, overhanging vines and drooping broad leafed palms. The garden was virtually swallowed up in the rainforest. The air was moist and heavy and water dripped from the trees as I followed Uncle Remus, who seemed to know exactly where everything was. He hacked with the machete and cleared a path, opening places where squash and pumpkins and yams grew. He deftly whacked overhanging limbs for plantains, breadfruit, guava and silk figs. We picked some kind of berries that stained my fingers purple for days. All in all, I bet I carried forty pounds of produce back to Teresa's kitchen. Uncle Remus also had a load over his shoulder. Mother Teresa bartered fruit and vegetables for fish and chicken when the van stopped on Saturday, and the bounty was on the table for meals. I can't bring her father's name to mind, but during our harvesting he asked me to speak with his two grandsons and arranged for us to meet at a beach off the beaten path the next afternoon.

Old man Remus had a Daihatsu sedan that had seen its better years many years ago, but he kept the motor in tip-top shape. The floor boards were patched with plywood and the passenger window didn't roll down. We went off road on a donkey trail to a stretch of beach on the south coast. Coconut palms towered overhead at tideline, the sand was brownish and coarse, debris tangled in the sea grapes. The surf was rough but the scenery was beautiful. Cassie had packed a picnic lunch and we bought Cokes at a roadside grocer at my suggestion. Teresa's father led us on a footpath along the beach and tree-line where we came to a cozy place out of the sun to relax.

Let me interject a quick word about Coke products in the islands. I've always been a Coke guy compared to Pepsi. I find it thicker on the tongue and syrupy, a bit on the flat side and slightly different than the bottled Cokes we buy at 7-11. Maybe it's the cane sugar consistency designed to be a better mixer for rum, but you can't beat an ice cold Coke on a sweltering tropical afternoon.

Uncle Remus's two grandsons joined us not long after we settled on a blanket. Cassie began laying out a wonderful picnic. The boys had ridden their bikes from wherever they lived, which seemed a good distance, and were bashful but friendly. I brought toys from home on every visit to the islands and pulled out a spongy nerf-like football with fins on the end that made a whirling sound if you threw it properly like Peyton Manning, and coaxed the boys to play catch after lunch. We started on the beach, but little by little our game went into the surf. Ankle deep, knee deep, the waves kind of knocked me around. We threw that crazy football back and forth until I was chest deep and thought enough recklessness and showing off, thinking it foolish not to head back to shore. A wave pummeled me upside-down and honest to God, it felt like someone grabbed me by the ankles and dragged me out to sea.

As I was having a bit of an episode, Uncle Remus was telling Cassie that the under-tow here was wicked and several tourists had drowned in the past year. I called to the teenage boys, who, of course could not hear me over the surf. I couldn't touch bottom and began to panic. I'm not a strong swimmer and my reaction was doing the very thing they tell you not to do in such a situation. I began flailing and fighting with all my strength to swim to shore, battling to find footing, and within minutes was completely exhausted. I made absolutely no headway, if anything I was farther out to sea. *So this is it? This is how I'm going to die? I never expected it to be like this.*

I can't say that I felt calm in the arms of Jesus and I can't say I felt fear either, I just sort of felt resigned to the facts. I didn't cry out to God to save me, in fact, I don't remember doing anything but trying to catch my breath and not drink sea water. I may have been in a state of shock, but it must not have been my day to die. As strong as the hands were that dragged me out to sea, something heaved up and shoved me back to shore. I tumbled blindly, tossed as though I had no substance. It was terrifying to be so out of control. Miraculously, I found purchase, my feet touching solid ground and ever so glad to be alive. No one knew of my dilemma. The boys kept tossing the nerf football and Cassie and Remus visited in the shade. When I joined them I think that I embarrassed Cassie. I jumped on her and wrapped her in a bear hug, looking like I'd been beaten to a pulp, dip in egg batter and crusted with Panko bread crumbs. "Touch Down!"

I announced, and laughed at my own joke, although my sides ached something fierce.

After relaxing and drinking a bellyful of Cokes, I invited the boys to take a walk on the beach. We ventured to a natural jetty and sat on the prow where waves crashed beneath us as crabs scuttled on the coral, a storm was brewing off on the horizon. It was a safe distance from the sea that I now had greater respect for. I engaged them with the gospel, asking simple questions, curious if they knew Jesus or went to church. I dug deeper, inquiring about their family and what their father did for a living. Their father left Granada to work for a Venezuelan Oil Company when they were in primary school and hadn't seen him since. The boys were both knowledgeable about the scriptures from their upbringing, their mother was a Pentecostal, but said they were backsliders. I shared my own failures where it was appropriate in order to relate with them. They were easygoing and spoke freely at my questions and prompting. I listened to their stories about being horny and rebelling and getting into trouble. I told them there was no need for worries because Jesus has a soft spot in his heart for horny guys who get into trouble. They prayed with me, actually, I had them pray for themselves before adding my two cents. They seemed honest about wanting to turn back to Jesus and promised me they'd go back to church.

Maybe it was because of those two boys that I didn't drown that day. If I see them in heaven I'll buy them a Coke and hope there's a nerf football in God's box of tricks. I'd love to hear Jesus' side of the story, as in my mind I was minutes from Davy Jones' Locker. My guess is that he was nearby, walking on water and paying close attention to me.

$\sim$

The day before Cassie and I were scheduled to leave Grenada, Mother Teresa put out a breakfast spread that rivaled Country Cupboard's buffet back home. The smell of bacon was intoxicating.

We often had fish and fruit for breakfast. The way mealtimes go in the tropics is different than we do in the states. They eat like a king at breakfast, a queen at lunch and a pauper at suppertime. We shared stories as at a king's feast and laughed, reveling in the joys we'd experienced together in such a short time. Teresa was either taken by my wit or stymied at our cultural differences, but she was always agreeable and accommodating, laughing at the strangest places in conversation. Cassie planned on packing and I begged time away after breakfast, promising not to get lost and be back by suppertime.

I wandered a path to a nearby village hoping to have one last encounter with a local. It was kind of like Forrest Gump's saying about a box of chocolates: "You never know what you'll get." My mother had an expression I often heard growing up: "Nothing ventured – nothing gained." I call it: "Poke and hope."

I met a pig farmer who was slopping out his pens and offered to shake my hand. His wife was a friend of Teresa and had heard about us. As we were having a casual conversation, I interjected a comment about the Prodigal Son from the gospels and said I couldn't imagine eating slop and husks. Half a dozen large pigs rutted for food in the mud within arm's reach, a sow nursed piglets at a dirty teat. His comments were brief but led me to assume that he might be a prodigal himself. He deflected my witness of Christ with an invitation to come back for supper and sample his wife's cooking, which I found humorous given where we were standing. He dumped a bucket of vegetable waste in a trough and patted his belly. It appeared that he was well fed. I couldn't commit but we parted with the Lord's blessing.

I proceeded wandering a path through the bush, enamored by the tropical ambience so strange and different than home. I'd forgotten to bring my camera. I found a hand pump on a pipe and worked the handle until fresh water flowed and stuck my head under the spout to cool off. My flip-flops and legs needed a good rinse from standing in a pigsty, and not being too smart, cupped my hands and gulped deeply to quench my thirst.

The next morning when we boarded American Airline 1372 to go home I began getting sick. The commercial flight taking eight hours with a layover in Miami wasn't fun, not any fun at all. I departed Grenada with fond memories that would last me a lifetime. Recovering from giardia would take months.

I wasn't impressed at all with Barbados; first impressions are rife with expectations. You hear and entertain stories from those who've been somewhere you haven't, the world travelers, seasoned tourist pointing you in the right direction according to their experiences. The people I've met that went to the islands did so for different reasons than I, extoling the thrills of nightclubs and resorts, snorkeling, shopping and partying weren't on my agenda. They'd just look at me when I shared that I lived locally, going native without the all-inclusive, that my purpose was sharing the gospel. If only there is an emoji to portray the expressions on their face it'd be priceless. I sought out everything I could find (no internet as yet), from the local library on Barbados and compared it to my previous visits to other islands. Every island has its own unique culture, cuisine, music, slang and accent like traveling from Boston to Gulf Port, Mississippi. In my limited experience no two islands were the same.

After Valentine's Day, Cassie and I flew to Grantley Adams International Airport of Barbados. When we departed from JFK it was drizzling freezing rain. Six and a half hours later we walked across the tarmac to customs like being in a steam sauna. We cleared customs and found a table outside in the shade and ordered some food to bide the time. Andy and his wife, Caroline were inbound from Trinidad within the hour so we decided to wait. All I had was a name and the address of our contact. We could have taken a taxi, but Andy was the one who made the arrangements.

A middle aged gentleman approached us, calling our name. He was the pastor of the church we were scheduled to hold meetings with. Andy and Caroline soon arrived and we all squeezed into a van, luggage strapped on the roof, and headed to the Parish of St. Thomas. Beyond the busyness of airport traffic, the road we took was less travelled. Everyone else seemed to be headed for Bridgetown and the resorts. The landscape was flat, open country and the sea was always within view with waves shimmering like diamonds under a clear blue cloudless sky. We passed small villages with a corner market, a gas pump, local Bajans sitting in the shade idling away the afternoon. Vast expanses of sugar cane towered on both sides of the road when we were up-country that obscured sightseeing. It was awe inspiring, the high dense green walls that gave me a feeling of claustrophobia and being pressing upon like when I was a kid lost in a cornfield.

The pastor wasn't a talkative man, only answering my banal questions and lame attempts at conversation without great elaboration. I wondered if he heard or understood me. The pastor turned off the main road and pulled into a sub-development where we came to carport attached to a single story block house still under some construction. This would be home for the next twelve days.

His wife had prepared a meal, and after showing us where our bedrooms were, we all sat at their dining room table to get acquainted. Everything was so formal, the high polished mahogany table and chairs, linen napkins and fine china that may have been Royal Albert, probably passed down from previous generations without a chip or ding in any of it. I'd seen it all before and made me puzzle how seemingly poor people had such priceless possessions. The house was clean and airy, the bathrooms spotless, a bookshelf gave me pause to investigate later. Our bedroom was small but there were windows with screens and a ceiling fan. I felt sort of snubbed that Andy and Caroline had the bigger and nicer of the rooms, but he's the apostle. Upon finishing our meal we were given our leave to take a rest after traveling. Cassie began to unpack and sort things out in our bedroom. She liked to nest like a mother bird and would probably rearrange things to her satisfaction. I changed into shorts and a tee shirt, my Reef flip flops, and went out to take a walk.

The area was flat, arid and desert-like, just the whisper of a breeze. Packed ground crunched underfoot with pebbly white coral, gritty sand and burned out brittle grass. I wandered around a development of modest homes in differing stages of construction. I'd get the tour later in the week after meeting some of the workers and see how they built things in Barbados. Some of the homes were inhabited and had landscaping of indigenous vegetation, flowering cactus and lush succulents. The bougainvillea and frangipani were in bloom and made me smile in appreciation of their magnificent presence against a drab background the color of sand. There were no shade trees to find relief from a bright sky that seemed close enough you could reach up and touch. The heat felt good after coming from winter weather in Pennsylvania and wearing a heavy coat only this morning. Wiping sweat from my brow and kicking sand from between my toes felt right. It was good to be back in the tropics.

The schedule for the next twelve days was tag-teaming a teaching series with Andy to a combined congregation of several churches. I'm not sure who benefited the most, the people who came out to the meetings or me. My talks generally lasted under an hour, Andy was just getting warmed up in an hour. We decided that I'd go first like opening for a big-name band.

Andy had a way of finding insightful truths from obscure places like 2nd Chronicles in the Old Testament, which was his opening message. He would unearth things I generally passed over without giving any attention to, stuff I found boring and of no particular significance. Andy taught of things hidden in the Word, decoding prophetic mysteries from a litany of obscure verses. How he did it I haven't a clue. He could wax eloquently and hold you spellbound for an hour on passages like when the Spirit of the Lord came upon Jahaziel son of Zechariah, the son of Benaiah, the son of..." You get it, right? Paragraphs and pages of verses droning on and on about who begat who were just words and names that I passed over speed reading. Andy spoke about history and genealogical continuity back to the patriarchs, of precedence and positioning, empowerment from blessings passed down and standing in the purposes of God for our generation. He put forth our role as being torch bearers, of having resolution to align ourselves with God's mentality being revealed in our present time. It was an eye opener to say the least and I vowed to pay attention to the verses I hadn't hi-lighted and passed over. An entirely new understanding of the Old Testament opened up to me.

I was challenged by Andy and the men who mentored him, Bertril Baird and Myles Monroe and others I'd heard speak at the Centre in Trinidad, apostolic men who shaped revival in the Caribbean if not worldwide. They had the spirit of a pioneer, pushing beyond boundaries and mapping out new frontiers, tearing down strongholds opposed to God's purpose, establishing deeper foundations in the global church. These were serious men, men of wisdom, prophetic men I was grateful to be in company with, but felt unfit to stand and minister beside them.

One night while we lie in bed, I shared with Cassie how inadequate I felt sharing the pulpit with Andy. That was putting it mildly. I felt utterly stupid, unqualified, way out of my league and wondered how I'd gotten here in the first place. Our topic for the conference was; "Establishing an Unshakable Kingdom." Andy was laying grid work, pilings, buttresses and watchtowers, heavy stuff. I felt like I was putting wooden pegs of primary colors into the right shaped hole like the game designed for ages 2-3. I wanted to feign an illness or concoct an excuse to return home. I wanted to quit, I wanted to hide. Cassie reassured me, of course, but in the pit of my stomach I still felt like a dunce.

At breakfast, Andy asked me to join him outside on the carport. I refilled my mug of instant coffee, tried another joke with our host who never really got my jokes, and found a seat in the morning sun with Andy sitting across from me. He had a glass of orange juice and his bible, wearing a thoughtful and serious look. I wondered if he'd overheard my conversation with Cassie the night before. He spoke as if I was his dearest friend and reaffirmed me in the most gracious manner. We talked about the series we were teaching, but it felt strained to me. Our usual manner was free-spirited, exchanging ideas, but he paused more often as though weighing his words before speaking. It wasn't like Andy. I had an idea he was sweetening the pot for some kind of bad news as my nerves vibrated with caffeine. I held my tongue.

Andy expressed that his hope on teaming up since our spark of connection when we met at Shekinah in Tennessee, would be that we'd grow closer in the Spirit and said he was blessed to hear me preach. He also said with great tact and aplomb, that it would be advantageous for me personally to step down for a season and devote time to study. I put my best foot forward and initially took no offense, answering that if it were possible I'd move to Trinidad and attend every meeting. I wanted to learn regardless of how deflated I felt at his comments. I know we should not covet another man's calling, but whatever gifting Andy and his associates had – I wanted.

He said that I was a gifted evangelist, a forerunner but not a teacher. He had great plans for us, adding a qualifying assertion that I needed to grow even my presentation of the gospel. His mention of my storytelling style and humor and conversational delivery was appealing to the common man, entertaining with allure, but my effectiveness needed to be honed with stronger insights. The bones were good but maturity was in order. His words stung like iodine on an open wound. Taking correction was never my strong suit.

Andy went on to invite me to join with him in Ghana for an upcoming convention and jokingly said that if I wanted to really push the limits I could minister to the headhunters. They would gladly entertain a blonde haired, blue eyed white guy with a singing voice. Very funny, Andy. What resonated in my soul was that he wasn't giving up on me and I shouldn't either, but I felt like I'd been punched in the guts and had my wind knocked out.

I made a friend in the church who took me on daytrips around the island when I was free. David was a short man who barely reached my chin and had a close cropped afro with a hint of red. He always wore a pressed long sleeve shirt, the crease razor sharp, with his business logo where a pocket would be. David had a new model flatbed truck and ran a lucrative delivery business. He made daily runs from nurseries to collect potted flowers and exotic plants. Bird of Paradise, Hibiscus in bloom, specialty floral arrangements, palms of varying species and size were loaded up and delivered to restaurants, resorts and hotels. I never knew there were so many different types of palms. Sago palms are so cool. I tagged along with David from Silver Sands to Hastings, from Bridgetown to Holetown delivering his bounty and helped unload at his directions. I was in lobbies and courtyards where movie stars stayed and upscale resorts on the west coast I never would have seen, camouflaged by flora behind walls and gated entryways. One day at Mullins Bay we'd just missed Barbra Streisand. It was better than paying for a tour guide.

David had a great rapport with his clients; he was charming, a crafty salesman with wit and a joke and introduced me to scores of people as his friend from "snow country." It was a great lead-in line to follow up if I was asked; "Where?" I chatted with managers and maître d's who shook hands with famous people and shook mine. In the lobby of a ritzy martini bar, the owner and I had a connection. I was given an invitation to return for cocktails and handed a Cuban cigar if I promised to tell him more about Jesus. The manner in which he spoke made me wonder if he was genuinely interested to continue the dialogue or just being polite. I'm sorry to say, I didn't follow up. Good grief. How many times have I missed an opportunity by not taking the time and accepting an invitation to make a friend?

David's wife, Maranda (I think), was twice his size both upward and sideways. They made an odd couple. We shared meals at their home a few times, but Cassie didn't particularly cozy to David. She said he had wandering eyes and made her uncomfortable. Maranda made me a bit uncomfortable. On more than one occasion she pulled me aside and felt compelled to talk about her sex life very explicitly; did I know the Kamasutra? She was so bold as to inquire if I talked dirty to my wife when we made love. I pled the fifth and wondered if they were swingers. Regardless of the awkwardness they were my friends, and I did enjoy getting away from the pastor's house. Andy was probably studying while I was off gallivanting around the island.

∾

I started out by saying that Barbados didn't exactly make me want to do cartwheels, but the trip taught me something very valuable. I realized my need to dig deeper - spiritually. It was obvious after Andy's talk that major demolition was expedient; my Americanized version of Christianity was shallow, need oriented, weak and pandering to likeminded people. How did Andy put it? "I was preaching a common message to the common man." Even though I tried not to take offense I knew that he was right. It was time for me to grow up in the Lord and put on big boy pants.

My need to grow up implied that my character and conduct, as well as my message, was deficient unto the day. It was well past the time to graduate from kindergarten and learning my ABC's. The high calling requires moving to the next level as in going up an escalator. The top floor is nothing less than exemplifying the nature of God. The inference is simple; to be a child of God, having his DNA by virtue of receiving his seed in our soul, we must look and act like him, like father like son, or daughter. Hopefully we mature in our faith as we grow physically by counting the natural years. Otherwise we are adults sucking our thumbs and still shitting in our diapers. Back when I had an amazing experience on a silent retreat at Dayspring by Merton's Pond and the revelation of God's love so overwhelmed me, I began to heal in my inner man. I majored on God's love and his desire to heal us deeply, not only in my own life, but it was what I predominately shared with others. I still endorse those two ideals – uncontestably. Love and healing are pivotal to a Christian's foundation and journey, but they are just the beginning.

The idea of being grafted into Christ has always lead me to believe in a union of two becoming one, like a branch of one type of apple cut and spliced into a differing apple tree, the joining of two distinct life juices creating a new species. Or better still, as in a marriage. Scripture refers to this poetically as the Bride and the Bridegroom, Christ and the Church. I give Jesus my humanity and failings in tattered garments of sin and selfishness, and in return he gives me a robe and new life and his divinity, if that's not too bold a word to describe it. I think of Michelangelo's famous painting *Creation of Man*. In particular I find it riveting how their fingers touch reaching from heaven and earth and connecting in the intimate moment of a joined life.

When Andy pressed upon me the need for spiritual maturity I didn't know where to begin. How do I escalate to a higher level? After nursing my immature emotions of being hurt like a fifth grader being scolded, it was on to praying for the next step. I knew there was more to this business of being a Christian other than having "fire insurance" and treading the well-worn path of churchiness and the status quo over and again. It seemed to me that lip-service was given to having strength and stature in Christ. Was anyone real, or is it just words? So many believers that I encounter who espouse the lofty concepts of the Kingdom of God, actually seem to possess little faith, hardly having enough power over their appetites to walk in victory. I'm not pointing a finger at obesity but allude to the appetites of the flesh in myriad of ways. Spirit-filled people struggle with compulsions and often juvenile habits. Aren't we called to overcome and take spiritual dominion over wanton desires and be free of obsessions? That may or may not suggest taking authority over your fork and not eating half a cheesecake at one sitting.

The writer of Hebrews in the New Testament said, "...it's a fearful thing to fall into the hands of God." A sobering word if ever there was one. It reminds me of Jay's comment, "You and me, we know too much." Paul exhorts us that when he was a child he talked like a child, reasoned like a child, but the time comes to put away childish ways. God's ways are not our ways. Change has to happen, and when it comes down to it, who do you suppose has to change? I'd put my money on me and you. But do we get that? Or is our paradigm more often than not focused on feeling good? Hedonism has many layers, hidden or otherwise. When the mandate clearly states that it's better to obey than sacrifice, we try to justify our weakness and maintain a semblance of happiness.

The fatness of the land that God promised us, meaning peace and joy, is more than just a side like at the buffet table at Golden Corral. The peace and joy that I'm convinced God means for us to have is being joined with his will and purpose and walking daily in accord, not getting goosebumps singing "Kumbaya My Lord." God is building something to resemble heaven on earth and he is more interested in my character than my happiness.

Andy provoked me in a good way under that carport in Barbados, miles and miles from home yet close to my heart. Once I got over being offended, I took his instruction to heart. When I got back home and unpacked, tossing a log on the fire and settling in my recliner, I thought long and hard. How much time had I wasted lollygagging, happy with B's? I may have had the heart and soul, "good bones," as Andy phrased it, but my mind needed rewired. I adapted a new prayer, simple and to the point: GOD - HELP - ME! Step by step I began to discover that the truths of God are obtainable, understandable, reliable and livable. I thank the Lord for his perseverance in provoking and instructing such a lame-brain as me. As a pragmatic seeking the bottom-line (and again you may fault me for being utopian in my beliefs), but to me, the Lord's Prayer is apropos and goes way beyond mindless, mumbling recitation. It's a reality waiting to be discovered.

*"...Thy Kingdom come, Thy will be done, on earth as it is in heaven."*

The downside of believing that God is presently establishing his kingdom on earth echoes ominous tones of vigilance and sobriety to follow instructions. It's a blessing and a curse both. It'll tear your heart out. If we're captured by the Spirit and see the kingdom for what it is, we'll never be able to escape or find a place to retire at ease. God's hand will always be on us, pressing us forward to the finish line. The upside is being partakers in what God is presently doing, living and breathing the life we were meant to live and breathe.

# 15

*Cassie* and I added onto our house in Lewisburg in the late 90's. I gutted the existing lower level walkout apartment to reconfigure and staked out a 20'X30' addition on the south side. The added great room had an open concept with a vaulted ceiling consisting of a spacious living room, kitchen and dining room. I scored old barn beams and distressed planks and the interior finish made you feel like you were in a log cabin. Cassie had a flair for decorating and our new addition could have been featured in *Country Living Magazine.* A mountain stone fireplace was the focal point, not a TV. My well-worn recliner was perfectly positioned to watch a fire burning and a peaceful reading sanctuary. A wooden porch swing hung from the loft inside our cozy abode for *sittin' and talkin'* on rainy days. The next spring I built on a deck and screened-in porch. We rented the main level to a 50ish couple who were wonderful tenants. They planted flowers, were always on time with their rent, and thank the Lord, quiet as church mice.

Cassie and I entertained a lot; that was the great thing about having a great room, the more the merrier. During one of our galas a discussion evolved and we brainstormed about taking a group trip to Trinidad. New Covenant Church supported us on previous mission trips and I think they were intrigued by our experiences. A group of thirty brave and daring friends boarded a charter bus for JFK via American Airlines to Port of Spain, Trinidad. I tried to prepare them as best as I could and hoped that my friends wouldn't only have the time of their lives ministering and experiencing the culture, but they would also receive the "spirit" of the leadership at the Centre. Andy had tact, I worried that Bertil Baird might scare them.

Of course, it was a major culture shock. We were placed in various homes scattered in differing locations, which may have been difficult for some being as everything was so foreign to Pleasant Valley, PA. I think it was best that we didn't all stay together. If change pushes you out of your comfort zone take a deep breath, it's good for you. When we gathered at the Centre for prayer and briefing of assignments, I heard them tell about creepy crawlies and lizards and the stifling humidity and heat, about primitive bathrooms and strange food. Everyone rolled with it, no one really whined, most of the time we laughed about it. What can you do but make adjustments to the circumstances you find yourself in? We designated four groups: teaching, evangelism, youth ministry with drama and puppetry, and technical support. I could go with any or all as my role was assisting more or less as a tour guide. I loved watching my friends do their thing and rejoiced at the response of the people they ministered to. There was a clatter of excitement and tears of joy at divine interventions when the miraculous happened (and many miraculous things happened), and their stories made me belly laugh when we all got together to share testimonies. It was a very busy ten day itinerary crisscrossing the central region along with sitting in at some meetings at the Centre under Bertril Baird's teaching. From the reactions I heard, he hadn't frightened my friends but lifted their vision and faith, as Bertril had done for me.

We took a day trip to Maracas Bay and most of us got sorely sunburned. It was one of the few times we were all together. I grew close to a couple who stayed with Cassie and me at Louise's home. Matt and Beth were dear friends to begin with, but by the end of the trip we were inseparable. Louise gave them the bedroom Cassie and I always stayed in as they were the "guests." Cassie and I had become family. We had a small bedroom with a tiny but functional bathroom in the lower level. Louise conducted some classes in the large adjacent room where instruments and sheet music and steel pans cluttered the area. I tapped my way around the design on the top of a polished fifty-five gallon drum shaped to play distinct notes with a little hammer, and marveled at the ingenuity and skill of Louise's students to blend and create such amazing music like an orchestra from primitive origins.

I usually met up with Matt to start the day, both of us were early risers and looking for coffee. We'd often gather in the dining room for the evening meal after returning from some kind of outreach. Louise took an afternoon break like clockwork. If we were present, we were expected to join her. Apparently the tradition of English tea-time is as sacred as happy-hour. I'll never forget the look on Beth's face when we came upon one another in the kitchen. She froze in place, suddenly seeing birds pecking under the linens covering food on the counter and gave me a look of horror or hilarity, I wasn't sure which. Yellow winged, long-billed birds rummaged after what happened to be our evening meal the maid had prepared. I shooed them out and wrapped the linens tighter. Later that evening, food was on the table in steaming bowls and platters along with a salad and fancy place settings. With a hesitant and knowing look, Beth smiled at me. The birds were our secret. Someone said grace and we ate a fine Bajan dinner without making a scene.

A group of us decided to venture out and boarded Maxi vans for Fredrick Street, the hub of Port of Spain. The plan was to hang out and share the gospel. Fredrick Street is seedy, loud and not particularly touristy. Bars and shops and beggars and wall to wall people bustled between the intoxicating smell of curry and spice, sweat and urine, an occasional whiff of ganja wafted in the sultry air. It felt primordial walking along the street under a hazy cloud threatening to take your breath away. Waves of colorfully dressed pedestrians crowding the sidewalks were interesting to watch. Street vendors and merchants hawked their wares, doubles and roti simmered on steam carts at the curb. Fabric and silks, ceramic East Indian idols and incense burners, cutlery and kitchen wares and blue jeans made in America adorned the windows of proud shopkeepers. Idle Trinnies and Rastafarians "liming" on every corner eyed us up, making you wonder if they were drug dealers or someone to be wary of and avoid. A raucous vibration of music blared from every other establishment creating an energizing atmosphere to put a dance move in your step. The distinctive rhythm of soca with a beat to tickle your tummy made you want to "jump up," calypso with a twist to "whine down." A lot of the popular songs were from the recent Carnival with lyrics that were politically oriented with slams against the leading party or were sexually explicit pushing the limits of censorship if you could understand it. Recordings of East Indian flutes and chanting, some dated American music from the eighties, Michael Jackson of all things, filled the atmosphere. Fredrick Street was a multicultural theater in surround-sound.

My friends went out into the crowd two by two at the least; long live the buddy system. They explored up and down Fredrick Street with determined objectives in spite of looking so out of place. It's hard approaching a stranger with the intention of sharing the gospel even in our own familiar hometown let alone being in such a foreign environment. I'm not sure how productive the endeavor was, but it promised to be a personal experience they would not soon forget. The women in our group had the best stories to tell.

At the risk of generalizing, Trinidadian men are like sharks seeking prey. Sharks have a small brain and only one thing on their mind; feed the hunger. Some Trinidadian men aren't much different. They're incredibly audacious, stealthy and bold, tactless and rude. Eyes filled with lust draws them to weakness, probably not unlike most men who get aroused but keep it private, or like a beggar scoping out an easy mark. Jill and Karen and Caroline stood as Joan of Arc and wielded the sword of God, managing to walk the length of Fredrick Street unscathed. I don't think that's embellishing too much. They were brave and strong and oh the stories they could tell.

As happens in the tropics, an afternoon storm rolled in unannounced. They came quickly with a vengeance and rolled out just as quickly unless it was hurricane season. I was with some friends on the sidewalk when a wall of rain descended on us, you could literally see it coming. When the intensity hit, torrents of water drenched everyone, the curb flooded and cockroaches streamed up out of the street drains, manically running up your legs. It was instant mayhem, the crowd yelling and seeking shelter under awnings and storefronts huddling close, some desperately holding plastic bags over their heads.

I ducked into an open door not realizing that it was a bar and found myself standing in a crowded room, soaked and bewildered, obviously noticed. I was hemmed in by a gang of rough looking characters who blocked the door. Immediately, I tried to get my bearings in panic mode with no escape, when I was tapped on the shoulder. I turned and gazed into the bare chest of a very dark man with nipple rings, heavily tattooed and scarred, and my eyes tracked upward wondering if he was standing on a stool. He was at least seven feet tall. I'm not making this up. His head was shaved bald with a sweaty sheen, he had large hoop earrings and yellow glaring eyes, a trace of a smirk cut his shadowy face as a razor's edge. He stuck his fingers in his mouth and whistled a signal in an ear-piercing pitch and the bar suddenly went quiet. He leaned down and said something to me that I took as a threat. I looked around in terror that stole my breath away, not surprised to see I was the only white guy in the place. None of my friends came in with me; we'd gotten separated in the frantic crowd outside. I hoped to God they were praying for me. The Zulu sneered and leaned closer, smelling of rum.

I have no idea where it came from as I'm generally a bit of a chicken whenever it comes fighting, but I replied by saying, "Greater is he that is in me than he that is within you," and stood my ground on shaky legs. I instantly realized my impulsive comment sounded like I was taunting him and should have weighed my words better. His laughter ignited a ripple effect in the barroom. I added; "What I'm trying to say is that David killed a giant with a stone and Samson slew the Philistines singlehandedly with the jawbone of an ass." He looked dumbfounded. Maybe he thought I was a mental case. I reached deep for a trump card. "Those who serve the Lord have kind of an advantage, don't you think? If God be for you – who can stand against you?" It was a desperate, rambling sort of attempt to explain myself and save my skin. When my Judgement Day comes it'll probably be on April Fool's Day. Words kept pouring from my mouth, nervously without regard, and I said that if I died yet would I live. I thought I should bend over and kiss my ass goodbye. The Zulu whistled again and the bar rebounded in raucous activity and noise like a freeze-frame film began to roll. He shook my hand and said he had to buy me a drink. He was impressed and said I had balls. No, I thought, I am one lucky traveler.

My hands shook as I accepted the offered drink and clinked glasses with the Zulu in a kind of comradery toast. I wanted to give him something to show my gratitude at not being beaten to a pulp or killed, but all I had to give were gospel tracts and a few granola bars. I unzipped my backpack and dumped the contents on the bar. Dozens of tracts were quickly snatched up and I spent around half an hour sharing my testimony while babying a glass of rum and engaged in conversations with guys gathered at the bar. Brian Hoyt, who was the last face I recalled seeing before disappearing in the storm, and several other friends stood at the open door. The rain had stopped. Brian was all eyes and white as a ghost. I met them on the sidewalk with relief on our faces, rounded up the group and walked to the bus stop to get back to

Tunapuna. I think we all agreed that we'd had enough excitement for one day.

Later that evening some of the gang lounged on Louise's front porch swapping stories about our adventure to Fredrick Street. I received a look from a good brother that put me on edge. As longwinded as I have a reputation to be, *that* look made me put the brakes on. Bob knew me well, my gift for self-aggrandizing and boasting in disguise of humility which he got a read on because of his own tendency to embellish, but the Lord dealt me a silent rebuke as if with a Taser. Let me pass along the lesson I'm still learning.

I grew up with the idea that it's better to give than to receive, as I'm certain you have, but I was also competitive. How can one root for someone else to win the race and deliberately choose second place? There is a maxim in the Kingdom of God with the basic tenet to prefer another. I want to be like Jesus, but I love the limelight, being the winner and receiving the trophy, getting all the accolades. Preferring another is a hard-won lesson for me to learn when I feel better qualified, which is subjective and probably in my own head. Who am I to feel better than everyone else? Such moments, when someone other than me deserves and receives praise, I tend to stand offstage and make comparisons. *Is not my performance just as spectacular or noteworthy?* Rather than bask in their victory and the moment of accreditation I'm guilty of holding a secret grudge. It's not a pretty character quality, in fact, it's utterly repugnant. The "look" I received from Bob on Louise's porch not only put me check, it was like stepping on a landmine. There's a rather odd verse that I'm sure is meant to encourage us but it's difficult for me to swallow. "The Lord disciplines those he loves." I need to get better at putting my brothers and sisters in the spotlight and quit gloating when they deserve a whole-hearted standing ovation.

A woman who had just gotten out of rehab dropped in to visit with Louise that evening. Carol was an international dancer of some acclaim, involved in theater throughout the West Indies and knew Louise as a music teacher, but I quickly gathered that Louise was more of a mother to her. Carol was in and out of a love affair with cocaine that was killing her on the installment plan. I was sharing my story when she joined us with a cup of tea and listened in. Out of the corner of my eye I saw her shaking her head. Carol asked where I was at on Fredrick Street and I described the place. She knew of it, informing me that the back door was on the harbor and the bar was notorious for drugs and murder. In a sober voice, Carol added, "You're very lucky to be alive." Louise huffed and grunted to clear her throat and let me have it, scolding me rather harshly and making me squirm in my chair. All my façade, the Don Quixote-like bravado guttered out like a snuffed candle. Cassie was none too pleased either. There was nothing I could say in my defense. They were right, it was foolish and reckless on my part, but as unrealistic as it might seem, could it not have been precisely what God arranged, an unlikely encounter to share the gospel with a Zulu?

In the end it was a successful trip. We all returned to Lewisburg in one piece, no one got sick and no one was killed. I know that Matt and Beth would consider going back and I thank Louise for her laughter and hospitality. On the flight back home I was sure that my friends would cherish their experiences in Trinidad, those moments of incredible grace and significance, vivid images and flavors, memories to last a lifetime. The best ones are personally engraved on our hearts and change us for the rest of our lives.

# 16

*Back* to reality as they say; home, work and church. My routine
was as predictable as the milkman who made deliveries to our
ice box on the front porch when I was a kid. I was getting beat
up by work and mentally weary. My heart wasn't in it anymore.
I started becoming unhappy at church for no apparent reason,
staying connected by nothing other than obligation. God, how
I loved these people, but I didn't want to be around anybody. I
began bowing out on the usual "after-glow" after church services
at Amity House for a hot fudge sundae with the gang. My home
life was stale and I wasn't sure whose fault it was. I'm looking
back for the most poignant word to describe my condition and all
I can come up with is the word: displacement. I could have said it
was disillusionment or disappointment, but it wasn't particularly
either of those. I thought that maybe I was depressed, having
feelings more often than not beyond the post-holiday blues
or like losing a close friend. There's a readjustment phase that
missionaries go through when returning back to their homes
from abroad, but I hadn't been in the field long enough to have
such a hard time with re-entry. However, something changed in
me with every trip I made to the Caribbean. Presently, the place
that I embraced and called home (good old Pleasant Valley),
where everything had always felt right and comfortable, was
becoming disoriented and on the verge of fracturing.

My mind was befuddled and everyday rhythms were like wandering around a corn maze or encountering warped mirrors at a carnival funhouse. Confusion reeled and gathered speed; at times it slowed my pace to a crawl. I fully expected to either hit a brick wall or step into a bottomless hole. There were better days when I felt refreshed as if standing downwind in a cedar grove, the fragrant cool air blowing on my face, daydreaming about pleasant things at home. I was often swept away by the distant aroma of curry and spice and frying fish, of a Maxi van's pungent smell while settling into a seat to enjoy the ride. I could fly like a hot air balloon over vistas of happy memories until it brought tears of joy and outright laughter. On the flip-side, I felt like an empty plastic bag randomly tossed about on the breeze, just someone's litter. It was difficult to tell which way the wind blew. I can be my own worse critic about my private life in hope that God knows me better, but his voice and nearness was wrapped in a steely silent shroud. It was up one day – down the next. I would remember events and fantasize the most elaborate scenarios and sail away, other times barely able to rescue myself no matter how recalcitrant. Displacement? I think that's the right word. I didn't know what to do about it and had no idea where I fit anymore. I wonder if I haven't felt displaced all my life.

I sought advice from my best friend, Jay. What we knew of ourselves we shared with one another. What we knew of each other we shared openly and honestly, speaking the truth in love. We would sit on the front porch at his farm or at my screened-in porch with coffee and a smoke and lay the whole truth and nothing but the truth on the table. I rambled. Jay listened. I'd ramble more and a pattern began to emerge. Mentally and emotionally I was angry in a puzzling and ambiguous sense, not raging-roaring mad, but more like a Weight Watcher hating their diet and obsessively checking the scale. It was paradoxical, my self-loathing and tendency to aggrandize. I felt like I was a walking, talking, functioning schizophrenic. Jay poked me squarely on the forehead like tapping out a telegraph. "Quit - beating - yourself - up. You know what God has put in your heart. Follow it." I heard him, certainly grateful for the encouragement, but this time it didn't connect.

～

I asked Mr. Hackenburg who owned the apiary down the road if it was okay to mow a path through his clover field to the creek. He had no problem with my request and said to go ahead. My retired neighbor, "Bob the Plumber" had a John Deere riding mower that I used on the agreement to mow his lawn. From the bank of my property it was a good seventy five yards to Buffalo Creek. When the leaves were off the trees you could see the signs for Wendy's and Dunkin Donut at night. It was the best of both worlds, a rural feeling from my backdoor through shag bark hickory trees and clover and a cup of coffee or a Frosty only a short walk away.

Buffalo Creek was rarely clear, it usually flowed like diluted chocolate milk from the run-off upstream. In the spring it overflowed the banks and flooded low laying land that closed the bridge on our road and made travelling the backway inconvenient. I found a cozy little spot where the path ended across the meadow, choosing a place where the creek came off some rapids and pooled. I cleared the brush and named it "Bethel," marveling at how perfect my secret get-away promised to be. I'd sit there for hours in a plastic lawn chair and just think and daydream, idling away an afternoon with a book, catch suckers or catfish if I was inclined to drop a worm. I'd take a thermos of coffee while Cassie put up leftovers and did dishes with the evening news on the TV, and go back to "Bethel." Sometimes I made a fire in a small pit that I'd dug and write in my journal or draw pencil sketches. I carved out my little corner of paradise and escaped to it as often as I could. Although "Bethel" never revealed Jacob's ladder with angels travelling between heaven and earth, I'd find myself drawn to the Lost and Found Department, rummaging through vaults of memories just as revealing as an angel could conjure.

It was flannel shirt weather (my favorite time of year), as I sat by the creek on a warm October afternoon. Red and orange and yellow leaves fell like confetti in the breeze and swirled on the creek as playful elves rowing downstream. I suppose you'd call it mental imagery or dream-scape, I wasn't having an acid flashback. Memories are unpredictable and mysterious, often taking us by surprise, and another eye-opening moment apprehended me.

I stumbled upon boxes of Super 8mm film reels that Dad was fond of taking and randomly picked one of the home movies marked: 1966. Spooling the reel in slow-motion through the theater of my mind, a hazy series of frames caught my eye and I was taken back in time. I saw my Dad holding a hand-printed sign on cardboard like a chapter title or someone in the crowd at the airport with a placard to receive an inbound passenger. The sign read; *Little League,* scrawled in his hard to read cursive, and that was where my mind went as Buffalo Creek gurgled by.

After the regular season closed I was chosen to play with the All-star team. We were in the semi-finals with hopes of going onto States, visions of going to the Little League World Series at Lamade Field filled our heads. I played first base and batted sixth, was one of three at bat with a line-drive double and an RBI. If I remember right, it was the bottom of the last inning and we were tied, looking at another chance at bat if we stayed tied. Our pitcher struck out the first batter. The second batter drove the ball over second base that the outfielder bobbled and he stretched it to a double. A lefty came up and I hugged the bag knowing them to be pull-hitters. Passing on the first pitch, he swung and popped up high just shy of being foul. I'd like to blame it on losing it in the sun but I can't. The runner on second base stole home and we lost by one run. If I had made the out it could have maybe saved the game. Our chance of advancing in the playoffs was over. I felt as though it was entirely my fault.

The film reel spools ahead in my mind and I'm back at home after the game. Just inside our front door you turned right to go upstairs to my bedroom. We were raised to take our shoes off when coming in the house and I was sitting on the bottom step unlacing my sneakers. My dad came over and leaned against the newel post without saying a word. He picked up my first base mitt and clouted me with it, the message wasn't subtle. I gathered my things and went up to my bedroom. I felt crushed.

～

Was God like my father, exacting and demanding? I was happy with B's but perfection was the standard, the expectation, the goal meriting reward. I was tired of failing. For Christ's sake, did I need therapy?

"Know and follow your heart," hearing Jay's voice in my head. "Displaced? Hogwash! We all make mistakes. Be free my friend."

I dumped out my thermos and peed on the fire, dousing it with creek water to make sure it was out. Once again, my niche on Buffalo Creek was a place of revelation. It makes me wonder if we all would do well and benefit from finding such a place, a secret getaway from business as usual, a sanctuary where memories collide with the promise of healing.

I'm not sure what the trigger is that entices me to enter the Lost and Found Department. Maybe it's a line from a song still playing in my head, the parting words of a friend or a stranger in the parking lot, a thirty second Pepsi commercial; pure happenstance? So much is discovered in spite of the reasons if I take the time to give it my attention. I'm happy when reminded of happier occasions and relive the good times, but even if it's a bad memory, I'm convinced that if something comes to mind it's probably important. There could very well be unexpected treasures waiting in the wings to discover, then again, it might aggravate an old wound that still needs healed, revealing infection under the skin. It's been nearly fifty-five years carrying the memory of that demoralizing moment, but the cognitive memory is as vivid as if it was yesterday. I prayed for my disappointed and frustrated father. I forgave that twelve year old gangly first baseman who didn't hit a homerun and missed a fly ball.

I walked across Hackenburg's clover meadow and returned home feeling a bit of resolve. At the time I was 46 years old and a wild hair twitched in my butt, as my old man used to say. I decided to run away from home for the second time in my life. Why the hell not?

Cassie went to visit her mother and sisters in Dayton, Ohio for a week. I made an honest excuse not to go along because of work. When she pulled out of the driveway I blew her a kiss and did a happy-happy dance. I convinced myself to go to the Town Tavern and get good and drunk. I needed to unwind. After calling Chris, a fellow who worked for me, and hitting the ATM, I found a barstool for several hours. Chris was shocked. He knew that I was a Christian and had a hard time comparing the talkative drunk sitting next to him to the man who prayed for the crew. I bordered on being kind of weepy and rambled at length about how miserable I felt at home. I went on about how temporal things like 2X4's and trusses and stair-stringers were meaningless, that in the end everything I did with my hands would burn. What lasts? What really mattered? Of course, Chris didn't know what to say, but humored me by listening and buying the next round.

Somehow I managed to get back home and recall wandering around the house envisioning what I would pack to run away. I popped in a Bob Marley CD and played it loud enough it must have seemed like a live concert to the tenants upstairs. I mentally itemized the important things I'd take, CD's and books and my favorite coffee mug and... I ended up passing out on the couch. Regardless of my state of mind (and yes, I was quite drunk), I knew I was going back to the islands for a long time. *That* was what was in my heart to do in answer to Jay's question. I'm sure he saw it coming long before I did. When I sobered up the next morning I called Andy.

# 17

*Cassie* and I ambled through everyday life with tension just under the surface like an invasive stranger had broken in and interrupted our mutual routine. I made my grand announcement one evening (being sober and of right mind), but should have thought before I spoke. Had I said, "I hope you understand that I have to back to the islands," instead of the demanding tone I used it may have gone differently. I added rather adamantly that I wanted to go for at least a year, maybe two. Cassie didn't rise to toast the adventure. Expectations are a bitch and my reaction was anything but pleasant. She was immediately indecisive about making such a long term commitment. I'm sure my sudden declaration was a bit of a shock.

The subject became kind of game between us, revolving around unresolved questions, both of us dealing with personal anxiety. Cassie could act as if nothing was going to change, scarcely giving it any attention. She typically deflected discussing the matter whenever I brought up it up. There were times that I was unflattering in my remarks and the silent treatment would start, but the proximity of the issue was always too near to entirely avoid. Sometimes we would find common ground and converse about how important going on a mission was, fondly recalling our experiences in the islands, but she always had qualifications. I believe she was trying hard to get her head around leaving home for an extended period of time, but Cassie never felt as passionately about it as I did. I was probably driven by self-doubting motivations and the need to prove something to God or reconcile with my past, but I'd like to think my motives were based on doing something right. If it was mid-life crisis I would have bought a red sport car and saved us both the trouble.

The incongruity of Cassie's look when we put our cards on the table was almost funny. We weren't diametrically opposed but almost. Compared to my occasional outbursts of blathering enthusiasm; Cassie's silence while making supper or sitting in the passenger seat when we were out was deafening. They call that the awkward silence and indeed it is. She shook her head whenever a touch of joy came upon me and I acted like a fool dancing around the living room with calypso music playing, or when I'd return from Weis Market with mangoes and canned coconut milk to add to my coffee or Coke. I think that deep down she was terrified at the prospect of leaving the comforts of home with such an erratic husband.

I began taking the long way home after work and finding more things to occupy my time when I was at home without actually being in the house; shop work, yard work, puttering. If that's something you're presently doing perhaps it's time to ask yourself some hard questions. We had a casual, amiable understanding between one another and kept it private. When we entertained for family events as well as at social or church functions we held hands and made a show that everything was peaches and cream. We got along finishing projects that needed done around the house. Staying busy helped us to avoid interfacing with each other directly, otherwise, without distractions, we'd inevitably hit bumps in the road. My heart was set on relocating sooner than later. An almost palpable shadow was dimming the light of our harmony. We didn't laugh as often as we used to, and as for our love life, what comes between obligatory and hardly ever? In many ways we'd become one of those married couples living as plutonic singles. Although I didn't exactly know what I wanted or needed, I was an obstinate, self-possessed idiot.

As I look back through years of foggy memories about those times with Cassie, I realize now that she understood me better than I understood myself. She gave me breathing room, or rope to hang myself, always praying for me. At the end of the day she agreed to go along wherever the Lord took us. Maybe she finally succumbed upon seeing it as another chapter in our on-going journey. We had 25 years of history following an uncharted road.

Cassie was with me through readjusting numerous times since leaving rehab; in my companionship there'd been major moves. We followed the wind wherever it took us from the beginning days of our first kiss to getting married in the backyard, countless evenings spent with Harry and Joann after meeting the Lord, learning the basics of faith at Crossroads Church, Jesus festivals and new awakenings, Lamb Fellowship, dancing and tongue-talkers, a coffeehouse ministry hosting a houseful of strange and needy people, all of it bursting with life and transformation. She'd been by my side clearing security to enter a maximum state prison facility when we served with Prison Fellowship, eyed up by inmates I'm sure. Cassie learned how to put a worm on a hook and start a campfire; she nursed poison ivy on her buttock after making love with me in a field. She was a trooper on countless trips that I know stretched her limits when we were in the tropics as she was sun conscious, slathering sunblock a quarter inch thick on exposed parts and had a phobia of bugs. Cassie wouldn't have experienced such adventures had it not been for my lead, as if any of them merits bragging about. Perhaps you should feel sorry for her. She could have married a millionaire. I'm happy she was with me at every turn in road. I'm fairly sure that if she hadn't been a part of things I never would have followed such a road.

I don't think for a minute that it was because I had worn her down and she just "threw in the towel." I'm certain my constant nagging and edginess and comparisons about trivial things that pissed me off were wearisome to her. I know that I behaved badly, worse than a moody child not getting his own way. No, Cassie didn't just give in. She had a deeper prayer life than me and I think she began conquering some of her own personal demons.

When Andy called and informed me that Barbados was the best option it wasn't like my heart sank, but it did sag a bit deflated. Trinidad was my first choice but I trusted Andy. He said a pastor friend of his was looking forward to us joining with his church; a young and growing fellowship in the network that was the best fit. On hearing the news it was as if Cassie had an earth-shaking revelation. I'm not sure what brought on the sudden change. The plan was to leave after the Christmas holidays for a year commitment. Cassie began making arrangements to rent our house and started packing. Her insight at making preparations was astounding.

Two large containers of household goods were shipped. I was able to add some basic tools and a few of my favorite things that I've already mentioned when I was going to run away. We stored our valuables, liquidated non-essentials at a yard sale, scraped our savings together and got all our ducks in a row. I sold my job trailer and an arsenal of tools, giving a stunning referral about my lead guy to the manager of the home builder I subcontracted from, and wished Johnny good luck with the business. I hoped that I'd never have to return to making a living with a tape measure in hand ever again. What a pipe-dream.

~

I went to Barbados in January of 1999, going a month ahead of Cassie to scout things out and lay some ground work. Trevor and Wendy Regret met me at the airport and from the start they were great at facilitating my transition to a new life. Trevor pastored the church called: "The Courts of Praise." The congregation of forty plus were locals from St. Joseph and Christ Church Parish, a closely knit body of believers from all walks of life in Barbados, families I'd soon get to know. They worked hand in hand as monies allowed and continued building a large block and masonry structure that would hold several hundred people with a dream to enlarge God's kingdom. At the time I arrived it sounded cavernous with an echo. When rain fell hard on the galvanized roof it was like ball-peen hammers pounding into your soul that made hearing what was being preached virtually impossible. Generally, the meeting-hall was sunny and pleasant with a breeze from large open windows.

Trevor was middle-age, an eloquent man, soft spoken with a subtle English accent, and had the same approach as Andy toward vision and teaching style. Bertril Baird had passed the baton upon getting ill, and Andy came under the tutelage of a new ministry in Trinidad lead by Dr. Noel Woodruff. "World Breakthrough Network" was a growing movement and Courts of Praise was in their web. Wendy, Trevor's wife was from the UK and more friendly and conversational about everyday life than Trevor was. I was more comfortable with her. Trevor was cut out of the same fabric as Bertril Baird and Noel Woodruff. I couldn't imagine him ever playing UNO or boogey-boarding in the surf. They had two handsome boys in college somewhere in the West Indies and a lovely but modest home. Wendy owned and operated a successful advertising agency in Hastings, Christ Church. She had located a little house for us and made arrangements for a car. I'd soon move into new digs and learn to drive on the opposite side of the road.

Home to be was centrally located a short drive from church, Trevor's home in Hastings and Bridgeton. Wendy secured a furnished bungalow through a client that was behind an older residence built by a wealthy sugar cane merchant when landowners had slaves. Mature palms, banana trees and overgrown gardens surrounded the walled property. The cottage behind the main house may have originally been servant quarters, but it was adequate, updated and more or less modern. It fit our needs and budget. Gerald and Denise were the landlords. Gerald was a doctor of some sort and his wife, Denise was an entrepreneur and a freelance artist. I was given the tour and told in no uncertain terms, of all things, to rinse every ware every time I drank or ate because of insect and what-not feces. Twenty years later and living in North Dakota, I still catch myself rinsing a clean dish before putting food on it. After getting giardia in Grenada I paid attention. Denise gave me a detailed roadmap of Barbados and a gate key and I was pretty much left on my own. The containers we shipped hadn't arrived. With only a suitcase, guitar and basics, I had a small laptop, compliments of Elvin, with notes and floppy disks of a novel I was trying to write, the story that I began at Merton's Pond on a silent retreat. I wanted to get serious about writing and spent most of my mornings on the patio outlining and slowly pecking away.

During the day I'd explore or spend time with Trevor. His assistant, Jan Browne was likeable when she wasn't in business mode, overseeing several hundred apartment units, laying down the order of things as a drill sergeant. Jan was a woman of deep prophetic insight and had me over for many meals when they all got together. Just sitting in their company and listening to conversations was a learning experience. I wandered around the small village of Lemmings in St. Joseph Parish where the church was located and introduced myself to locals in hopes of make some friends. I never could locate the pastor from St. Thomas Parish who hosted us on our first trip.

I'd lie in bed at night and listen to the insect's insistent buzz and the tree frog's melodic mating calls vocalizing mournful complaints at not getting lucky. Dogs barked in chain reaction from afar and usually died out around 2 a.m. I became accustomed to the night sounds like living near railroad tracks and not hearing the trains anymore, but the green-face monkeys raised the bar. Their night-time pillaging for bananas from the trees around the bungalow made such a racket!

The monkeys would rise when curious or provoked and stood on hind legs as tall as my waist, skinny and nasty, probably rabid, and glared at me like I was the intruder. Sometimes they were naughty and slung a handful of shit or mashed up bananas at me out of spite. You did not approach them. As if on some prearranged plan (I began to think they were deliberately being devious), I would be jolted awake before the cock crowed when one would jump and land with a loud thump on the roof and give me a scare. Three in particular became familiar. I called them Moe, Larry and Shemp, the stooges, and was pretty sure they knew what the middle finger meant.

Church kept me busy; worship team practice, Tuesday night teaching service, Wednesday morning prayer service, Friday's luncheon service for leaders, a surprise guest speaker, etc. I'm glad they were called services and not clubs or I would have been clubbed to death. The Sunday morning service started at eight so families could rest and enjoy the day, but it often went till noon. I seemed to fit in and made friends rather quickly. Michael, the lead guitar player on the worship team and his wife, Maria became close friends, and because of them I learned my way around Bridgetown, more or less.

The kids in the village taught me how to play cricket, which I sort of got, but no matter how hard I tried not to swing the bat like an American baseball player I'd slip up. They'd hoot and holler and wag a finger as if scolding me. I started a game-night on Friday evenings as an outreach, board games and improvised games and a home-made shuffle board court in chalk on the basement floor of the church, served cold drinks and store bought cookies. In-between games I'd take fifteen or twenty minutes to share a devotional each week. We sang choruses and jumped up on fast songs, yelling and stomping our feet and having a time of it. Sometimes I dressed up playing various roles in modest homespun costume, telling stories of Jonah and the whale like Ahab in Moby Dick with a cardboard hook taped to my arm and a patch over my eye; or David slaying a bear with a sling shot to save the sheep. I played a leper with spots and regretted dotting my face with a red dry marker that didn't wash off easily. It was pure joy, those Friday evenings, and I watched the group growing with childlike excitement. They were the best company and made me feel like a kid. God, how they laughed! Occasionally I was invited to share a short message like reading a five page novella aloud during Sunday service and tried to stay sharp and ready when called upon, but I think Trevor was testing me out. Little by little, Barbados was growing on me.

≈

Shortly after Cassie arrived it became apparent that we still had issues to work through. They were swept under the rug but obviously dragged to Barbados tucked in-between the layers of each of our baggage. The space between us became crowded and there was no place to run. A lingering sense of unease and uncertainty lurked under the surface when were by ourselves. The feeling of wanting to escape from her that I had in PA still plagued me, as I wondered if it did with her to avoid me. But here she was; in my bed, her toothbrush on the bathroom sink, the scent of Red Door perfume in the air and another place-setting at meals. I'd made the bungalow comfy and homey, arranging the humble furnishings and kept the place clean, happier to be on my own. It took days to clear the debris and brush to create a yard, careful not to get bitten by some menacing insect when I should have worn gloves, and set up the patio for entertaining or chilling out to my own liking. Seeking solace like doing yard work back home and avoiding Cassie was an idle and often redundant attempt at escape. There was no garden to tend to, though I was planning on one, and what meager leftovers the monkeys left of the bananas was hardly worth the work. With no TV and the only books we'd brought from home, conversation was either strained or enjoyable. If we didn't make the effort to change up the routine we'd just be stuck with each other on an endless carousel of consensually disassociating and being comfortably numb.

We were on a budget that allowed little wiggle room for gallivanting off needlessly, but we did cheat and take occasional day trips to sightsee. I'd bought an older jeep, a hard top Daihatsu that showed some age, opposite drive of American vehicles with a four speed stick-shift that was easy on fuel. I'd take us on journeys around the island wherever the road lead without a plan, refusing to look at a map. We often got sidetracked on the scenic route, which was what I called it, but Cassie said that we were lost. I'd never admit to it. How could you really get lost in a country only 166 square miles in size? The county where I now live is ten times bigger.

I was put off on my first trip to Barbados with a stinted opinion of its lack of attraction, but how wrong I was. Barbados is a lovely island with stunning beaches on every point of the compass, the Atlantic to the north and east, the Caribbean south and west. The seas are different in such vivid contrast. Parts of the interior are colorful with hanging vines in flower and fruit trees, I acquired a taste for tamarind and ginger. Of course, there is sugar cane, which means slave history. You can tour little museums and landmarks of shacks and hovels and get a glimpse of the hardship and way of life the slaves endured a century ago. The Chattel Village on the west coast where local artists have exhibits is a gold mine, as is Harrison's Cave or Gun Hill to hike the highest point in Barbados. Downtown Bridgetown is metropolitan, worldly in its own right, touristy with Cave Shepherd and duty-free shopping, eateries and pubs and night-clubs that offer live island music and every venue beckons you when the sun sets. A picturesque beach is always in view, private or public and were allowed access. The gardens and old missions and churches where a photographer would have a field day or a painter could spend hours trying to capture it on canvas are worthy of an all day visit. Resorts and hostels tucked secretly in coves have such allure; Sam Lord's Castle with its pirate history, Bathsheba, which is so postcard-like where I stepped barefooted on a spiny sea urchin that hobbled me for a week, and Mullin's Bay where you could jet ski and swim with sea turtles gave me a sense of awe and pleasure.

We bought kites and hiked and lounged in the shade watching the waves and sea birds, or find a café and people-watch while sipping a cold Coke in peaceful quietness. I can't say that it was always paradise, but knocking around Barbados there were times I heard whispers of hope and beguiling possibilities somewhere in my being. There was chance that Cassie and I might find a place of grounding if we stayed at it.

As I reflect back on those days, it's likely that my perspective was or is jaded, I may have been wrong for years about my inner issues and anxiety between us and fabricated a paragon of my own making. Cassie's story could very well be quite different from mine. If, what a sad word, but if we'd gone to marriage counseling who knows where we'd be today?

From the start of our relationship I realized that Cassie was an intuitive woman with extremely jealous eyes as volatile as nitroglycerine. She picked up on something about Denise, the landlady that bothered her. Before Cassie arrived, I volunteered to help Denise with projects and crafts. As I said, she was an artist. Along with her impressionistic paintings of seascapes and tropical scenes in water colors, she also sold wooden nick-knacks and shadow boxes at several consignment shops. I'd cut frames and sand and matte pieces of art while listening to her jabber off the point about mindless things in her French accent that totally lost me. It was funny but frustrating, as Denise didn't seem able to carry on an entire conversation about anything of depth and made me wonder if she was bio-polar. I wished that I'd known a little French to at least know if she was being pompous or insulting. Jesus was an anomaly whenever I brought up the gospel, which she gave little attention to. Denise was around my age, a white Bajan of French origin, attractive in a Tom-boy kind of way and I never knew for sure if she was being flirtatious or not. She was so full of herself and high maintenance that it was nauseating, short doses of Denise went a long way. I paid her little mind, staying in my own world and routine, but I have to admit, I did have fleeting fantasies.

Cassie was a tigress when it came to her man and kept her claws sharp, figuratively speaking. Whenever she and Denise happened to engage one another (which was rare), the discussions were curt with politeness sprinkled in to keep the pot from boiling over. Within a few months after she'd arrived, Cassie located a new place for us. Her comment was, "If I have to live on an island I'd like to see the sea." She could have added a proverb along the lines of an adulteress' smooth ways to ensnare a godly man. Like I said, Cassie was a jealous woman. She located a ground level, one bedroom flat for $400 US a month and we moved far away from the clutches of Denise whatever her last name is. It was a good move. Au revoir, crazy monkey house. Bienvenue, Sea View Road.

～

The property Cassie found was in Chancery Lane on Seaview Road, a small community just a short drive to the airport or the fishing village of Oistins. It was a large stucco three story house owned by a gynecologist who lived in NYC. His brother, Jack Pilgrim was a local Bajan who managed the affair. The house was on a hard turn in the road with a wall that bordered the lot and a driveway that swept around to the back. There was an almond tree, small palms, papaya and dwarf orange trees and room for a garden that I wouldn't be very successful at. I don't mean to paint such a glamorous picture about the place to make you think it was a postcard island paradise, although having a sea view was a huge plus. Compared to the bungalow that was in the country and shaded, this property was open space. A field of wild grass lies between the sea and the house, brutally beaten by the sun, scratchy on bare legs and flip flops when on a walk. Being so close to the sea dwarfed the lushness that could have been amazing if not hindered by salt spray and hot winds. I tried being a gardener and watered the flowers and veggies I planted but it was futile and better left to Mother Nature. Our apartment was on the ground level, a small but airy one bedroom that came semi-furnished with a washer and dryer which was such a plus. The little patio had a sea view no more than a hundred yards across the field. Casuarina trees, scrub brush and sea grapes bordered a strip of sand at tideline. Here, the east coast is rough with sharp coral so it wasn't a swim beach, but it was scenic and secluded. Cassie walked there every morning to pray and get her exercise before the heat of the day.

I discovered a lovely cove within a thirty minute walk called the Kayak Club where competitions were held for wind surfing and sea-kayaking. An outfitter rented equipment, and when you wanted to wet your whistle after venturing out, a makeshift bamboo bar offered snacks, cold beer and drinks. Cassie bought me a nine foot surf rod for my birthday and I fished from the bluff. A local fellow named Garfield, who was dark as midnight with a starry bright smile, taught me how to stun and catch live bait and the ins and outs of fishing in such rough seas. He often came to the Kayak Club as he lived close-by and we became friends. I caught a three foot Reef shark one night and Garfield went crazy when I landed it. He pounced on the writhing shark like a rodeo rider, pummeling its brains with the five gallon bucket he'd been sitting on. I had no experience to gut a shark other than gutting a stock trout and he was on it in a heartbeat. He asked me if I was going to keep it and I answered with a shrug, "I don't have freezer room, you take it." Garfield had a large family and the know-how to portion it like a butcher. I met his family and enjoyed an amazing shark dinner with all the Bajan side-dishes and played games with his five children, number six still nursed at momma's breast. Garfield rededicated his life to Christ and our fishing together became all the more enjoyable. The bay calmly pooled at high tide on the reef like warm bath water almost chin deep. It was a wonderful place when I wasn't fishing to soak and think and pray, letting the sea soothe away my stress.

Mike's Mini Mart was an easy walk unless I had weighty bags to carry back home after shopping. It was a great little grocery store that had local produce and everyday necessities. Banks, the locally brewed beer, along with Carib (the Budweiser of the Caribbean), was two dollars a bottle in Barbadian, a buck in green backs, and well stocked in a large chest cooler. It's nice to hear your name called in greeting when you enter any establishment, it means you've become a local, a regular, and the owners soon knew me. I was a big fan of chocolate biscuits, Crisps and New Zealand cheese. You probably thought I was known for buying beer. I admit that I'd sit on the patio and chat with the locals with a Banks in hand. Mike's Mini Mart was a busy place for local gossip, a bus stop on the coastal road to Bridgetown, and a get-away from Cassie when I needed a different perspective. I'd make an excuse to get eggs or bread and make a half day excursion of it. The regular fellows that I was on a first-name basis with had a magical way of making me laugh.

Another great thing about living at Chancery Lane was the neighbors. I never had the occasion to meet anyone up-country at the infamous monkey house other than Gerald and Denise and hadn't made any new friends besides church friends. John and Lorna Wilson lived next door and we instantly developed a very close and open friendship. They had a lovely home and a large gallery with a sea view where we spent countless hours sharing stories and discussing everyday things to esoteric subjects. I'm sure our laughter was heard across the street. John owned an auto supply business in Bridgetown and has my greatest respect. He liked a good cigar and debating politics. Lorna was a socialite, a Nubian Queen, and I affectionately referred to her as a witchdoctor. Lorna was into holistic living and was an incredible cook when she cooked. Mariah, her maid, who had an amusing and delightful character, did most of the work. Lorna may have dabbled in oils or acrylics back then, but since has become an accomplished artist. Her paintings are in galleries and available on-line. She has a talent that I didn't know about when we were neighbors. As she encouraged me about writing, so I, too, tip my hat to her. John and Lorna were engaging conversationalists, entertaining and supportive of my, what can I say? Poverty? I was treated lavishly as one among their family.

Pete and Linda Lautenschlager lived across the street. They were Canadians from way up north in Sudbury, Ontario. I wondered what they were doing in the tropics besides thawing out. Pete was a short, stocky white guy, sort of opinionated and loud and liked to quote George Carlin. He was entertaining but sometimes gave me a headache. My god, was he a talker. Pete had dual citizenship from marrying a Barbadian and could work legally. I went along to some of his job sites and he taught me the tricks of tiling. Pete was an artisan when it came to tile work, meticulously laying patterns and creating custom mosaics that rivaled anything prefab from Home Depot. Linda was a light-skinned Bajan and the perfect mate for Pete. Her sensibility and calm even-keeled demeanor kept Pete from being more outrageous than he was. Linda was an RN working part-time and minded two adorable, rambunctious kids. Her oldest, Kiyan was five at the time, Noah was just a baby. Kiyan had a lion-like mane of sun-streaked golden locks around his deeply tanned oval-shaped face and bright inquisitive brown eyes. He never wore a shirt or shoes. Kiyan was a spitfire like his dad. I enjoyed hanging out and sharing meals, taking walks together around the neighborhood or to the sea. Pete would call when coming down my driveway; "Yellow!" It was never hello, but it was a welcoming voice all the same, the call of a friend coming to visit. I gave up counting how many times he said; "eh?" Canadians ya know. We were a tight knit group, this "Seaview Road Gang," and they made my stay in Barbados unforgettably memorable.

I was asked to teach a series on Tuesday evenings at church that made me feel useful in an adult arena. Trevor was getting to know me, although he was guarded about who he let speak from the pulpit. He was an excellent teacher but held the reins and at times I thought was a bit overbearing. What I'm trying to say is he had an agenda that emanated from Dr. Woodruff, the apostle of WBN in Trinidad who he was accountable to. A nagging concern about authority issues tugged at me, control and the hierarchy so to speak, of expectations to align (submit), oneself to the mentality that came from the top. I noticed how more folks than not in the congregation sounded like Trevor. I get that. It's not mind-control or cloning, but adapting to the soil God has planted you in. If you're committed and walking in community and fellowship, it's a given that after time we take on the verbiage and principles of the leadership and join them to facilitate their vision, or else we wouldn't trust them, at least I wouldn't. I tried to get with the program.

There were times I felt rebuffed and actually ignored by Trevor when in a group setting, it was as though I were invisible, a shadow at best. Granted, I still had acceptance issues, but I never begged for attention. I realized that Trevor was a busy man, but come on! I was a guest in his country. I'd treat a guest with respect and strive to make them comfortable, buy their favorite snack, offer another blanket. It made me wonder if I was being set aside because I didn't necessarily fit the mold and walk and talk exactly like the rest of them. I took it as a snub that angered and hurt me both and justified Trevor's seeming lack of tact by thinking he was teaching me some kind of valuable life skill. We got along in casual settings, but why was "church" a testing ground? I bounced like a ping-pong ball between being hurt and angry on one side of the net to embracing tough love and learning character on the other. Needless to say, it was with some trepidation that I embarked on my teaching series.

"Hearing the voice of God" was my topic for the next three sessions. I know, it sounds kind of presumptuous on my part to tackle such a subject. I felt that the message fit in with the trend of establishing God's Kingdom on the earth, which was the battle cry of the hour. I used a visual example as a warm up and had two volunteers sit back to back on chairs, each with a handful of different cut-out shapes of colorful construction paper. One would make a pattern at their feet and try to communicate it to the other to duplicate it without seeing it. The lesson was entertaining to watch and was never a perfect, recreated match. The congregation seemed to enjoy it and heartily laughed. I shared from scripture the imagery about God's design of the Tabernacle to Moses, my point being the necessity of hearing God's voice to accurately implement the pattern and build accordingly. I expressed that the ability to rightly hear is a hard-learned process and that we often make mistakes or even fail, needing a do-over. I concluded with a handout of the Holy of Holies for the next week and thought that overall it went very well.

The next Tuesday evening was part two of my series and I felt well prepared, geared up and ready to go. Before I went to the pulpit, Trevor asked me to stand in place like a crossing guard holding me at the curb. He went to the pulpit (that I've come see as a throne), and for the next hour I was grilled, chastised, corrected and rebuked. They're all just nice words to say that I got my ass chewed out. Apparently, God is quite clear in his instructions and his people intrinsically hear and know his voice. My message was somehow contrary to clarity and accuracy, not to mention that I'd said we sometimes failed. My object lesson with colored paper patterns fell flat and it seemed to me at the moment the wrong thing to have done. I felt belittled and more than put in place. It was very hard to swallow and not interject a rebuttal. If I gave an ass-chewing to a coworker I always took him aside, never in front of the crew. Was I being made an example for his followers to take note of? Was Trevor drawing a line to imply that he was the boss? After Trevor seemed to right the wrong I'd made, he bid me to come forward and continue my teaching. I could have fainted dead on the spot. Not sure if I'd passed the test or not and trembled with emotion, I walked to the platform. On the way I gathered two folding chairs and set them up back to back without saying a word. It may have appeared as a deliberate act of obstinacy to Trevor's rebuke.

"This is our positioning before being in Christ," I said in a clear and rather pronounced voice, pointing at the chairs facing opposite directions. My blood pressure still peaked and I nearly added that was the intended starting point last week, but I bit my tongue not wanting to take issue with Trevor. At seeing the look on his face it seemed like I was opening a can of worms.

"We're facing away from God," I said, and turned the chairs to face one another. "This is our position in Christ. We are in the proximity to not only see his face but to hear his voice." I remember taking a deep breath to get centered and stuck my toe in the water. "It may take our lifetime to fully know and understand, but yes, God makes his ways knowable to us if we have an ear to hear. The apostle Paul says that we see in part, we know in part, we prophesy in part... until the fullness of time has come. Then we will know perfectly." I was tempted to add a sarcastic remark that some people already think they know everything. Trevor nodded and I took it to mean we were in agreement. "So, if you will allow me, a humble and flawed man to continue, I think I have some ideas that will encourage you on the journey."

This is all in hindsight and the best way I know to express how that evening went down. I didn't foresee my topic or the way I presented it as controversial, nor did I imagine it would be grounds for testing that in my opinion shouldn't have happened in the first place. In retrospect, maybe ear candles or a pick axe to dig out doctrinal earwax for an object lesson would have been more amusing than colored paper. I folded my notes and bible, unsure if my message met the standard, but in a way I didn't care. I felt like I had given the subject my best shot. Trevor came forward and I half expected round two and another black eye. He shared the announcements and ended the service with prayer. Among the announcements for the coming week I was slotted to continue teaching my series.

It was a quiet and longer than usual drive back to my apartment after service. I replayed my rebuke a hundred times, my head ready to burst, and debated about stopping at a rum shop to imbibe in a little medicine. I had to chill out or explode. When I got back to my flat, I walked across the street before calling it a night. Pete liked Mount Gay rum mixed with orange juice and made me a drink. He listened to me rant, and although he didn't understand the spiritual gist of it, I think Pete felt my pain. Lorna would get an earful in the morning.

# 18

*I'm* not sure why I haven't made mention of Cassie's daughter. Molly was seven when I came into the scene, awkward as was at the time, but we grew to love one another. She never called me dad but I know she respects me. The background and history are too complicated to articulate at this point in the story, so it's with some variance and hopefully your forgiveness to skip over details.

Molly, my step-daughter, was married for a few years when we went to Barbados. She and her husband wanted to start a family but had all but given up on having a child. They went to specialists and did the fertility routine. Molly miscarried. They went through the revolving door several times with disappointment. Molly and Elvin were considering adoption when she became pregnant. She called long distance with a sobbing voice, hopeful yet scared to death, and Cassie caught a flight back to the states within the week. She'd be in and out to assist and minister to Molly as well as taking care of emergencies and needs on our property. Cassie was gone more than she was by my side.

I thought at times it was a convenient excuse; leaving to tend pressing needs back home, but I know that Cassie struggled when she was in Barbados. She often felt like a fifth wheel and didn't exactly know where she fit in. Perhaps Jan and Wendy could have done more to include her. Her experience was so different with Louise in Trinidad, those days passed with happy busyness. Here, she dealt with boredom and loneliness. Cassie battled the sun, the heat, reacted to any kind of bug and maybe troubled by being in the minority as we were among the 15% white population. It took some getting adjusted to. I don't know the depth of her angst, but I know that she wasn't a happy camper. A younger couple from the UK lived on the second floor above our flat on Sea View Road; Paul was a gourmet chef at one of the high end resort and his wife was a stay at home mom with a couple of young kids. We played games and partook of wine and munchies on their balcony and were entertained. As I recall, Cassie was very fond of the woman. I think her name was Mary and they got along like peas and carrots. But regardless of having someone to visit with, Cassie would fly state-side and be out for extended periods of times. It could very well have been me she was avoiding and having a hard time with. I can't say that I understood her urgency to run home at every red flag, certainly not from a mother's point of view, but I gave assent and prayed for everything to turn out all right. Molly hung on and went full term and had an adorable little baby boy.

I continued my usual routine (being such a creature of habit), writing in the morning and adding pages to my on-going novel, "Merton's Pond." I'd venture out for the afternoon and visit with folks from church, spent time lending a hand to various building projects in the church. Friday game night with the youth was growing. We were considering hosting VBS before the year was up and bring a team from home. I attended nearly every service at Courts of Praise but wasn't asked to teach anymore. However, Trevor allowed me to write a monthly newsletter with feature articles and interviews with guest speakers for a small circulation. I called it: "The Living Stones Chronicle." Dr. Noel Woodruff held a three day teaching series at Courts of Praise and I had the opportunity to spend some time with him. I felt uneasy at our luncheon for a taped interview, but Dr. Woodruff was accommodating and cordial. He knew of me through Andy, although vaguely by name, and invited me to visit WBN whenever I was Trinidad. I wasn't exactly sure if I liked him or not.

One Tuesday evening during service, a Bajan woman stood to share her grievances about racial issues in the church in so many words. She lived in Lemmings within walking distance of Courts of Praise, a mother of four and a neighborhood tribe that she looked after, many of whom came to youth group on Friday night. It was uncharacteristic of her to speak out so boldly. I'm not sure what prompted her but had my suspicions.

A group of white Bajans began attending on Sunday morning service, mostly younger people who were entranced by Trevor's reputation and teaching. They were so full of life and likeable. We shared refreshments and fellowship after service in the guava grove behind the church, having wonderful discourse about the Lord and life in general. I was surprised when several of the girls came to the Kayak Club where I happened to be fishing. They were fun and carefree as cheerleaders, playful and prancing in the shallows in their bikinis which disturbed my fishing. Go figure. They had a watermelon and we shared stories about the Lord while spitting seeds in the surf like having a contest.

Anyway, the black sister who raised the objection about race said they were cliquey. I thought it was ridiculous. Those young people were innocent and loved the Lord and enjoyed being among us. I'm not sure what inspired me, if it was inspiration or gas, but I rose to sit in the empty chair between the angry woman and a sister sitting next to her. Meaning no disrespect, I smiled and said, "Aren't you glad there's icing in the middle of an Oreo?" It raised a chuckle. No wonder Trevor kept me on a short leash.

Being sensitive and tuned into the plight of the under-dog, I've seen degrees of prejudice all my life. Anytime I feel a vibe that threatens to put a boot heel on anyone's neck makes me cringe. I saw it in shops that were owned by a wealthy white Bajan merchant and on job sites with a boss barking at laborers and in homes that had maids. It could be subtle, but the attitude of servant and master that was inherent of England's rule and standard of position, class and privilege trickled down through generations and still had an influence in Barbados. I suppose there's inequality based on color or education or family standing regardless of being predominately black. There's an unspoken, unwritten standard accepted by bigotry and greed or entitlement, an unfortunate part of world culture since the beginning of days. One lords it over – one is subservient, from South Africa to America, and yes, Barbados is no different. Evident not only in the secular world in subtlety or with blatant bias are the stains of prejudice that taint and divide people even in the church. The animosity goes both ways. If there's any place on the planet to get it right, for God's sake, let's get it right in the church and declare to the world that we are all one in Christ.

I began riding the vans more often to save gas money, catching a ride from Mike's Mini Mart to run errands in Bridgetown or to the fishing village of Oistins where I banked and grocery shopped. A video store rented DVD's for a buck, but you had to like movies pirated from five years old. The times that I drove, the ladies at the wharf would recognize my jeep and jovially engaged me with friendly banter; apparently I'd become a local, or loco. I was never sure if they got my name right. We laughed a lot and they always gave me a sack of flying fish or an occasional fillet of fresh caught swordfish or yellow tuna wrapped in butcher paper. Yummy!

I started noticing a certain intrinsic beauty in dark skinned women when I was out and about, their sultry eyes, thick lips, supple curves and round hips, the way they walked. There was something behind their demeanor that whispered the exotic, an uncanny allure that made me turn my gaze. I never considered being with a woman of color in my life but it began to intrigue me. Of course, I'd be solicited by hookers when I was in Bridgetown who assumed I was a rich tourist, but paid them no mind. I kept my integrity, which was hard won, yet my eyes were wide open. I entertained fantasy scenarios like being the stud in some Hollywood movie, the classic portrayal of an island romance. I was lonely, being tempted more and more for a woman's touch and fell asleep or woke up aroused, replaying the fantasy over and over in my mind in vivid detail.

~

It wasn't a chance encounter and certainly one that I should have ran the other way from but didn't. I was working for John and Lorna doing some remodeling and house painting. Lorna had a friend who stopped in occasionally and I became aware of Monica right away. She was slender and shapely and carried herself as if she was a queen in a slow gait, swaying her hips and body in a graceful manner as if music played in her mind, smooth and rhythmic and enticing. It wasn't as if she was putting on a show, it was the way my mind worked. She worn long braids down her back untethered and wild, catching the breeze as she sauntered down the driveway. Monica had a coy smile, desirable lips without the coloring of lipstick, and deep brown oval eyes conveying that she didn't have a care in the world. She was wearing a clingy, yellow gingham sundress that accentuated her curves. I was enamored. I felt like a Peeping Tom sneaking inconspicuous looks, not wanting to take my eyes off of her for one second. Believe it or not, by nature I am shy, especially around women, but I made a point to introduce myself and tried flirting with Monica throughout the afternoon. At first she shrugged me off. Maybe I wasn't what she was interested in, being a slightly older white guy with paint splatters on my face, but I didn't feel rejected. I could tell you in detail what Monica looked like from behind when she left and walked back to her car after visiting with Lorna, but I'll keep that image to myself.

The next weekend, Lorna had a birthday party for her

daughter, Amber, and Monica happened to be there. Of course, I was invited. Throughout the evening I made an effort to chat with Monica alone but it didn't seem to go well. I discovered that she wasn't married and casually tried to conceal my wedding ring. I took her stand-offish coolness in stride thinking that she just wasn't much of a talker. The next day, while having coffee and scheming with Lorna on a design for an arbor over their front entryway, Lorna commented that Monica was interested in me. Really? I was surprised.

I could tell that Lorna didn't want to get involved, knowing that I was married and a Christian, but she was aware of the weird stuff happening in my life. She didn't know much about Courts of Praise other than my stories and seemed reserved about making any negative comments. It wasn't hard not to read between the lines. Lorna was sensitive to the judgement I expressed about church and her suspicions reflected mine. She was sympathetic about my struggles with Trevor as Pete had been. She knew Cassie, but they didn't really get along all that much and I'm not sure why. Lorna was so inviting and friendly. She was a spiritual and moral person, observant and sly of eye, and I thought that maybe she intimidated Cassie, which was unmerited. And here I was, alone again, which was another thing Lorna watched being played out. I tried to be flippant and nonchalant when she mentioned that Monica had shown interest, over-compensating my racing heart to down play it. I said that I'd like to take her out sometime and left it at that.

My phone rang the next morning.

"Hi, it's me." Monica's sing-song voice enchanted me.

Without dragging this impassioned story out (I'm not writing a romance novel), we ended up going out a few times for dinner and drinks. On a day when we were both free she took me on a drive up the coast to Speightstown on the west coast where we had pizza, her treat. Our conversations weren't particularly intellectually stimulating; Monica wasn't verbose or highly educated but a practical-minded woman. She was interested in my life, where I came from, what I did, and I felt at ease to share candidly about anything she asked about. She seemed rather guarded to reveal much information about herself but I didn't pry. I realized very soon that she wasn't a Christian and hedged on going into any detail about my background.

We met at St. Lawrence Gap at a club called "After Dark" and danced until the sun came up. That's how Barbadian's party. The natural turn of events fell into place rather quickly. Monica and I ended up in bed with sweat pouring like rain, savagely devouring one another. The morning seemed to never end. Everything was different, her features, her responses, her taste. We took a breather to shower and wolfed down food and drank fresh squeezed juice between bouts of climactic ecstasy. It was like we both had an insatiable appetite. I was ruined.

You're probably asking yourself how a married man who was a Christian missionary could or would do such a thing. I have no excuse. I was weak, careless and impulsive. Did I have regret? Guilt? Shame? It tore me up inside. But I was infatuated and crazed out of my mind. Everything with Monica was unmatched in my experience and exhilarating. I was a young bull again. I wondered if she put a hex on me.

The twist in all of this is that I had liquidated and sold off or given away most everything we'd shipped to Barbados and in five days was scheduled to return home, my visa about to expire. It was a whirlwind affair.

The afternoon I was to be at the airport we met for what I thought was the last time. I tried to say goodbye to Monica. The last thing I asked her was what she would do about what had happened between us. She cried and said she would just go back to her miserable life; that she would miss me and think of me. I found myself overwrought with emotions of deep compassion. I hardly knew her but I could imagine living a life that was miserable. As crazy as it was, in such a short time I began to care for this woman and it un-nerved me. It wasn't all about sex.

I sat in a window seat on American Airlines with earbuds playing steel pan music in my head and choked down a lump in my throat the size of Gibraltar, concealing my tear-streaked face. I felt such emptiness in the pit of my stomach that I could have died. Looking at the inevitability of going back to my life as usual was daunting. I'd basically have to start over, having burned my bridges and credibility as a husband and a missionary. I didn't want to go home, although I wasn't sure where was home even was. I wanted to stay in Barbados with Monica. The clincher was my conscience. I can no more lie and keep a straight face than levitate. I knew that I would confess my infidelity to Cassie sooner than later. I knew it would burn the house down to the ground. Maybe that's why I did what I did. Maybe I'd wanted to do it for a long time but was a coward. I know it was a really deceitful and horrible thing to do to a good woman who faithfully loved me, and I'm pretty sure a shrink would commit me to the crazy house for throwing away a good life. In the year I spent in Barbados I'd lost almost forty pounds, was brown as a nut and had aged beyond my years. In spite of what I'd hoped for in going to Barbados, to redefine my life and spiritually flourish, I was in many ways half the man I used to be.

# 19

*When* Cassie picked me up at JFK it was pushing ten o'clock at night and typical January weather. What a wake-up call. The wind was biting cold, pelting my face with sleet as I pushed a luggage cart to the car in ankle deep slush still wearing flip flops. After spending a year in the tropics I shivered even with the heat blasting in the car. I wasn't up to driving or talking and it was a long and quiet four hour trip back to Lewisburg, making a stop to satisfy my Big Mac Attack. Cassie, I'm sure, was concerned by my morose attitude but she didn't prod. We settled into our old house that she'd set up with the basics, planning on getting things out of storage in due time, and spent our first few days walking on eggshells. I was drinking heavily, sometimes cracking open a Yuengling Lager before noon, outwardly defiant as to say, "Go ahead, just try and give me a lecture." I was a walking time-bomb about to explode. Cassie gracefully turned a blind eye. I suppose she didn't know what else to do, allowing me time to clear my head and readjust. Since leaving the airport she knew I was having a difficult time and it wasn't getting any better as the days went by. The drinking, I'm sure, was a vain attempt to forget, or at least numb my guilty conscience. I didn't know what to do with all the questions and second guessing going on in my head, do I confess or wait it out? I was conflicted by weariness of heart and anxiety burned in my guts at keeping a secret. Why didn't I just spill the beans and get it over with?

We nearly had a head-on collision one morning. It was still dark and I was mistakenly driving on the wrong side of the road wondering why everyone coming at me was flashing their lights. I must have been in Barbados in my mind. We had coffee with Wyatt and Gail and later had brunch with Ron and Joy, the folks who home-schooled and sheltered their kids on a visit to the coffeehouse years ago when Ginger who was allegedly possessed had turned up. Ron could still put me to sleep with his monotone and Joy asked endless, moronic questions, plying to gather fodder for gossip. She was a busy-body. Our visit was as phony as could possibly be. And so it was with many other friends we spent time with who inquired about Barbados. I felt hollow relating stories that should have been glorious testimonies in the telling. Being a hypocrite paralyzed me; perhaps hypocrisy is the bitterest of all the things I've swallowed in my life.

There was no intimacy between Cassie and me, I evaded kissing her thinking it'd be the ultimate insult. In a half-hearted way I tried to get pass the weight that hung around my neck to express my feelings of residual love to her, but it was just going through the motions. I've done a lot of really shitty things to Cassie in our 26 years of marriage, things I'm ashamed of, but the afternoon I abandoned her on an impulse and caught a bus back to JFK was the worse. I called that evening from the airport and informed her of what I'd done, where her car was parked, and said I was going back to Barbados and why. What an underhanded and gutless thing to do. Not even an: "I'm sorry" or "good luck." I just ran like the hounds were on my heels without any regard to the consequences, or was it another wild hair up my ass like dad used to say?

∾

Early morning sun streamed through a New York skyline. I hadn't slept all night wandering around a near empty airport like a lost ghost. Time moved in slow-motion as if God was giving me time to reconsider going back home. My bags were checked-in hours ago and I had my boarding pass, killing time, sipping my umpteenth cup of coffee while mindlessly thumbing through a discarded newspaper, when someone tapped me on the shoulder. Jay looked me square in the eyes without a word and grabbed me by the arms with vise-grip hands. It was a total shock. What immediately registered to me was the level of his sadness, there is no way I can describe it. Elvin stood beside him with a stern look that masked his concerns and angst. Cassie had called my friends and they'd driven through the night across Pennsylvania to JFK in the hope of rescuing me. Wyatt and Gail and another couple who I adored and did prison ministry with were also in the airport, but somehow we'd missed each other.

They pleaded with heart wrenching words to come to my senses, my God-given senses and not the burning in my loins. Jay and Elvin weren't preaching but were certainly insistent and touched multiple issues near to my heart. I knew they loved me, I knew what they said was true, and it was hardest thing I've ever done to hold fast even if it was the thinnest straw I ever grasped, but my mind was made up. I was going back to Barbados and that was that. I'm not sure if Jesus Christ had been there in person I would have been swayed.

When the announcement over the intercom interrupted our discussion with the boarding call, I rose to go to the gate. I faltered, feeling torn in half, not so much because of what I was doing to Cassie but what I was doing to all the caring, supportive friends in my church that had blessed me and stood by my side in so many ways. I looked Jay and Elvin in the eye, dry-mouthed and stupefied, trying to find equilibrium and venture some kind of reasoning why I had to do this, but I couldn't render any plausible reason. There was no adequate way to express my resolve. I remember thinking deep down inside my soul that it was spiritual suicide. We embraced and parted ways. Jay hung on tight and wet my neck with tears. I didn't look back for fear that my knees would buckle.

~

Monica lived with her mother and a large extended family, all under one roof. She was the one who drove, her daytime hours were a full-time job running errands for aunts and sisters and the children. When I called her from the airport at my arrival it wasn't just a shock, it interrupted her routine. She told me it would be a while but was on her way. When we met, I read apprehension on her face, or was it total disbelief that I'd come back? She didn't beckon to kiss me until we were in the parking lot away from the crowd and then only tentatively. When we arrived at Seaview Road to the flat I lived in less than a week ago was already rented out. Monica said that she couldn't take me to her house because it was complicated.

I spent the first couple of nights with Pete and Linda and slept on their couch, not exactly what I was expecting. John and Lorna took me in for a season when their company went back to Toronto, but in a way I felt as if I was putting everyone out. There were friends at Courts of Praise I could have called, but it was awkward even to consider because of what I had done. Trevor and Wendy knew what had happened, thanks to Cassie calling them in the hope of intervention. They never came to look me up. What does that say about your pastor? Only one brother from the church made the effort to visit me.

Philip Edwards was a friend I'd met at Courts of Praise, a barrel-chested man like Gordy with the nickname of "Banks" after the local beer. He had a reputation from years gone by of drinking a whole keg. Philip owned a major international import-export business of container ships and maritime transport. It was great to see him again, a most welcome face even though the current circumstances were uncomfortable. He treated me to lunch at Brown Sugar, a high-end eatery at the Hilton. We'd shared so much life in Jesus with one another, our testimonies were similar and he had a sense of humor that out did mine, but presently I was spiritually bankrupt. He was a fairly new Christian and I felt bad about being such a basket-case. Philip had a 36' catamaran and we sailed on the west coast, trying to talk things through and figure out where I would go and what I would do. He was sympathetic with my dilemma but quite guarded. I suspected that he had a skeleton or two in his closet. Philip said he'd like to assist me but his hands were tied because of his wife. Michele and Cassie had become friends at Courts of Praise and Michele was a loyal sister in the Lord on Cassie's side. So, I found myself at loose ends. I didn't have a whole lot of money and the credit card was nearly maxed out. I didn't see as much of Monica as I would have liked to. The times we did spend together were short and furious, no sooner did we get naked than we were washing up and getting dressed. Monica always had a schedule to keep, I didn't have any schedule.

A few months passed without any memorable occasions to make note of. I drank a lot of rum, bought small bags of ganja from Rasta's and idly wandered the beaches. Lorna offered me her car for daytrips to town. I'd hang out at Accra and treat myself to a cup of coconut-raisin ice cream at Chefette's, browse the shops for a good paperback novel and overall felt like a wanderer among tourists. My routine was a blur of boredom and semi-detachment with worries eating at the back of my mind. The saving grace was my writing. I began a collection of poetry with pencil sketches to occupy my time. It was rewarding in part, but the ability to concentrate was gradually growing impossible. I worked under the radar as an illegal doing small renovations where the location was remote in order to make a few bucks. If one was caught without proper work papers it meant deportation and "NO ENTRY" stamped on your passport. I kept thinking there had to be a better way.

Monica and I went to a small resort on the south coast not far from the Kayak Club where I fished with Garfield. We spent the evening together at the open café that had a great view of the bay. Our conversation was strained with long quiet moments. I babied a Long Island Iced Tea and picked at an appetizer. Monica traced a finger around the rim of her ice water and nodded when I asked any questions of importance, offering little in the way of dialogue. When I suggested that we get a room to loosen things up, Monica informed me there could be no lovemaking. My heart sank, thinking that she was about to announce that our affair was over. Her face became awash with tears and obvious anxiety. She informed me that she'd had an abortion the day before and was still bleeding. I was floored. Yes, she confirmed before I asked, it was mine. Her rationale was that we were just beginning a relationship, adding that she wasn't sure if it would last. She hoped it would, but who knew? A child complicated things. The rug was pulled out from under me. Anger and disappointment choked any words I may have been able to form, disjointed words circling like wary hornets in my brain. Suddenly, whatever resolve I had in returning to Barbados evaporated and seemed fruitless. I felt used, betrayed, confused and empty. My spirit died.

To continue another day with my cockamamie "Hollywood Island Romance," would be like walking a high wire without a safety net. If I chose to set this startling revelation aside and resume our relationship as if abortion was of no consequence, I had neither balance or footing nor the will to attempt it. Monica tried reasoning with me, but I became evasive and stood like a stranger facing the sea with my back to her, concealing my anger and pain.

I had thought that a little love with this woman was a dream worth pursuing, that it didn't matter how I got it or what it cost, that this plunge into unknown waters would bring happiness into my life. The idea of having a son or daughter never entered my mind, but I would have leaped at the opportunity to have a family of my own in Barbados.

Waves crashed in the dark distance, sweat chilled on my skin, my heart hammering as if it'd explode. I felt adrift, forsaken by God and lost at sea. The irony of the real becoming unreal or the unreal becoming real mocked me. I had no heart to embrace Monica and resigned myself to forgive and forget, which took years to get over, and move on with my life. I remember buying a postcard before we left the resort, something I would post back home to remind myself of the second worst day of my life since being raped as a teenager, but I had no home address to post it to.

# 20

*Elvin,* God bless that man, picked me at the airport. We made the trip to Lewisburg in comfortable conversation, which I found to be of great relief returning to the land of forgotten dreams. I expected an "Elvin-like" rebuke, as I was caught in the crosshairs and guilt and "I told you so." He softened his approach with a generous dash of grace, speaking the hard truth. The last we'd seen of each other was when I ventured from reason and boarded a flight to Barbados. He didn't throw my infidelity or stupidity in my face, he was reticent yet gracious. I didn't assume to find total acceptance and reconciliation based on his favor or influence with family and church, but Elvin was an advocate who saw the homeless spirit within my soul crying for another chance. It doesn't take being bombarded by many words to become convicted when you carry millstone around your neck. Like a slow trickle from a warm spout, the fewer the words and the greater the love, even the hardest of hearts will thaw. Elvin's love sustained me when under my feet was shifting sand.

I ended up staying at a motel behind Perkins for privacy sake rather than take Elvin up on his invitation to stay with them. I wasn't ready to see Molly, nor she me. Cassie worked at this Perkins as a waitress 27 years ago and gave me a Valentine's heart on a red napkin beside my pancakes when we were living together.

My first couple of nights back in Lewisburg felt strangely foreign. After renting a compact car, I went to my bank and opened a line of credit for twenty thousand dollars that wouldn't take long to burn through. I began re-establishing myself from ground zero, putting a plan together to find an apartment, deal with debt, start contracting... and wearing a frigging nail bag again. My pipe-dream to be a New York Times best-seller and living in Barbados was a brazen reality check of failure if not a joke.

∼

Jay reached out to me and once again we began meeting at Dunkin Donuts like old-times, although shifting nervously in our seats. He didn't make mention of our encounter at JFK on the morning I defied reason and throw it back in my face. He felt my pain then and he felt my pain now. Jay bucked the prevalent attitude in church on principle and probably prejudice in my behalf. The love between us was sorely tested but held fast. Leadership and friends alike ostracized me. News of my actions may have been shared from the pulpit or not, but the grapevine was certainly active. The innuendo was clear: I had fallen from grace, I was a reprobate, and I was back in town. I'd run into people who knew me at Walmart or Weis Market and some of them turned their cart around upon seeing me and walked the other way. My so-called friends who called themselves Christians treated me worse than a sinner. I guess I had it coming, but talk about being hurt. In a town with a population of less than five thousand and having lived there for twenty eight years with history, it's hard not to encounter someone you know. It didn't take me long to grow weary of groveling and trying to make excuses. I needed some place just to hole up and find my bearings.

Jay had a bottomless reservoir of grace, pouring buckets of blessing and not hot coals on my head. It was like healing oil ran down my chin when Jay ministered to me. After many years, he's still pouring out libations of blessing on needy people; he can also pour you a perfect pint of beer and make time to hang out. Sometimes I wish that he poured a little more grace on himself. Jay was a giver but suffered his own needs privately. I possessed little to offer in return, not a lot of grace pooled in my soul, but what I did bring was curry, Bajan hot sauce and island vanilla.

Lauren, Jay's wife and their two boys who call me Uncle Dirk to this day, were open-armed and made me feel like I was part of the family. Lauren was a graduate of Bucknell where she'd met Jay and was gone all day teaching high-brow calculous (that was Greek to me,) at Penn State's satellite college in Williamsport. Their oldest, Andrew, favored his mother in personality. He was a private kind of guy who could disappear in his bedroom for days on end playing video games. He didn't initiate many conversations unless I pushed his button, and when we did talk he was given to sharing stories like his dad, detailed and long-winded about whatever was happening in his world. I wondered where his niche in life would be. He was in college for a season but I've lost track of what Andrew is doing now. What a gifted kid with a promising future.

Matthew, the younger brother, had the nickname of Pooh. He was free-spirited and wore Grateful Dead T-shirts. His hair was long and frazzled and frizzy like his dad's in an Einstein-like way. I was partial to him. He was entertaining and a genius in his own right as his brother was, more astute about alternative music and the arts. Matthew hunted, not just on the first day of buck season but for anything interesting that rang his bell. He grabbed life by the balls. Our comradery as fellow seekers was quite the marinade, tangy with earthy overtones to tease the palate. I listened to his take on things spiritual that he cloaked in words not so Christian-like, but he always made me think he saw the real deal. I read a book sometime back called *The Tao of Pooh* by Benjamin Hoff that made me think of Matthew's paradigm. The profundity of insight in that little book captures the imagination and raises thought provoking ideas, as were many of our conversations. Matthew figuratively sails the high seas, sometimes getting dragged ashore to learn yet another hard lesson. It's probably a good thing we didn't know one another back in my junior high school years. I hope he finds whatever it is he's searching for.

Jay and Lauren had a spare bedroom with a private bath and came to an agreement to embrace me as family and deal with the backlash of our peers. They would certainly be under scrutiny for opening their door to me. I can hear Jay saying; "Damn the torpedoes – full speed ahead." As lost as I'd felt being back home that first unsettling week, rambling around Jay's farm unsure what my next step was, I began feeling like I was part of a family. It was as though I was rescued, a drifter without a country. The times we spent together were rich, but when I was on my own, it was an underground battle waged between guilt and hope. I can't say that every day was a good day, but enough grace quenched my soul to sustain me.

Jay's 52 acre farm sprawled pleasantly with woods and hills and fields. When I sat on his front porch with my first cup of coffee, I was often taken by the dawn breaking as a Monet painting. I recognized the path from the barn to a pasture where a few horses grazed, and one morning, I decided to set off with absolutely no premediated plans. Along the way, raspberry and blackberry bushes were budding with the promise of rich pickings. Robins pecked for worms, undeterred by my nearness, a pair of mallards flew low for a landing, an opaque silvery-blue sky cast a shadow walking beside me in tandem. A rutted tractor trail ran uphill to the cornfields that bordered the property line where an apple orchard lured deer to graze and buck rubbed the trees. It's no wonder that Jay always got his buck on the first day of deer season.

The view from the family room picture window was a Pennsylvania postcard. Trees bordered the road and a narrow creek flowed under a wooden bridge to enter Jay's property. You had to take it slow on a rutted, pot-holed lane to the house. High grass and cattails hid frogs along the bank of a sizable pond, whose forlorn love songs serenaded us in the evenings. A simple dock bleached grey by the weather leaned at a slant. Cabela binoculars rested on the window ledge, tempting you to pick them up and magnify and dial in on the magnificence outside. I observed birds and ducks of all kinds in the wetlands provided by a government grant intended to re-establish dwindling waterfowl and watched a black bear rummaging for berries one evening. Wildflowers and butterflies made me dizzy. Without going on, you can see that Jay's farm is a little piece of paradise. For me, it was an oasis in the desert.

I cut a walking stick the heft of a pool cue and whittled it clean of bark and to a point. Jay told me there were snakes on the property and showed me pictures of blacksnakes he'd caught, some were 4-5 feet long. He asked that I not kill them as they ate farm rats and rodents and were his friends, but snakes and I do not get along. Thankfully I did not encounter any. Anyway, I had a walking stick, and was slashing at some brush to make my way to the treehouse Jay and I built years ago when I had kind of a flashback. I was literally wading through thick brush, working up a sweat and smelling like fresh cut grass and honeysuckle, but my mental frame of mind was back again in the Lost and Found Department. The walking stick had become a homemade wooden sword.

*"Zorro - Zorro - Bitsity!"* I know, what's bitsity mean? I was a six year old kid so who knows? My mother tells the story about my swashbuckling days when I was Zorro charging into the kitchen, hollering: "Bitsity!" I remember wearing a mask made of black construction paper with eyeholes cut out, strapped around my head with a rubber band, a towel tied around my neck for a cape, a very dashing Zorro indeed, according to mom's recollection.

Dad made my brother and me swords out of plywood and we got to paint them with whatever paint he had in the basement. My sword was mostly green, Sparky's was yellow, both the colors of our house. We dueled each other until getting scolded that someone would get hurt or poke an eye out, and took off plundering and vanquishing imaginary enemies in the backyard and along the neighbor's arborvitaes next to the sandbox. Sparky and I were invincible. Maybe that's what bitsity meant; bravado, conqueror, spoils to the victor.

I found the old treehouse was still sturdy. It had weathered and turned a bit grey and mossy over time and swayed slightly in the breeze although soundly turn-buckled between three trees. Jay had envisioned and designed it. We built most it with a chainsaw and three inch screws over a few weekends back in the day. It was a secret place that offered magic and peace of mind if you took the time. I sat on a stump on the makeshift porch, looking down some fifteen feet to the narrow stream and laid aside my trusty sword (the walking stick), inhaling all the life around me.

I looked up through the treetops and saw wispy clouds in a turquoise sky, picture framed by a dimpled curtain of hardwoods in my periphery; both the permanent and transient filled my vision. Basking in repose and feeling a sense of weightlessness, I sighed deeply and could have taken a peaceful nap. That which is everlasting and heavenly, like the sky above, was God-given and could not be taken away. For the first time in a long time I felt consoled in the arms of God. What is made of the earth, the surrounding trees that reached above the creek, was like the patchwork of years of trial and error making up the very fabric of whom and what I am, and like me, changing with the seasons. A long lost quietness bathed my soul.

The old treehouse seemed like holy ground and I wondered if I should kneel or take my shoes off. Happiness and contentment could be mine if I fought to recover my faith. I wasn't a terminal case after-all. If I could only believe again there may be a new beginning. Dare I harbor such hope? I was a survivor, a fighter, Zorro with all his bitsity.

# 21

*I* moved to State College to start over and for two years my business slowly gained momentum. I'd cut price tags off so much new equipment it was ridiculous and regretted selling everything to Johnny to go to Barbados. I bought a used Chevy 2500 crew-cab, hired a crew and subcontracted from the sister company of Harris Homes in State College. Between weekly payroll and making payments on a three year loan, along with rent on a townhouse with bills and business expenses, every month that went by I fell deeper into the abyss of debt. For years, Cassie was the administrative one and managed our household budget and all the business bookkeeping. I never knew anyone who could stretch a dollar like she could other than my father. I could build you anything you wanted but I was a piss-poor accountant. It got to the point I hated getting the mail and answering my phone. Long story short, two firsts happened in my life. I was evicted and ended up filing bankruptcy. What little pride I had went down the drain.

I hobbled back to Lewisburg, found a small apartment and hooked up with an old friend who owned two large antique markets in town. Craig Bennett offered me work, and with the help of a crew we remodeled the old Pennsylvania House chair factory into an indoor mall like a Victorian village. Mock storefronts gave one the feeling of going back in time. The spaces were divided for antique dealers, collectables and crafters, and Roller Mills Street of Shops became a hotspot for tourists. It was a delightful project to work on and Craig and I became much closer friends.

During that time we had our one and only family reunion at Worlds End State Park, a scenic place where we had many picnics growing up. My brother and sister-in-law came in from Colorado. Sparky threw me an offer to team up with him, and with anticipation I packed up all my worldly possessions, yet again, and drove across the country. It was the best option on the table.

I landed in Loveland and worked for my brother who had his own business as a successful remodeling contractor since moving from Florida. We had a pretty good run of it for a few years. Getting reconnected with Sparky is one of the best things that ever happened to me. He was a great tour guide and made my transition to Colorado most enjoyable. Besides working together, we swapped stories while fishing for rainbow trout and took road trips in the high country to places like Estes Park and Mt. Princeton Hot Springs. On a pleasant fall Saturday we wandered up and down Pearl Street in Boulder, watching the weird and wonderful that only Boulder can offer. Sparky called it the *Peoples Republic*. I'll never forget the scenic view from "Oh my God Pass" on the way to Tommyknockers Brewery in Idaho Springs. After driving a steep narrow dirt road without guardrails to the summit, we stopped for pictures at the edge of the road, looking down a thousand feet to tree-line. Rarely did a weekend go by that Sparky and I weren't playing games like when we were kids, but the games were now adult oriented. Instead of chocolate milk and cookies, I developed a taste for IPA's and hard pretzels.

Sparky's oldest son, Eric lived two hours south in Colorado Springs and carried a contractor's license. I'd join Eric on jobs to fill in down-time and ended up moving to the Springs. We built a spec house in Woodland Park (my framing forte a definite plus), which led to several others, along with townhouses in Denver and travelling to Park and Summit County to build a few log homes. We had the honor of building a magnificent log home for the Greisen's. Steve is a film producer and his wife, Nelly Ward Greisen is one of the three members who made up the Christian band, "The Second Chapter of Acts." Nelly was impressed that I not only knew of the band but had a number of their CD's. "How the West was One" with Phil Keaggy is my all-time favorite, *The Easter Song* is a classic.

I'd like to think that Eric and I were friends, but at almost half my age he was a difficult man at times to get along with. I'd been my own boss for twenty eight years and was now signing the other side of the check, a rather difficult thing to adjust to. He was six-four, 285 pounds at the time and had played college football, so there was no way I'd ever put him in place by arm wrestling. I wish to be kind, but nephew or not, he was in the top ten of the most narcissistic men I've ever known. He referred to me as *Uncle Buck* (as in the John Candy movie), which I didn't find particularly flattering. We had engaging spiritual discussions on the long road trips, me in my hobbled spiritual state, and Eric made a decision to follow Christ. I doubt that I'd get any of the credit, as if it mattered. He and his wife began attending a non-denominational church in a strip-mall which I visited on occasion, and his know-it-all demeanor even creeped into his Christian experience. Eric's wife had a Christian background and could be very pleasant and hospitable, but she was a bit materialistic and sometimes borderline haughty. I felt second-class, in that whatever Christianity I possessed (years notwithstanding), didn't begin to compare to theirs and often felt like I was being politely humored. I may be overly sensitive to conservatives and have it all wrong. I'm happy that they know Jesus, I just wish they were a little more humble. We butted heads like elk in rut season, Eric could make me so mad with his condescending attitude and demands, but I'm confident that he and his wife love me.

I've probably given them reason enough to lack respect. They're doing fine and I'm glad that Eric's business is thriving and his family life is golden. Maybe the older we get we'll learn to lay aside petty differences, unless politics drives a wedge between us. That's a new issue in these last four years I wish none of us had to contend with.

A lady friend or two crossed my path while I was in Colorado but nothing serious enough to entertain marriage. I certainly wasn't in any hurry to wear a ring. Connie was one of those women. She was a social worker involved in many charitable organizations in the city, she was also an addiction therapist who liked red wine. I joked that she studied me as a case number to write curriculum. Connie introduced me to her friends, Jim and Barb Saunder's, who became my closest friends since leaving Lewisburg. Jim was a retired Air Force Chaplin and taught psychology at CSCU. Barb was the personal secretary of a three star general at Schriever Air Force Base. How I've made friends with people of such high esteem over my lifetime is beyond me. They kept me buoyant, entertained and optimistic.

Jim and I played guitar together and we all went camping or snowshoed at Breckenridge. We tossed lawn darts at picnics in their backyard and carried on an ever deepening relationship. They treated us with killer seats to a Chicago and Doobie Brother's concert in Denver and dragged me along to several plays at the college theater. Whenever Jim preached at the Lutheran Church, filling in or as a guest speaker somewhere in the city, I'd attend to support him and saw the true side of his passion. We enjoyed grilling on their patio and spent time in their hot tub, telling stories and watched fireworks from the Sky Sox Stadium bursting overhead. Jim had a yen for concocting specialty drinks; frothy, fruity, colorfully layered and very potent. He was an ordained minister but a very entertaining bartender.

I mention Jim and Barb because they were friends in the long line of friends who came into my life at a critical time and offered me love and acceptance. Jim was intuitive, patient and gracious, other than Jay the only man who knew my heart since leaving Barbados, and not just in a clinical way. He didn't judge me by my failures. He saw the ember of Jesus still aglow somewhere in my soul and blew the breath of encouragement to keep it alive.

I think that I may have a knack for writing and am hopeful (or delusional,) to be a published novelist someday. Writing has become more than a hobby for me since becoming a single man. From Merton's Pond to Barbados to Colorado was inspiring. While working fulltime for Eric I managed to complete two novels, each one taking approximately two years to write and screaming for publication. They're good stories, but you know what they say: practice makes perfect. Whether they ever make it to actual book form or not was never wasted time. I enjoyed the writing process as well as hiking and camping on the backside of the Maroon Bells near Crested Butte making notes and creating a story about an off the grid cult, taking my stab at abusive church authority. Neither were the countless hours I spent wandering around Manitou Springs taking photos and talking with weird and interesting people doing research for a coming of age, dysfunctional family story. Merton's Pond began twenty years ago and is on the back burner until I find the muse to revive it. The imagery and ideas often calls for me to come back. It's been rewarding to create and write stories, much better than watching TV. As a reader, I'm always looking for something original, an engaging storyline and interesting characters. I think that Mrs. Ludwig, my teacher from second grade would be proud of me.

It may have been Connie or Barb who pointed out that every one of my protagonists was a "seeker" of sorts, a wanderer who wrestled with more questions than having answers, the enigma of faith always in question. I don't spend a lot of time self-analyzing, if it were so, I'm sure that I could come up with a convincing self-analysis, but maybe it wouldn't be a bad idea to see a therapist or a hypnotist and figure out a way to connect the dots. Honestly,

I don't find it odd that there are unresolved issues still lurking in the basement that emerge in my writing. Such is the effect of spending time in the Lost and Found Department. It's kind of come to my attention. I have to say (jokingly), that writing has kept me out of rehab.

~

Jay was navigating through conflicts at home that were both confusing and troublesome. The sudden upheaval of events unforeseen had led to separation from Lauren, his wife and anchor of many years, and brought chaos to paradise on the farm. Sometimes a change of geography is just what we need in times of strife. Reflecting and healing and getting away seemed to be expedient for Jay. Before hitting end on our phone call I said, "You're always welcome, come to Colorado and breathe fresh air. I'll keep the light on for ya."

There are two sides to every story and I only heard Jay's side. I still have a great friendship with Lauren and look forward to spending an afternoon together hiking or sipping Chardonnay on the patio and getting caught up. She's like a sister who I'd want to know why and how things happened. Jay was my closest brother and was under the gun for alleged impropriety in his church. I mentioned earlier that counselors walk a fine line, that affairs can happen even if they're only emotional. It's dangerous business getting emotionally involved with anyone of the opposite sex. Jay had the heart of a counselor and was simply ministering to a married woman about the deeper walk with Jesus at her request. His emails to the woman were discovered by one of his sons, the text of which was his undoing. I've read them. The picture he painted of the garden of the Lord, resplendent and life-giving would be insightful for the Body of Christ. I encouraged him to publish a coffee-table hardback with illustrations. It reads as beautifully yet suggestively as the Songs of Solomon, but we embrace the imagery of Solomon. That's just like Jay. He's forever weaving illustrious imagery and flowery words when telling stories, especially when recounting prophetic visions. Jay maintained his integrity, but in the court of opinion he had crossed the line. He didn't. He needed to get out of Lewisburg for fresh perspective and baling water out of his battle ridden boat. I could relate with his feelings of being judged and misunderstood, but of all the better times of year to host his visit and show him around colorful Colorado, I wouldn't have chosen winter. I'm not a big fan of cold weather nor do I ski.

Jay was inbound to DIA on Christmas Eve on a late flight, and although it excited me to see him the timing kind of irked me. Sitting in the reception area where everyone arriving in DIA has to pass through, it didn't take long for my tune to change. I was captivated by seeing soldiers returning from Afghanistan or wherever they were deployed, reuniting with their wives and children. Watching them embrace made me smile while choking down tears. I saw grandparents with gifts and balloons and kisses for their grandkids, boyfriends and girlfriends with backpacks wrapping up in unashamed hugs, anxious to hit the slopes and snowboard after spending the night playing an indoor sport. It was an emotional roller-coaster ride, witnessing their warm and joyful reunions. I didn't begrudge Jay for coming in on Christmas Eve after-all. Being at DIA was better than watching a holiday Hallmark movie alone and crying in my beer.

A well-dressed dark haired woman was also watching the goings-on. I'd seen her change her seat several times while inching her way closer to me. We flashed a smiling face with raised eyebrows as if understanding our mutual situation of being at the airport on Christmas Eve. She'd leave her coat draped over a chair and wander, restlessly checking her phone and the arrival schedule, and came to sit beside me after some time. Maybe my seat was better for viewing, as much as I'd like to flatter myself that I was a babe magnet. The scent of sweet, fading perfume and a wool coat dampened from snowfall and being in an overheated room allured me by such womanly essence. Her openness was refreshing as we chatted and we had an instant connection, laughing and relating and getting one another's jokes. We exchanged business cards and offered the standard line with a handshake: "Let's stay in touch." When her people came in from the Dominican Republic, she jumped up overjoyed to welcome them in fluent Spanish.

Jay nearly fell over himself when he saw me. We were both giddy with exhaustion (it was pushing midnight), and talked excitedly on the way to my apartment in the Springs. The only restaurant we found open on Christmas Eve was an IHop. We had pancakes and tapped our spoons in rhythm with Christmas music playing overhead, the waiter being very gracious and joking with Jay as an out-of-towner. "You guys ought to go to a pot dispensary and get Rocky Mountain high. Merry Christmas!"

We spent the next four days experiencing not the old grace that we used to share like warmed up left-overs, but a fresh and invigorating grace we neither of us saw coming. The highlight of our visit was hiking up the Crags on the backside of Pikes Peak on a sunny day fully prepared to snowshoe. When we reached the summit I felt as if I'd accomplished two things. First, I was winded but had made it. You can clap your hands if you'd like to, I did. I made it without having a heart attack and being air lifted to a hospital. Secondly, I'd made the trek with my dearest friend, which was a godsend. I never would have done it without him. Jay's visit made me climb a mountain. We each had our own chart to course, similar in so many ways, and viewing the panorama from the summit where the winds blew fierce we found affirmation from the heart of God and resolve to continue our extraordinary journey.

Jay met my brother and Colorado family at Christmas dinner at Eric's house, bearing homemade cranberry and nut bread and told stories as only he can tell, truly a treat for all of them.

~

I began corresponding with the woman I met at the airport on Christmas Eve. Her business card was tucked in with my collection of souvenir magnets adorning my fridge door along with pizza coupons. I entertained the memory of her liveliness and interests every day I went for coffee creamer. We started by taking the easy steps, texting was in the future, and shared daily emails back and forth. Her name was Alicia but I called her Ali. I guess that's what we "east coasters" do; we tend to clip the name. Sharon is Cher, Kevin is Kev. Bob is, well, Bob. She said no one else ever called her Ali but she liked it. We met in Denver at a posh lounge and had drinks and were both quickly enamored by the unusual rapport we shared. She was talkative and energetic and engaged with me in conversation like we'd known one another for years and were getting reacquainted. I'm guessing that Ali was ten or more years younger than me. She possessed an alluring glamor and elegant poise without being pretentious. Her wit and insight was intelligent and entertaining, fun and very conversational. First dates can be agonizing if one party does all the talking about themselves, but we drew each other out effortlessly.

I gazed across the table into a face as beautiful as a Madonna, framed by shoulder length dark hair and riveting brown eyes that paid attention as our conversation emerged. Her questions were thought out and made me feel easy to answer in response. We both tip-toed a bit, the polite dance around disclosing personal things, but Ali was open and obviously felt safe with me. I was captivated by glimpses of intimate moments that she shared from her life, backstories that tickled my funny-bone. I liked that we were being real with one another. Ali wore a thin string of pearls that rose and fell with her breath when she laughed. Her full lips glistened after sipping her drink and I yearned to kiss them. I had a difficult time not staring at her lavish cleavage as she leaned in to tell me about the kayak she planned to purchase and how fun it would be being out on the lake. Ali was a professional woman who worked as an interpreter for the Denver court system. She had two adopted daughters who were then in their early teens, and if truth be known, it was Ali who kept them fit and young.

It didn't take long until we started spending time together on the weekends. She was an outdoor enthusiast who loved hiking and biking and ate kale chips and made crazy smoothies. Ali also liked Modelo Especial from the bottle. We hiked Red Rocks Amphitheater and posed for pictures in the museum. She came to the Springs and we went on trails I never knew about in the Garden of the Gods on a glorious spring afternoon, singing a Jack Johnson song. We enjoyed the benefits of companionship without commitment in one another's beds. Ali rocked my world at a time when I was convinced that I was damaged goods.

She invited me to her church at Easter before taking me for a meal and meeting some of her friends. Mile Hi Church in Lakewood was an ecumenical gathering I wouldn't have considered visiting even if I'd known about it, but it was an experience that touched me deeply. Picture a lovely stew, a blend of colors and flavor, celestial essence and magic; then imagine East meets West in heart and mind and spirit, global religions combined in the same kettle. The worship flowed between flutes and harps and chanting, harmonies of praise to the Creator in words that I embraced. I was mesmerized. Choreographed dancers with banners in fluid motion like swans without lyrics spoke to my open heart. The speaker was illustrious and painted a picture in words about the "Spirit of Life" which I interpreted as the risen Lord. It was a magical Easter message.

Ali asked me what I thought of the service as we walked across the parking lot to her car. I choked, holding words close to my heart for fear of weeping and appearing foolish. No matter what you might think, questioning if I'd become diluted in my Christian theology or even deceived, I believe that deep calls to deep. I felt the touch of God, and that, my friend, cannot be argued.

I've met few people who possess such a positive outlook on

life. Ali was always bubbly and full of gusto. We've stayed in touch going on eight years and not seeing each other, but every time we talk it's like picking up where we last left off. In a world that buffets and beats me up and tries to grind me to dust, she makes me feel light-hearted and somehow more alive. Ali is the poster child for Live-Laugh-Love.

# 22

*My* folks moved from Florida to the Austin area where my baby sister, Jody and her family lived at the time. Dad found a contractor and built a new limestone ranch home mortgage free to enjoy retired life. The day before Sparky and I arrived to help them move in, dear old dad wanted to get a step ahead and start shuffling what he could from the storage unit. Mom was directing him behind the U-Haul van, the ramp was partially released, and when she motioned for him to stop dad hit the brakes and the ramp extended like a shot, pinning her to the macadam. It fractured her knee bone. When we arrived she was in a wheelchair, pale and helpless, her leg extended on a foot rest in a cast, not able to even make coffee.

They settled in and it didn't take long until you know who had gardens and landscaping per her idea. Mom pointed a finger and felt so bad she that she wasn't able to help. I don't think the old man begrudged digging and planting to follow mom's directions one bit. If anything he probably pointed out where the squirrels were and made sure his old BB gun would be handy on the patio.

My pop wasn't a big fan of the Dallas Cowboys, being a NY Giants fan, and he rubbed it my brother-in-law's nose whenever they lost. Their golf clubs collected dust but they stayed active and took daytrips or enjoyed puttering around the house. I visited the folks on holidays when I could, they traveled every year to see one of us kids, so it was kind of on a rotating schedule. Thanksgiving Day on the first year they were in their new home was the first in many years that a lot of family sat around the table and passed the gravy.

I especially enjoyed treks up and down Sixth Street in downtown Austin. What an eclectic party scene; totally *Austin-Weird*. Jo and her husband took me on a pub hop and we listened to every kind of live music imaginable. On that same visit, we all headed to Fredericksburg in the hill county, a German village that was quite touristy with history and charm, great restaurants, wine from local vineyards, schnitzel and strudel and sausage, not to mention the many fascinating gift shops. Dad was a handful to mind, as he'd had a colonoscopy just days before, and would wander off on his own doing whatever dad did. I recall frantically searching for him when an hour passed and he hadn't returned to where we agreed to meet. There was a good reason for being delayed, of course. He ran into a shop owner who told stories about Fredericksburg's history and being of inquisitive character and talkative, Dad had lost track of time. With a mocked sheepish look and a shrug he handed us a bag of miscellaneous flavored salt water taffy like they were the Crown Jewels. Bribery was his specialty.

On one of their trips to Colorado my brother and I took Dad on a weekend to camp in the mountains. We hoped to recreate an infamous adventure at Worlds End when we were kids. Whenever we went to Worlds End to picnic or watch the kayak races from the spillway or take a dip in freezing cold spring water at the swim beach, the camping adventure with my father is among the high points of my childhood memories.

Dad started a campfire of kindling that Sparky and I gathered with a baby jar of gasoline. Fumes hovered and built up in the concrete fire ring, and when he'd toss in a kitchen match our fellow campers were awakened by a kaboom and giggling from two young boys. He made us breakfast, fried potatoes and eggs in a cast iron skillet over the fire, and as he seasoned the beautiful sunny-side-up eggs the lid came off the pepper shaker, so we had blackened eggs. Sparky was mischievous, being a typical ten year old, and drank too many cans of pop. Remember Kickapoo Joy Juice? If you do you're showing your age! Sparky peed in his sleeping bag, perhaps because he was afraid to go outside in the dark forest. He also fell in the creek when we were skipping stones and catching tadpoles. Dad's cot ripped in the night, landing him on the ground with a string of curse words I'd never heard him use before. I nearly got my hand broken when the car door slammed on it in the parking lot by accident when we went to fetch ice at a kiosk. It was a fun-filled weekend howbeit comedic. We all looked the worse for wear with black sooty faces, Dad with two day stubble on his chin and us boys with scores of bug bites. When we returned home and Mom saw our smiling faces, she shook her head in dismay and shooed us to go and take a bath.

Sparky and I knew this present camping trip in Colorado was kind of a reunion between father and sons and may very well be the last of its kind, which unfortunately it was.

Jefferson Reservoir with a backside mountain view near Breckenridge was quite spectacular. Sparky and dad got there ahead of me and chose a site in a grove of aspens and set up camp. His pull behind camper was perfectly positioned to access the picnic table and fire ring and give the old man elbow room. I arrived and managed to set up a two-man tent thinking it was the best spot just before it rained. We around a smoky fire after a rainstorm passed and weren't able to cook the steaks and sides as planned. We had a gourmet meal of pimento loaf and cheese sandwiches, chips and Coors (to keep Dad happy), and listened to him tell long-winded tales. My sides ached from belly laughing, reliving so many mishaps and adventures of us boys growing up. Dad was a kid at heart and sometime in the evening he sneaked a rubber snake in my sleeping bag. He wasn't disappointed by my reaction. I'm sure Sparky put him up to it, knowing how much I was afraid of snakes. In the morning, I awoke fairly soaked to the skivvies. I dragged everything out of the tent and hung it on rope between trees, my sleeping draping and dripping; so much for my perfect spot. I thought I'd never hear the end of it.

We fished off the banks of the reservoir and went four wheeling for an afternoon. When we came to the trailhead in a high meadow for a break to stretch, it was picture time, and took the traditional photo per Sparky's request; our drawers pulled down and mooning the camera. I have that moment in a frame on my mantel, capturing Dad in his Gomer Pyle hat and colorful boxers, glancing sideways at me. I'm poised with my cargo shorts at my ankles and my ass hanging out in grey boxer briefs, standing on the four-wheeler and looking his way. I wish I could recall what he said. It might have been something like; "Hope you're wearing clean skivvies."

～

Dad was working on the family-tree at the time, which took us to Leadville, Colorado. He hoped to find records of a distant uncle of ours. William Lundy, on my mother's side had pioneered in the silver boom in 1879 – 1890 in the region. We stayed at the old Delaware Hotel and stomped around during the day, up one side of town to the other, from the county courthouse and library to the cemetery and museum in the attempt to locate any information about Uncle William Lundy. I have to say that the old man was tenacious. He was like a kid in a candy store, engaging anyone from the librarians to locals in hopes of garnering some tidbit of info. Mom and I would wait only so long and wander off on our own when Dad started telling stories. In a gem and rock shop, even the clerk wearied as dear old dad embellished tales of William Lundy, a pioneer from Pennsylvania who he should have known about. The clerk did when dad left the store.

My folks retired early in the evenings as the altitude (10,151'), was hard on them at their age and coming from flatland Texas. They promised to meet me for breakfast which meant being on time at 6 a.m. I enjoyed scouting out Leadville on my own and found Rosie's Brewpub where I scored keys to a locked gate at the old mines outside of town from a local fellow after telling him my story. When we breakfast the next morning, it was a surprise and my treat to take the folks up a dirt road past No Trespassing signs to King Solomon's Mines.

I unlocked the gate and swung it clear, feeling quite pleased with myself, and found a place to park. We walked a hard-pack dirt road in an open area of old head frames, derricks and ancient equipment rusting into oblivion, retaining ponds of colorful toxic waste water still pooled from the mining days. I'd call that an environmental disaster, irresponsible and inexcusable for not being taken care of. This was Colorado, the land of tree huggers.

I could tell that dad was impressed by my bringing them here. Of course, he knew everything there was to know about mining and there wasn't much he didn't know about the era of the silver boom. He should have been a commentator for PBS. If he didn't know the facts, it was amazing how quickly he could concoct the most believable spiel on the spot, which was probably a complete line of bullshit.

The mines didn't offer much backstory about William Lundy, but I took a roll of film and had them pose. Dad found records and photos at the courthouse that authenticated his research. A very patient and pleasant assistant walked him through micro-films of old newspapers and data on a computer for hours. I have photo copies of William Lundy's Railroad Restaurant and Boarding House that he ran and owned from 1887 until he died in 1891; it's a great story of another time in our family history when railroad companies and miners clashed during the silver-boom. I have copies of Lundy's obituary and advertisements from newspapers in grainy black and white that I show off to my friends. Sparky and I almost merited "Pioneer" tags, which is quite prestigious.

There aren't a lot of license plates in Colorado bearing that historic notoriety, but apparently Uncle William Lundy was too distant a relative for us to merit them.

What I found on that visit was a new relationship with my father. We became buddies in those days that passed too quickly but pleasantly. A bond solidified between us when we rode the scenic train to Climax Mine on a sunny Colorado afternoon in an open car. We trudged the streets of Leadville, browsing shops and bookshelves of local history, spent the evening sharing stories over dinner and drinks. We actually hugged a few times.

But times passes too quickly as we turn the calendar month by fleeting month. I don't mark days off with an X like when I was in jail, but I'm astounded at the passing of days as another year sneaks up unannounced. Holy smokes! I lived to toast in 2021. Where's the time go? It's like Ground Hog Day but different. One can get the feeling that we live forever. I thought that my folks would.

The dreadful day came ten years ago on a Monday morning. It was and still is mother's tradition to clean house on the first day of the week. Dad knew the routine after fifty six years of knowing how to dust and run the Hoover. Their new limestone ranch home that he was so proud of still had that new house smell of carpet and fresh paint. I don't know exactly what my father was doing but he collapsed. Mom called 911.

I missed my usual call on Sunday and happened to call just moments after the paramedics had arrived, not having a clue what was happening. Mom was in a panic and couldn't talk, only saying that Dad hit his head falling to the floor and abruptly hung up. I guessed that it was his heart and whispered a desperate prayer. Within the hour, Jo called and informed us that Dad indeed had a major heart attack. When Sparky and I received the news we broke every speed limit from Colorado to Texas. Sister Jo called several times while we were on the road keeping us abreast of the latest developments. Dad was on life support to keep his heart beating and it didn't look good. Sparky and I arrived at Round Rock Hospital before midnight just in time to say goodbye.

I was stunned to see my father lying incoherent in an ice bath, my Superman, the Amazing Hulk, my hero all but lifeless and nonresponsive. When I saw his pale face my heart flat-lined. Every hope I'd hoped and every prayer I prayed speeding on the highway, envisioning that I'd clout him on the shoulder and say, "Come on Dad... get over it, we need you," drained out of my soul and left me feeling utterly helpless. When the inevitable happened, it was heart wrenching. The expulsion of air from his lungs when the tubes and plugs were pulled froze me place. I thought it was in that moment dad's spirit left his body, floating like ethereal vapor into eternity where he'd receive a new heart and wait for us to join him. I hoped that he heard my last words. "I love you, Dad. See ya on the flipside." I didn't break down when I kissed his cold cheek good-bye; I was numb and vainly tried being a comfort for Mom, hugging my brother and baby sister. Missy and Jill were on speaker via cell phones, and though not being actually present, they were with us.

I wandered down the hallway and found a men's room, locking the door of a stall and collapsed on the commode. I could barely breathe. A cry exploded and echoed in that metal enclosure like pulling the pin on a hand grenade; "God-damn-it Dad, why'd cha have to die? We were just getting to know one another."

We convinced Mom to sell the house and move back to Pennsylvania where she had some family and more support, and miraculously the house sold within a week over asking price. Missy and Jilly were close, as well as Aunt Faye and Francie, mom's sisters who each were characters in their own and brought a variety of colorful backstories and understanding, both of them having lost a husband. Within a year, Jo and her family left Texas and moved back to Williamsport. Mom grieved so deeply that I worried about her mind, but she's a tough old bird. Her world crumbled after knowing only one man in her life who brought abiding joy, married for 57 years, eight children and lovely homes. They had built a life to last forever and she lost it in a moment; how she stayed so strong is beyond me. I miss my dad, but no one lives forever. I cannot begin to fathom my mother's loss.

When the downturn caught up with us in Colorado, I seriously debated about moving back to PA to be closer to her. Although we talk every Sunday it's concerning to me to visit more often than budget and time can afford, which is a piss poor excuse. It isn't enough just sending cards and knowing her grief, sharing stories and trying to hug her through a cell phone. I told her to call even if all she needed to do was cry. We've done just that. We're different now, each of us. Our relationship has changed from that of a mother and her son. We've become close allies, or more like friends, walking through loss and loneliness and trials with both of us seeking some kind of release from sorrow. I'd like to take her out for breakfast to one of her favorite places, but the nearest Cracker Barrel to me is in Bismarck and she's too far away.

As the fates would have it, or if you prefer: "as God wills," Sparky's brother-in-law called and solicited us to come to North Dakota and build him a commercial shop, adding that there was work out the wazoo. There was an oil boom going on that I had absolutely no clue about. The Bakken? Who pays attention to North Dakota unless you were in the oil field? It was never on my bucket-list. We were starving for work in Colorado so why not give it whirl? Little did I know that North Dakota would wind up being my home.

# 23

*I've* been in North Dakota for almost ten years, counting by how many times I've set up the Christmas tree. Perhaps I should have said it was how many winters I've experienced, but my brain may have gotten frost bite by negative temperatures that can plummet to minus fifty or better. That means its 85 degrees warmer in my refrigerator than it is outside sometimes. I'm not sure if I'm bragging or complaining. The snow actually sounds different at negative twenty-plus, not when it's falling but under foot. It's as though a plaintive cry comes from the sole of a boot, a whinny, high pitched eek-eek squeal. The sound of tires on a snow packed road echoes the same weirdness in the still frozen air. On a cloudless day when moisture crystalizes in the atmosphere, a glowing ring circles the sun like a celestial prism that the locals call Sun Dogs. As I'm writing this section it's a Sun Dog kind of day. A new term to me is the rime effect, which is when fog or moisture turns tree limbs sparkly silver and every surface to a hockey rink. May I remind you that I relished the tropics?

Sparky, Eric and I agreed to go to North Dakota on a promising phone call to make some money. I went ahead to scout and found it was indeed promising, and my brother and nephew followed shortly after. We arrived, to our surprise, in the throes an oil boom much like the California gold rush. The highway between

Williston and the town of Ray where we first came to build Pat Lajoie's shop (Sparky's brother-in-law who I didn't know before), was a surreal landscape. At night you could see hundreds of flares from drill sites, the burn-off of natural gas like an open torch flame. It looked like a city skyline off in the distance. Being so close to the Canadian border, on a clear night you could see the Northern Lights if you were lucky, and in my mind it was a much better view than gas flares. I'm not obsessively pro-climate change, but I believe it's an issue and it makes me wonder what Mother Nature thinks about the emissions.

There were sprawling mobile units called man camps that housed thousands of rig hands; fifth wheels, trailers and pull behind campers. The oil companies set up prefab housing like motel rooms at strategic crossroads along the highway. Halliburton and Hess and all the big boys were present.

Countless drill sites with pumpers going full tilt, huge pads with mega storage tanks and ranks of pipe, cranes setting up work-over rigs and wide-load semis hauling equipment that took up two lanes, it was drill-baby-drill and a never ending panorama on a dangerous highway that I travelled daily. I think the jury is still out on fracking and it gives me concern about the detrimental effects on the aquafer for future generations. In my mind, oil comes in second place. Clean water is a priceless commodity.

I saw a map of the underground pipeline system, layered in multi-levels defying geology more complicated than an Air Traffic Controller in a major airport has to monitor, a virtual web that boggles my mind. If that visual worked on my head too much it'd kept me awake at night, envisioning blowing sky high like Hiroshima if something went wrong. Maybe I watch too many movies where stuff blows up, but pipeline ruptures are concerning. Semis and crude haulers, pickup trucks from all over the country of every imaginable kind and condition ran the county roads and US Highway 2 as well as Route 85 south to Watford City. I played an amusing game tallying up the different out of state license plates. The traffic was different but as crazy as Denver rush hour.

Railroad tankers miles long transported Bakken crude to refineries, and you not only waited at RR crossings, you waited forever in line to get fuel at gas stations. Forget about scoring a quick lunch at a drive-thru "fast food" joint; aggravating and impossible to accomplish without having a meltdown. Waiting was never one of my strong personality traits. The grocery stores and Walmart were either overstocked with pallets in the aisles you could hardly get a cart around or out of stock on the essentials. You stepped over filth and litter in the parking lots, rubbers, cigarette butts and vomit, unimaginable debris carelessly discarded by disrespectful assholes from out of state. I saw men sponge bathing in public restrooms. The Strip Club did a thriving business as did the escort services. I heard that hookers were coming from Vegas because the money here was better. Hardly a day went by that some kind of altercation *didn't* make the newspaper, a stabbing or shooting, a drug bust, but the local media kept it low key. Go figure. Oil companies rule the world and are in bed with politicians and banks, the perfect ménage a trois. Oil money trickles down to local economies that are indebted to stay the course or suffer the consequences otherwise. Broadcasting bad news didn't fit the criteria. Thankfully, the county cleaned things up after some time. Getting up to speed on the volume of traffic, house needs and infrastructure became the top agenda both residential and commercially. There are two seasons in North Dakota; winter and road construction.

It sounds like I'm complaining but it's my observation as an outsider. For me, it was culture-shock every bit as drastic as going to the tropics and changed the status-quo. Had I not gone to North Dakota, I might be working in Colorado Springs as a greeter at Walmart struggling to make ends meet. I'm not sure I would have been hired, as it seems they only hire happy people who can put up with Walmart-crazy people. At the risk of being hypocritical, we made good money as the result of the boom. I for one was grateful that Sparky's brother-in-law called and threw us a bone.

We spent nearly three months building Pat's shop, which was a high-end 40'X44' commercial building. Pat was a trucker with three Kenworth's (Lajoie's Trucking), and operated a winching business doing rig moves and hauling oil field related equipment. Not only was his shop organized and outfitted with every piece of equipment and tool imaginable, bottled Budweiser by the case was stocked in his beer fridge. Bring a gas mask if you weren't a smoker. Pat's new Man Cave was the hangout for many locals and truckers after the bars went smoke-free. I met the likes of Frenchy, Quiggly and Shorty, all of whom told funny but coarse jokes. I didn't like hearing the "N" word or slams against Obama but bit my tongue, four to one odds were not in my favor. I hung out at the Man Cave on occasion, often thinking that I was being tolerated with a cautious eye, but I'd impressed Pat with my building skills. We liked one another in an awkward way. I didn't smoke two packs of Marlboros a day and didn't fancy Budweiser nor was I a trucker. Their language was foreigner to me. I didn't wear FR gear, steel toed boots and Carhartt coveralls, neither did I wear tie-dyed shirts, but I was odd man out for wearing shorts and being a liberal. As a writer with a vocabulary that didn't use the "F" word five times in a sentence, I opted just to listen and nod my head.

Sparky and Eric stayed in Sparky's small pull-behind camper during the project. I bunked in Pat's spare bedroom in his trailer. We took turns cooking meals and tried our best to be accommodating. Pat's wife, Pam, wins the prize for being a go-getter and the perfect partner for Pat, being familiar with trucking and his personality, and took care of the books. She was talkative and a fellow gardener I learned a lot from. Generally she was sweet, until the times she wasn't so sweet. I dreaded the evenings when they were in a mood as the result of something between them that lit both of their fuse. But overall, the Man Cave was a cool place to hang out.

We worked 18-21 long days and would spin back to Colorado for a break, calling it the end of our shift as did countless other men from out of state who had the same routine working in the oil patch. I think we out-numbered the local residents at one point during the boom. Many locals were not happy about the changes out-of-staters brought to their small town dynamics, but the land owners who had mineral rights and wells added profitably to their bank accounts.

When our much anticipated break came at last, Sparky and Eric blasted back to Colorado. I didn't always make the twelve-hour drive to Colorado Springs where I still kept my apartment. I had a passport, and being so close to the border, explored on some of my breaks. I went to Regina and Moose Jaw, Saskatchewan playing the tourist for Easter holiday. Not much memorable to tell about that trip, it snowed, everything was closed for the holiday and I hadn't prepared very well. I got lost, endlessly navigating downtown Regina enough times to drive myself crazy. The saving grace was finding a coffee shop with ambience and good pastries and an Indian deli that had curried roti. I discovered a pub across the road from my motel within walking distance where a silver-haired gang of Canadians was like finding old friends at Happy-Hour.

I was intrigued by our northern border, and on another trip arbitrarily chose a place just because it sounded like something from the Lord of Rings. Gimli on Lake Winnipeg is a small resort town where Harrison Ford filmed winter scenes in *"K-19: The Widow Maker."* A marina and shops and great restaurants were a welcome change in my North Dakotan routine. Lake Winnipeg is ranked as the eleventh largest lake in North America and made me feel like was at the ocean. I meandered around town and chatted with folks from all around the world, returning several times to a restaurant on the main street for their pickerel dinner and brown bread that was like cake, an amazing Norwegian treat. A larger than life bronze statue of a Viking in the park was a photo op. I drove along the lake road like driving along a sea road, waves of blue-green water as far as the eye could see, inlets and parks and sandy stretches with a captivating view. Pubs and beachfront properties added interest to my round-about tour, along with a huge Curling Club. Honestly, I don't pretend to understand how it's an Olympic sport, but Canadians take curling very seriously.

Vacations for me are simple; it doesn't take a lot to make me happy. I enjoy just being someplace new and having time to relax, indulge in breakfast buffets, browse gift shops and bookstores, the spontaneity of going and doing anything I wanted, and most of all, meeting interesting people. The only event I scheduled at Gimli got canned. A morning phone call informed me the charter fishing trip I planned was canceled due to weather. I was pissed and lurched from bed to throw the curtains aside, eased onto the balcony for a smoke, and was pelted with chilly rain that came off the lake in sheets. Everything moored in the marina bobbed and rocked from wind and whitecaps like a lunatic choreographer set them in motion. The fog became thicker as the morning passed with some breaks in the rain, but not a promising day to be outside.

My spirits weren't entirely dampened. After a late breakfast I set off with binoculars and my camera, a map and a Swiss Army knife in the pocket of my rain jacket. After a leisurely drive up the lake, I pulled into an empty parking lot at Hecla Island and sipped the last dredges of a go-coffee and decided to head out. Signs marked the way in Norwegian and English with multiple paths to choose from. The rain slowed and I set off upon seeing a faded sign; *Moose Country*. It was a grand experience, feeling like I was in a foreign country following an imaginary Gandalf and hiked a good ways. I took a few snap shots of pelicans and geese, odd twisty driftwood, cloud patterns, wildflowers and mushrooms. I was fascinated and kept scanning the distance through chest high brush for wildlife. I was alone, the only adventurer foolish enough to be out in this weather. When I heard thrashing not more than thirty yards away and saw the rack of a bull moose above the brush, it dawned on me that I wasn't alone and how ill-equipped I was with just a pocket knife and high-tailed it for my truck.

Showered and a bit bored and restless, not into TV, I went down to the hotel bar looking for excitement and pulled a boner on impulse. Somewhere a party was going on. Balloons and banners and all the telltales of a wedding in the hotel where I was staying pointed me in a direction I would probably have not entertained. But when the live band started playing *Old Time Rock and Roll* by Bob Seger, I discreetly wandered in from the covered patio, drink in hand, and checked out the crowd in the ballroom. I recognized a few faces from the breakfast buffet and was waved in to join them on the dance floor. Fellow revelers at Gimli grabbed my hand and made me laugh like we were all in some magical place having a grand time. I'm not sure how many women I danced with or how many of them were married, but bowed out before the party ended, buzzed and already feeling sore muscles that hadn't been used for a long time. I need to dance more.

At breakfast a gentleman nodded at me from across the room and asked if he could join me, and of course, I welcomed him. He brought his coffee and a book he'd been reading to my booth. I'd been making notes of my trip in a spiral-ring notebook and daydreaming, my mind miles away as the sun warmed my face through the window. We shook hands. His name was Jeffery Burgess from Portage la Prairie, a middle aged stocky fellow who seemed pleasant, casually dressed with a tan turtleneck wool sweater and a Winnipeg Jets ball cap cocked back on his head. Jeffery was an optometrist looking to buy real estate on the lake. I noticed his book, a copy of Albert Camus *Exile and the Kingdom* which I'd read and was tucked among notable authors on my bookshelf. Jeffery mentioned that was a writer. His assumption that I was a writer, that he'd somehow intuited, gave us a kind of instant connection. "What are you working on?" is an open-ended question writers ask of one another.

His work in progress was non-fiction and Christian oriented, of which he made no apologies for, addressing what he called, "coddling weakness in the church." He was tactful at describing the basic premise of the piece he was writing; emphasizing his relevant point with focused eyes that bore into mine, that many believers preferred milk over meat. I got that, but hoped his approach to readers was graceful. He was rather adamant, expressing how the message in churches was more often like managing a household of children needing attention, discipline, fed and burped. I became uncomfortable and nearly choked on my coffee, not having the heart to tell him I was a Christian and that I had preached that very thing, but had become one among the meandering flock of needy sheep. I admired Jeffery's forthrightness, the easygoing cadence and said that I carried my own cross of doubts and precautions, glibly agreeing with him.

Jeffery paid for my breakfast and left his business card. I remained glued to the seat, spellbound by the inexplicable truth and interruption of my morning. It was like getting splashed in the face with cold water, a wake-up call that only God could have arranged.

∾

I longed for a big city experience and Winnipeg had tons of culture. I went to a jazz festival in the art district that I'd seen on the Internet. After driving around lost in a large and strange city with most of the signs in French, an absolutely agonizing time, I was tempted to forget the whole business and head back to North Dakota. A coffeehouse caught my eye and I found a place to park, it was time for coffee and finding my bearings. I discovered a hotel after wandering around blocks of inner city businesses and retail shops called Mariaggi's 231 that had a catchy sign as a "theme" hotel, and settled upon a price after haggling with the manager for a room. I dropped my overnight bag on the floor of make-believe little Mexico. The African room was across the hallway. Asia was somewhere. Maybe the North Pole was on the top floor. The suites were obviously designed for sexual liaisons. The canopied jetted-tub surrounded by Mexican tiles and Day of the Dead artwork was particularly interesting.

Mariaggi's was within walking distance of the band shell where jazz musicians from all around Canada were scheduled to play for the weekend. A pub across the street called *The King's Jewels* had an amusing illustration on the overhead sign. A reclining king wearing nothing but a crown discreetly hid major parts with a shit-eating grin and a pint in hand. They served amazing Indian food and an English Style IPA. It's funny how I end up stumbling onto the most amazing places after getting totally lost and frustrated in a city I've never been before. Although I was bashful at first, sitting back and taking pictures at the jazz festival, I cozied up and made new friends in the mosh pit. Ha! And at my age! If a horn player in the rhythm section careens up and down the scale like Miles Davis, why not make sure your shoes are tied and join the chorus line? I spent two nights in Little Mexico without companionship, but my experience in Winnipeg is unforgettable. One of the gems was coming upon a book in the *free-to-use-please-return* bookcase. "Siddhartha" by Hermann Hesse was not only interesting reading but a copy I was tempted to steal.

I hit some of the highlights in North Dakota on my breaks from work to places like the Turtle Mountains to go fishing at Metigoshe State Park where I caught buckets of bluegills and rejoiced in seeing forests and hills that reminded me of Pennsylvania. I drove to Devils Lake to meet a "blind date" as the result of an on-line dating site that proved very disappointing. Renee was a stunning redhead but she was dwarf-like, barely coming to my chin when she stretched to greet me with a kiss on the cheek. She gave me the tour, which included every bar (I think), in Devils Lake. By the time midnight rolled around, her speech was slurred from tossing back Seagram and Coke for hours. I babied short drinks of vodka and cranberry juice, heavy on the juice, and most of the time didn't finish my drink. I wasn't interested in a party-girl and should have made the trip to fish for walleye.

Since then, I'm suspicious of photos on dating websites that don't reveal anything from the face down or offer more background. There's a funny local quip that says there's a beautiful woman behind every tree in North Dakota, which is hysterical. The landscape here is kind of bleak and there aren't a lot of trees. Many of the women my age, and I mean no disrespect, are thicker than a tree trunk. Not particularly my preference. I know, I'm an ass. Call me shallow Hal.

Of my favorite getaways was a long weekend I took to Fargo. How many of us have seen the classic dark comedy by that name at least one time? I exited the interstate highway and pulled into the welcome center in Fargo for a pit stop and what do you suppose was in the lobby? The authentic wood chipper from the movie, complete with costume and a copy of the original script and I nearly peed myself laughing. It was also the weekend parents brought their kids back to NDSU. I had one hell of a time finding a room and paid dear for a double. I encountered a scalper selling tickets to a Creed concert and drove up to campus. Not only did I feel like a grandfather, but the scene was so raucous and loud I left early with a headache. I happen to like Scott Stapp's voice and lyrics and have their CD's. It's no wonder my hearing is shot, years and years of concerts and loud music have taken their toll.

Little by little the work schedule wore on everyone. We did the bounce between work and home for a year and a half, dozens of trips back and forth to keep this routine going. Eric pulled out first. His wife was fit to be tied that he was missing so much family time, Pop Warner football with his son Blake or Taylor's dance recitals. Money isn't everything. Eric and I rediscovered friendship and I missed his snarky comments and slap on the back when he was gone. We sure pulled a lot of hours together on jobsites. Sparky hung on until his heart wasn't in it anymore and left to rebuild his business in Colorado. Although his wife was a workaholic, the strain of separation took its toll. Other than the stories he tells in his local pub, I don't think Sparky misses North Dakota all that much. I decided to stay. There was indeed work out the wazoo and we had established a good reputation as remodelers. Pat bought a late 90's trailer with promise of a garden, so the housing arrangement was compatible to be on my own although the rent seemed exorbitant. I packed up all my possessions in Colorado and moved, yet again. I'm getting too old to keep doing this!

~

I slammed North Dakota and degraded it about simple and everyday things, constantly making unwarranted comparisons to Pennsylvania and Colorado, but I slowly began seeing beauty in the northern prairie. You have to have the mentality to make the best of wherever your mail is delivered and create a home or go totally crazy.

As dawn gradually breaks on the eastern horizon, my heart began to welcome the promise of a new day, not necessarily like having an epiphany, but tentatively, although with a generous dollop of expectation. I longed for a sense of contentment and feeling at the end of the workday like I was going home. I hadn't felt like I was home for a long time.

North Dakota offered more to be discovered than first impressions; there were gems that caught my eye. Fields beyond end captivated me with awe when canola is in flower. It paints a yellow sea that moves with the breeze like waves on the landscape, the same with flax, when its tiny blue flower is as thick as carpet. Acres upon acres of sunflowers track their golden faces following the sun. This region is one of the nation's largest producers of grain with wheat and barley and durum, so remember that the next time you toast bread or eat a bowl of cereal. That's all well and good, geography can be pleasant anyplace in the world, but it's been the people I've met who influenced me to see the hidden beauty inherent in this vast land by and large been forgotten. The Lakota's and Sioux saw it centuries ago when buffalo grazed beyond counting on the endless prairie. Teddy Roosevelt spent time in what is now Medora and found solace in the Badlands. I was trying really hard to adjust when I came upon a woman who opened my eyes to appreciate being in North Dakota.

I came upon Mia through "Our-Time," an on-line dating site for the over 50 crowd. I was delightfully surprised by everything about her even before we met. Momma Mia, was she was a good looking woman.

Mia was fresh-faced with light blue-eyes that sparkled, short blond hair and sweet mousey lips. When Mia smiled, as she often did, she had a way about it that was both teasingly innocent and devious. I tried describing her to my brother and said she kind of reminded me of a young Meryl Streep. Mia is voluptuous, of Bohemian origins and would have made a fine gypsy. She's my age, but has beaten the odds at showing her age, possessing a youthful exuberance that must be the result of good genes and the clean life she's lived. As a lifelong resident in Williston with generations of family history, a career elementary school teacher (now retired), and a large family and broad circle of friends, she's well connected and respected. I've had the privilege to meet her family and many of her acquaintances. Nearly everyone I've met since being in North Dakota is Lutheran and has Norwegian roots, which in my experience has been a friendly experience. As everywhere in the country, there's a unique accent which is quite noticeable; don't cha know.

Before I met Mia my routine was work, eat, drink and sleep seven days a week, one day was no different from the next. Mia got me out of the doldrums and became my "social coordinator." We were at item at weddings, birthday parties, backyard picnics and fireworks on Independence Day, Mia's schedule included me for all kinds of get-togethers. She liked to dance and was very good at it, and whenever I slow-danced with her it was sweet as honey. I had some of the best Christmas's and holiday feasts with her family. Mia loved to entertain, and when the fun and games ended there'd be a pile of dirty dishes and cleaning-up. I swear she used every pot and pan and utensil in the kitchen. Our time together was comfortable and I began to find a sense of normality. An unexpected sprout of something inside me pushed with determination as through cracked concrete. It felt like love seeking release.

Weekends were made for traveling and off we went to the International Peace Garden on the border of Manitoba where the gardens indeed give you peace. There were shopping trips to Bismarck that I could accomplish in half a day when Mia was just getting started. It'd be Red Lobster for me, Hobby Lobby for her; both an incredible treat as we didn't have such amenities on our side of the state. I tried lutefisk at an event when she took me to her Lutheran Church. I'm game to try anything once, but apparently I'm not Norwegian. Hufda. Lund's Landing on Lake Sakakawea and the Lewis and Clark trail are memorable, not to mention the many summer events in small town for a Saturday outing.

Crosby hosts the annual Threshing Festival where century old steam driven tractors with iron wheels chug down Main Street. My dad would have loved it, as he would have enjoyed our trip to Writing Rock; an ancient petroglyph of a phoenix that Native Indians carved in a boulder out on the plains. There was Old Settler's Days at Alexander where the firemen dug a pit, burying quarters of beef in burlap sacks to cook for two days. The unveiling (dug up with a backhoe), made for the best B-B-Que sandwiches I've ever had.

Our outings were never like going to the Met or a Broadway show, but the traditions and old fashioned way of life was a wonderful change to any big city's pace. I was moved by the patriotism and respect I witnessed at parades when the flag was unfurled and the National Anthem was played. Hats were removed, hands placed on hearts and the veterans honored. Rarely did a weekend go by that we weren't off someplace. I'd relive and reveled in our experiences on Monday morning, my heart light as a bird and whistling a happy tune as I went to work.

Mia and I went to Pennsylvania to visit my mother and strolled down memory lane as I played the tour guide. We ran into Stu, one of my old cronies who lived across the street from where I grew up. He was loading bags of grass clippings into a small pull-behind trailer. The Rennick's house hadn't changed for 60 years. Mia was taking a picture of me sitting on the front stoop of the house I grew up in and Stu recognized me; "That can only be Dirk." I thought, my God, he looks like Keith Richards and walked across the street to shake his hand. Stu's an old hippy and still plays the bass in a honky-tonk band; our reunion tickled my funny-bone.

It was nostalgic for me, making the tour from Bennett Street to the elementary school, a lap around the Little League field and on to the high school. We had an emotional moment at the monument to TWA Flight 800 when 230 people died in the crash; 16 students and 5 adult chaperones in the French club from my hometown were on board. I knew many of the family names chiseled in stone. The statue of an angel seemed to radiate holy honor like a seraphim keeping watch, speaking unspoken words of peace and comfort.

~

My mother absolutely adored Mia, they hit it off like they'd known one another all their lives. On that particular visit it happened to be very close to my mother's 80th birthday and Mia planned a surprise party. She gave instructions to the baker about the cake and inconspicuously passed out invitations to dozens of seniors in mom's building. We decorated the common dining room with flair and balloons; I bought enough pizza to feed an army. What a surprise it was for dear mother. After getting mildly scolded for embarrassing her and making such a scene, Mom cried and said that she'd never had a birthday party in her life.

Mia is one of those rare people who are insightful and thoughtful about things that usually didn't cross my mind, noticing and appreciating the little opportunities to make someone's day a bit brighter without a sense that it's a sacrifice. I have no idea what she spends on Hallmark cards in a year. I'm glad she blessed my mother in such a wonderful way.

I rarely said the words, "I love you," although it was always signed on a holiday or birthday card. Mia felt the same way. "I like you - a lot," was a shared joke between us. Our relationship was fun and certainly active, but for some reason I never had a deep feeling that there'd be permanence between us. Mia was divorced and single as long as I was, both of us independent going on 16 years. Maybe we were both so accustomed to being in control of our own worlds that it was too much of a chore to change whenever our routines or personalities collided. The idea of opposites being attracted has great inspiration and is certainly exciting in the beginning, but it's generally what's opposite that sneaks in the backdoor and muddies things up after time.

The reason I've gone to such length telling you about Mia is because she was salvation for me at a time when life tested me to the max. Had it not been for the few years we spent together I'm not sure if I'd still be in North Dakota. I don't know where I'd be but I have no regrets. Before meeting Mia I was anxious and miserable, depressed and drinking way too much. She gave me a sense of equilibrium and a great deal of happiness and turned my head around to see that life could be good.

I think of her often and deliberately drive by her house when out running errands, hoping to nonchalantly drop by if I happen to catch her outside. We've done a pretty good job of remaining friends after the break-up.

～

Two things have always drawn me with interest wherever I've travelled, old hardware stores with creaky wooden floors and locally owned bookstores. I'm a sucker to spend half a day wandering up and down aisles in a hardware store checking out tools, wind chimes, garden supplies, any number of oddities, but a brick and mortar bookstore, used or new grabs my attention like a kid at the toy store. It didn't take long to find a great little bookstore on Broadway in Williston.

I met Chuck Wilder, the owner, and discovered a tight circle of friends. Books on Broadway became like a Mecca, giving me a sense of connecting to people and things that I loved. I'm trying to learn Mahjong as the gang enjoys playing whenever we get together. I've hosted parties and have been at Chuck's table for most major holiday meals, elaborately set with a fine fare of food and a wonderful group of friendly people so diverse and talkative. I'm enthralled listening to their stories and the tales about the local history and sharing good reads with one another. I found another reason to get rooted.

My work has been steady through word of mouth and the wages have been very good. Fortunately I've had happy clients and more times than not, the projects grew. I joked that I felt like a Pennsylvania dairy cow getting milked for all I was worth. I moved to Williston from the trailer in Ray and rent a charming craftsman style house built in the early twenties with a nice yard that's still in progress. If I was ever in a crisis or need, it's a relief to have people I can turn to. My Nodak friends are honest and loyal to a fault and will give you the shirt off their back. Once they got to know me and warmed to my quirks, I began fitting in, as awkward as it was at first. By that I mean bucking the mentality of a small and closely knit town as an outsider trying to integrate during the oil boom, which wasn't something locals were entirely pleased about. It was a bit of a challenge but I think my charming efforts were well placed.

My writing routine has continued in the morning and free-time and I have two more completed manuscripts on the shelf. After nearly twenty years that's four completed novels, not to mention the starts and stutters of other pieces, but who's counting? To me, every word put on the page counted, spieling out stories that I virtually lived and loved to write. Maybe after I'm dead someone will find and publish my work and then I'll be famous. No joke intended. The stories that I write are what may be called Indie/Alt for lack of a better genre, or maybe "shit-for-brains-reading," as the fiction I write is outside the norm. Wanting to be a serious novelist and somewhat OCD, not to mention how lonely a writer's life can be, I inquired about starting a writers group in Williston. Chuck introduced me to a woman named Jackie Keck.

Jackie led a small writers group called Scribblers that it had fizzled out, and after having met we revamped it. Chuck offered to host our Friday evening meeting at the café in the bookstore. What could be more perfect than a writer's group meeting in a charming bookstore? It was like stepping back in time, a veritable emporium of vintage and eclectic ambience with cozy booths and a bar of dark stained maple, its patina aged and warm. Antiques and memorabilia, travel posters and framed artwork capture one's attention everywhere you turn. Games and puzzles arrayed on the tables are entertaining, and if you're thirsty or want a munchie, old-fashioned sodas and gourmet bakery goods are available, as is Thai tea and uncontestably the best coffee in town. I always run into a familiar face or meet someone willing to visit and swap tales. I've spent a fortune on hardbacks, paperbacks, special order books, cards, calendars and art supplies, but I'm not complaining. Books on Broadway has offered me more joy than I could have imagined. As for the cost, my advice is: afford yourself the luxury of whatever little things make you happy.

The writers group took off with a bang and was fun as well as instructive. Surprisingly, there are diamonds in the swamp of oil country. Clair Eide is a Vietnam veteran, a local and true to the roots Norwegian, and even though he's a legend in his own mind, he's a published author of short stories. Rachel Kelly, the author of the *Colorworld* series lived here when I first arrived, and her critique and helpful insights took my work to another level. If you like mystical fantasy along the lines of Dean Koontz you'd enjoy Rachel's series. Doreen Chaky is another. She is published through Oklahoma Press with her book *Terrible Justice,* a historical account of the Sioux Chiefs and U.S. Soldiers in the Upper Missouri in the mid 1800's. Google it if you're a history enthusiast. Her current project is about lynchings in North Dakota and sure to be a best-seller. There were a few college students who graced Scribblers, also a handful of out-of-towners related to the oil boom that dropped in with their poems or short-stories. Fred MacVaugh led a writers group in Sidney, Montana and works part-time at the bookstore. He's my buddy and knowledgeable about literature, a fellow "Dharma Bum," as in being a fan of Jack Kerouac. Fred is the curator at Fort Union and a brilliant man who I wish had more time to write. His work is very good, although I don't possess the wherewithal to properly read the cadence of most poetry. I rather prefer hearing some poet read aloud from the classics or their own work. These are among some of my acquaintances in the literary world in my neck of the woods who have kept me sane.

And now, back to Jackie Keck.

I've never had a close female friendship other than having a girlfriend involving physical relations. Jackie and I were friends, nothing remotely romantic, but the closest of friends in my recent history who in a sense compared to Jay. It seemed that God chose to join me to a woman who had the heart of Jesus with interests in common more than any man I've met as yet. We had an instant connection and stimulated one another not only with our writing but a reciprocal understanding of spiritually.

Jackie was an old hippy eleven years my senior who was in DC as an assistant journalist for some newspaper during the turbulent 60's of the Vietnam War and the Civil Rights Movement.

Coming from farm country in Iowa she had grass-root ideals, one in a handful of fellow Democrats I know in my part of North Dakota. She was brilliant and savvy, not a mean bone to speak of, but she did have a propensity to be mildly sarcastic. Jackie helped legislate on a state level, volunteering and rallied behind all the right causes, a staunch supporter of Heidi Heitkamp at the time. I liked that about her. We never debated politics.

Jackie was kind of troll-like, short and round with frizzy grey hair and wispy whiskers on her chin as grandmothers are guilty of having, but that's not to say she was ugly. An innocent, childlike lovely face radiated life that spilled forth kindheartedness as a welcome sunbeam. Her endearing persona and the twinkle in her eye is what greeted you, that and a Bic pen tucked behind her ear as though it was as necessary as putting shoes on. Her life wasn't an easy one, coming from poverty as a youth and losing her husband through a drastic act of suicide a few years before I met her. She kept a long-distance vigil supporting her oldest twin son Robert and his family, often taking Amtrak to Seattle, but lost him to leukemia. Jackie's exuberance wasn't because life had treated her well or fairly, but because she possessed an unshakable foundation in her spirit and a strong belief in God.

We shared our daily lives together whenever we had opportunity; Lonny's for breakfast or at Go-Go Donuts, Applebee's with a coupon for buy two get one free. Besides discussing what was happening with Scribblers or the local news and chit-chat, we also shared whatever we were writing with one another; her on-going memoir titled: "Iowa Child," and my work in progress. Jackie was a tremendous support about my spin on writing. At the time I was in the middle of an old-world fantasy story about a boy on the cusp of manhood set in the year 1200, a Viking-kind of plot. Jackie fell in love with my characters and coaxed me on We'd rendezvous somewhere for coffee or just sit in the backyard in nice weather and have "Happy-Hour," reading each other's work to one another. Jackie was a great out-loud reader,

I'm sure her children have fond memories growing up under her magical spell. We'd make stir fry and drink wine and pontificate into the night about spirituality from the bible to the poet Rumi or whatever Native American phrase she'd quote from heart. It was always an engaging discussion that uplifted us both, but what captured my attention was the cunning glean in her eye, a smile, a sarcastic comment that poked fun at liturgy. "We must believe in fairytales," she said. "It's non-negotiable."

I remodeled her kitchen and you would have thought that I'd recreated the Sistine Chapel by her reaction. We travelled to Sidney, Montana for the MonDak writers group and ate nasty East Indian food at a place off the main street I wouldn't recommend but was our tradition whenever we were in town. The aroma and spices made me think of Trinidad that was table talk and made Jackie laugh at my stories. "Fire ants?" That tale nearly made her pee her pants.

Jackie was an accomplished musician with a great range of voice, singing classic folk songs off the cuff and knew every hymn in the hymnal line upon line. I remember a time after we had too much wine and Goggled the words to *Puff the Magic Dragon* and we sang it so the whole neighborhood could hear us. Jackie played the piano but was well known for the French horn in City Band. Music was part of her fabric. Sometimes she even sang what she wanted to say, improvising a rhyme as an old hymn to make a point. You had to be there.

Jackie was part of half a dozen groups in Williams County. "Out of the Darkness" was a suicide support group that was near and dear to her heart. She was elbows deep in GIFTS, the charity Saturday evening meal at the Methodist Church, and networked with so many other organizations I couldn't begin to keep up with. Jackie ran on high octane.

I think the thing that most affected me was her optimism. She had good and bad days. Her soul was deeply wounded by her husband's death, but somehow Jackie stayed afloat and positive.

Of course, tears were shed on my shoulder, but so did mine on hers. There were times when I would be reading something to her I had just written that was close to the nerve in my own experience and I'd choke up and feel embarrassed at losing it. Generally the words and feelings I expressed were something about my shaken faith in rambling prose from my guts, questions about God's forgiveness for screwing up and thinking that I was beyond grace. Jackie would dish up more than enough grace to fill my void like a true Methodist at a church supper. "Be sure to save room for pie," she'd say with a wink.

That summer, Jackie took a marathon trip to Estes Park, Colorado for a family reunion and extended it for a month or better on the road through Nebraska and Iowa researching her memoirs. She took enough pictures to fill a sim card for all it could store. I enjoyed the slide show, but you how that goes, so many stories behind every picture and not enough time. I don't know if subconsciously she knew it'd be her last trip home or not. When she returned to Williston, Jackie's back bothered her and she blamed it on spending so many hours in her Subaru Outback that she named "Green Sue" and countless strange beds. The pain grew and became nearly debilitating. Chiropractors and acupuncture didn't help. The writing on the wall was scary, something was seriously wrong. Jackie wasn't one to take prescription pills and managed the best she could until finally going to a doctor. The discovery was a total shock. A mass of cancer tissue was wrapped around her spine and hip like an octopus, tendrils reaching into her lungs, inoperable.

Jackie's approach at first was holistic, consisting of a green vegetable liquid routine and detoxing, all of Mother Nature's herbal remedies. She had rosy cheeks and put on a smile, but quickly began shedding weight. Her determination for inner healing through diet and meditation and spirituality was exercised diligently. She believed in it. I tried to be supportive but was skeptical. How could I argue with an old hippy set in her ways? I wanted to scream: chemo, but Jackie would have nothing to with it. The MRI's freaked her out, so under-going radiation treatments was out of the question. It got to the point that she lived between lying in bed and shuffling to sit in her recliner, never able to get comfortable.

A visiting angel came to her home, practically living there, and facilitated showers and meals, doing light housekeeping and tended to her needs. Gail is a saint. I met Jackie's brother, Tim who came by train from St. Paul and stepped and fetched for whatever Jackie needed. He was a gracious and a wise man, knowing when and how to defect a minor crisis and interject a joke to lighten the mood. Tim is Jackie's only sibling and shared stories with me about the two of them growing up on the farm in Iowa. It was an honor getting to know Jackie's family, her sons and daughters-in-laws, especially the grandchildren, whose artful little helping hands and stories decorated Jackie's life with joy. I wish I had met Jackie's daughter, Vail, her firstborn before sickness invaded their home. It was later when I was sitting in the funeral home that Vail's words of hope and kindred spirit of her mother's life brought peace to all of us. She had a beautiful voice and sang many of Jackie's favorite hymns, bidding us to join in. I knew most of them, at least the first verse, and observed the family participate while I sat in a puddle of tears.

Jackie's stay at home only lasted six or seven weeks and she had to be relocated to Bethel Nursing Home for appropriate care. There was nothing wrong with her mind but she lived in excruciating pain, barely able to walk. And then, the pain mitigation began. I saw her chart of daily meds, morphine tablets on a schedule that could knock out an elephant. The word hospice seems to soften the jolt of reality, but it means the sad downhill slide to the obvious. It became a hard journey to maintain assurance and hold fast to Psalm 23.

Jackie and I continued visiting, sharing stories, prayer and hope. She kept prompting me to write my memoirs, expressing frustration at not being able to finish "Iowa Child." She said my stories had such flair and uniqueness, that I had lived such an interesting life it would read like a fictional book. "Amusing... never a dull moment. Truth is stranger than fiction," she said. It would work as a testimonial and she saw it in the hands of guys in the County Jail or those who attended GIFTS, even the "pew warmers who needed a kick in the pants." Her prompting intrigued me. Perhaps my life-story *could* help others, so I took her up on it and began typing like a maniac.

This story you've been reading was never intended to go as far as it has. At first I did it to amuse Jackie and would read her pages at every visit. It brightened her day and made her laugh, especially my early childhood days that she could relate with. She often pleaded with me to stay, but it would get to the point in our visit when she would groan in pain and hold her breath, give a little shiver to fight down nausea, trying to be brave. I'd bow out with a funny quip and a quick prayer of comfort and a kiss on her cheek, promising to be back.

I was surprised to find that Bethel Home had Wi-Fi in the rooms. Her sons, Samuel and Wesley installed a Goggle voice activated Internet connection. A nurse came in one day with Jackie's daily meds and to take her lunch order. She was a big woman, maybe Nigerian by her accent, wearing purple scrubs. I had an impulsive flash and said, "Goggle, play: *The Purple People Eater* song." It may be before your time, but it's one that folks like Jackie and I are acquainted with from back in the 60's and we sang along. *"One-eyed-one-horn-flyin' purple people eater."* It was hysterical. Jackie lit up and we had a grand party. The nurse was a good sport and played along, hooking my elbow and dancing around the tiny room.

It was uncanny how time passed so quickly. With no rhyme or reason, from one visit to the next, the dynamics of our time together changed. Jackie gradually talked less. I'd like to think she was still alert in her mind, but then, one day words began to fail her altogether. I growled about North Dakota's archaic laws and ultra conservative viewpoint concerning medicinal marijuana when it has proven beneficial advantages. My friend was an old hippy who suffered and it would have made complete sense. I often thought if she could indulge a magic truffle and hum along with instrumental Celtic music that she so enjoyed it would have set her mind at ease, rather than drooling down her chin in a zombie-like state the pharmaceuticals produced. Yet, Jackie strived to stay cognitive. I felt so bad for her when I knew that she wanted to say something, screwing her face up like sucking on a lemon, clinching her eyebrows, frustrated that she couldn't connect thoughts and words. I'd hold her hand and asked her to squeeze it in simple responses of yes and no and it kind of worked. She'd point for a Ginger Snap that I'd break into pieces and feed her, hold her sippy cup of cranberry juice so she could drink and wiped her chin. I prayed for her before leaving on every visit and kissed her cheek goodbye, assuming that I'd see her again.

It was the day before she died when all hope was tested, although I didn't know it at the time. I wavered, feeling led to share things with her like a priest would, I suppose; the looming ultimatum. I've never journeyed through a valley like this before, never held the hand of someone while trying to find words to speak about the difficult things, about dying, about eternity. A Chaplin stopped in, as did one of the Catholic priests in town and Pastor Ross from Jackie's church, but our paths hadn't crossed for a while. I hem-hawed and rambled reaching for words to express hope. Jackie shifted on the pillow to face me and gripped my hand with such strength, eyes open, keen and focused like I hadn't seen for weeks. Her look of determination to say something made me lean close, hoping to hear her voice even in a tiny way, but instead her mouth remained unhinged and speechless, a trickle of tears leaked down her cheeks. I could only imagine what she wanted to say and prayed, although it was more like talking to Jackie than to

God. I hoped that God was listening.

~

Before Jackie got sick she enjoyed taking Amtrak to the west coast to visit her daughter-in-law and the grandkids. She took lovely pictures (her little digital camera sure got a workout), of Montana and Idaho landscape. Making that trip is on my bucket-list. I loved her stories about the people she'd meet along the way. Jackie always returned home in good spirits and brought back treats from Seattle to share.

I sat on the edge of the bed in her overly-heated room, waiting for some God-breathed moment to happen, for the sky to part and show us some light. I was hoping that God would inspire me with something meaningful to pray, even perform a miracle. I owed Jackie more than glibness or something said by rote. An image came crystal clear in my mind as sovereign moments often do.

I envisioned Jackie standing on the platform at a train station, a small worn suitcase at her feet, shielding her face with a hand while looking down the track. She hummed an old Methodist hymn that I couldn't readily place. Music was always a powerful medium between us, and out of the blue, an old Curtis Mayfield song came to my mind. I tried singing it to her as a prayer until my voice broke.

*"People get ready, there's a train a'coming, don't need no baggage, you just get on board... All you need is faith to hear that diesel humming, don't need no ticket, you just thank the Lord."*

The next morning as I was checking Facebook, someone had posted that she'd died. I don't think I've been the same since. There's a hole in my heart and a strain of music in my head that's too distant to clearly hear, but unmistakably a French horn.

As I began writing this so-called memoir, in a way I was writing it for Jackie to help keep her alive. She has given it back to me with her seal of approval. As cathartic and crazy as it's been, coming to terms with Jackie's illness and my buried memories while writing them on paper, some things in my soul have been healed or are beginning to heal. It would not have happened without her remarkable persistent prodding and encouragement, that from the layers of raw soil I might tumble forth and shine like a diamond. To have someone believe in you is life-saving. Even after Jackie died, her voice sings in my inner ear to stay the course.

~

Pastor Ross was so gracious and eloquent at Jackie's send-off service. Instead of giving the regular eulogy and reciting the obituary, he told tender stories he knew from Jackie's life and her family. At one point, Pastor Ross asked the crowded church to stand when he mentioned various aspects of how Jackie had touched each of us in the community. Those who knew her through "Out of the Darkness" were asked to stand. A significant number rose to their feet. Those in City Band, church functions, the Books on Broadway crowd and those who were part of this group or that or just had coffee with her responded. I looked around and saw that the entire church was standing, hearts thrumming with emotion, those of us whose lives Jackie Keck had blessed.

She was buried March 5, 2019 on a cold morning with crystals of dew adorning the tree limbs like winter in Narnia and laid to rest with a Bic pen tucked behind her ear.

# 24

*It* feels like spring and I'm sitting out back in a T-shirt enjoying the sunshine. The geese are happily honking homeward by the droves and the robins are back. I swear Ruby and Rudy Red Breast remember me from last year, hopping within a few feet as if we're old friends. I talk to them like one would talk to a dog, but don't hold your breath that I'll teach them any tricks. I'm seeing a crop of dandelions popping up and the lilacs are budding. It's been a long time coming; I wasn't sure winter would ever end. An old-timer told me it can snow any month of the year in North Dakota. I hope he was pulling my leg.

I write early in the morning before work, being such a creature of habit, and print out a hard copy of pages in the evening to read over and revise. This project has come full circle and it's time to wrap it up. Hemingway is quoted as saying: "Write drunk – edit sober." He's been known to edit uncountable times. I don't pour beer on my cornflakes and I rarely if ever get drunk, so I guess I have it backwards from Mr. Hemingway. I do enjoy a cold beer after a hard day at work as in the old-school way. I'm not a bar guy, preferring my own Happy-Hour routine. It's my time to relax and wind down, get my ticker in rhythm and be one with the world. Such is the lifestyle of a melancholy writer. I'm especially pleased if I have written something of substance that won't get tossed in the garbage and wonder about some of this story. If you've read this far you either deserve an award or a smack on the back of the head.

$$\sim$$

I live caddy-corner from Everson Funeral Home, so if anything bad happens I don't have far to go. The old Hess office is across the street and I can see the Elks from my front door, getting a mouth-watering whiff when they're charbroiling steaks as they're doing this fine spring evening. I'm two blocks from downtown and love it, what little downtown there is. From my sanctuary in the backyard I look at the north side of the county municipal building; the courthouse and all the various departments that keep the city in civil order, the place where one pays their parking tickets, which I have several times. It's also headquarters for the State Police, Williams County Sheriff's Department, local police and Canadian Border Patrol. A steady flow of law enforcement drives past my house and I get weary sometimes with blaring sirens at all hours of the day. We're not on a first-name basis like when Chief Early accosted me when in I was sowing wild oats as a juvenile pitching ice balls at streetlights. I'm sure the local cops know me as the guy who sits out back with a clipboard in his lap.

I've met the DA and some clerks who've stopped to compliment me on how much I've done to the house and the flowers out front. I recognize the women who routinely take their lunch break power-walking around the neighborhood when I'm doing yardwork. The parking lot is a-buzz with lawyers and office staff. The folks called for jury duty never look happy. It's an entertaining place to live and I've often joked that I live in the safest place in town and probably didn't need to lock my doors. It's nice to be on the right side of law, but I have a deep-seated phobia; cops always have and still make me nervous.

The new county jail facility is also within view. I put up with the noise and dust from construction for two years, the endless grinding and beeping of heavy equipment, contractors milking the system for government money. I've seen the ambulance arrive on occasion for an inmate, sirens blaring and lights flashing, probably not a false alarm, but everyman gets his just due and hospital attention. I reached out to a fellow who frantically paced around the block in negative temperatures without being properly dressed, looking for his ride back home and may have saved him from frostbite. A young woman who was just released without family or friend to pick her up looked like a lost puppy. I extended the offer to Abigail as a Good Samaritan for a meal and a bed for the night while we figured out what to do and get her to safekeeping. It seems to me that the county jail just swings the door open and escorts an inmate to the curb; here's your hat – there's the door.

I've witnessed a variety of visitor's activity for the jail. For example, a minivan will find parking and someone's wife or mother will struggle with small children in fair or inclement weather making their way to the visitor's entrance where they wait forever to get clicked in, almost like they were the prisoner. Girlfriends dolled up in short skirts or trailer-trash looking women in sweats wearing $200 sneakers with an IPhone to their ear, making their way to the dreaded door. From such a short distance I've vaguely overheard heated discussions via cell phone, vented frustration with expletives and heartbreaking discouragement. I have to say, I've seen a lot of crazy stuff living across the street from the county jail.

Seeing it causes me to daydream about the times when I was incarcerated and my heart goes out to the inmates, especially during holiday times. I wonder if they realize the drama their families or spouse or girlfriends are going through that I get a glimpse of from the outside. Do they understand there's no one else to blame for whatever capacity or reason they're wearing county issue clothing and assigned a number and a cell other than themselves?

If you're currently an inmate reading this book, let me tell you that I love ya bro, but it's time to face some facts. Granted, maybe it was a screw up and just a stupid mistake. Pay your dues, and please, learn a lesson. During your "vacation" in the county jail it's been difficult to pay the bills at home or be there for the kids, and that's what hits me in the guts. I worry about the effect incarceration has on the children; the fractured home life. This is an eye-opener to me, a different perspective from Prison Fellowship days when I ministered to the inmates. Oh, the mayhem families suffer! I've seen toddlers pitching a fit in the parking lot, mothers trying to cajole them or holding an umbrella over a stroller in driving rain, racing to the visitor's door just to keep it together for one more visit. I can only imagine what is happening in their homes with daddy gone.

Do those guys have a clue how much they're missing? Family picnics, birthday parties, making pancakes or grilling wieners for the kids on the weekend, Easter egg hunts, walking the dog, but missing out on the everyday joys for months or years that can never be retrieved. Many go through the proverbial revolving door, in and out for the second or third time, hopefully the last time, paying fines and restitution that takes a huge bite out of the family budget. How many times does it take to become embarrassed that your sister is put out and has to drive you everywhere because your license was suspended for another DUI? The family norm is like a game of Jenga. Which piece will collapse the house?

There's another reality that goes on inside the jail walls. I know how it is hanging out with the guys in county, sitting around the table with a handful of cards bragging about exploits in crime, dumbass public defenders, how much weed we smoked or sold, the party days, all the one-up-man bullshit. It's like a dog marking his territory. If you're wearing county issues I have to ask; who's the big dog now?

I heard it before I saw it, a bass woofer from a block away. A compact car pulled next to the curb and a young guy proceeded to sit there listening to the rap artist for what I thought was forever. It's cool to have a killer stereo system in your car, but really? Be respectful of the neighborhood and turn it down. Sorry if I sound like a grouchy old man. I was certain he was there to visit a friend or brother in the jail. You paid your fines on the other-side of the courthouse. Maybe it's a snap judgement, but when I saw his black T-shirt with skulls, tattoos from sleeve to wrists, a stiff-brim Raiders hat turned backwards and his cocky swagger to the door, I prayed for him. I prayed for whoever he was visiting. A thought crossed my mind; *birds of a feather flock together*. To me, the demeanor he exuded read like a billboard: "Peter Pan," the kid that never grew up and thinks the world owes him a favor.

I have a nephew who's spent the best part of his adult life in the state penitentiary. Jr. is 35 going on 16 and another Peter Pan who never really grew up. He got fat and bald and has a criminal record longer than his leg, felonies included. His charges were always drug related, so there's that issue; the quicksand of addiction. He didn't learn to play by the rules and habitually broke his parole, in and out time and time again, sometimes for a long stint. Jr.'s a gentle bear but his appearance is kind of scary looking with tattoos even on his face and neck. I'm not bashing tattoos, I have one and understand that it's a personal choice; however, there is an identity of excessive tats associated to felons or gang members as much as I regret having to say so. I love Jr. with all my heart, he's made me laugh at his charming chatter and stories, but he's one hell of a conman and that's the thing that concerns me about these guys. It's the mentality behind their lingo, the cavalier look disguising a don't-give-a-shit attitude, doing everything under the sun to play the system. It's a common characteristic that I see as an adaptation from habitually finding acceptance in a certain crowd. My take on it is that's exactly what has to change, unless you like prison food. It's a choice, maybe a hard one, but separation from so-called friends is necessary for real freedom. Change the crowd and how and where you hang out and you might be surprised at the benefits. The mind (control panel), is in need of rewiring in a drastic way to change thought patterns before the tongue and actions follow. Meeting someone who's sober with virtue and knows how to listen and offers solid guidance, or getting involved in a positive group rather than playing Grand Thief Auto with ex-felons would make a world of difference. Get right in the head and life will change.

I can't help but think of Jackie's prodding that my testimony had some value to the guys I've just mentioned. Yes, I can relate and sympathize, but it's not just the incarcerated and disenfranchised that are lost and hoping to catch a break.

You can be coasting on auto-pilot and still be vaguely lost, living in a $300,000 house with a cushy job, respectable and outwardly happy. The Peter Pan syndrome is evident if you look close enough at the lifestyle and toys many adults possess, and that's not to say it's wrong to have wholesome fun or a hobby. But status and possessions are no substitute for genuine contentment whether you have a boat or the latest travel mobile home and a Corvette parked in the driveway. I feel sorry for the payments some people must make to keep up appearances. Quite simply, in my opinion, being driven for anything temporal is kind of a letdown after the newness wears off. It's not unlike spoiling our kids with enough stuff to make the basement look like Toys R Us. How many items become yard sale inventory or get posted on eBay? Being truly content is a rare and priceless commodity in our present world of anxiety and generally not found in "things." I apologize if this is a buzz-kill, but I'm passionate about finding a quality of life based in inner contentment.

There are countless successful, middle-class everyday warriors who've slugged along and have a secure lifestyle but still struggle with quiet despair and uncertainty. It's only natural to overcompensate by spending more at the mall to feel good. But what do we do in the middle of the night when something unexpected turns up? Crisis has a way of finding all of our backdoors. It can be any number of things besides being hauled off to jail in handcuffs. Take for example getting a call from the hospital informing you that your son has been in a car accident, or waking up with a tear-soaked pillow worrying about the test results of a biopsy from a lump on your breast, or your teenage daughter who hasn't come home for three nights and you can't get in touch with her. Maybe it's count-down time to foreclosure on the house and you're so eaten up with fretting about it you can't sleep. What's your first response? Is it prayer, some dire inkling that hopefully God has everything under control? Or do you stick your head in the sand, buy something new, repaint the living room or devour a can of Pringles streaming a movie on Net Flicks? Diversion tactics are endless and often anticlimactic.

I don't mean to be harsh, but reality smacks us in the face, and rarely do we stop to ask ourselves the hard questions even if we knew the right questions to ask. The bottom-line is highlighted in flashing neon lights; "What will it take to make me happy?"

I've been the guy in a crowd of family or friends who couldn't recall very much of the past whenever the conversation meandered down memory lane. I always wondered what was wrong with me. It amazes me that my sisters can remember details, like what they got for Christmas at four years old or the new clothes they wore on the first day of school. As my story evolved by writing it, memories returned that often inundated me. I'm not sure how that works, but every page revealed multilayers as though the curtain was pulled back; what I did, how I did it and why, although the jury is still out on answering the why issue. A thread of thought emerged that exposed my innate tendency to only go as far as was necessary and comfortable, and at the risk of sounding like a broken record, ever since elementary school I was happy with B's. Not only was my education and relationships problematic, my walk with the Lord was stinted by choices, however colorful and exciting, but certainly not completely what God would have hoped it to be. I failed many times. I don't believe it was always flippancy or hedonism on my part, moments of weakness and rebellion no doubt, but sometimes I think God let me down. I know that sounds wrong somehow, but it's honest.

I still see myself as a kid poised on the dock, ready to jump head first into a pond. You may be bold and do a somersault off the edge, cannonballed at the least, but that idea terrified me. I'd roll up my pant cuffs and waded in. Looking back as an adult and a bit self-aware, I realize that for me, it was about getting in over my head and who was in control. I'll be daring to make the jump from where I presently sit and confess that for years I've been so close yet so far from total abandonment to the Lord. It makes me wonder what I might have been or done had I'd given him full reign. Maybe it's not too late. I sure I'm the only one who feels this way; so if you're like me, an uncertain seeker sticking a toe in the water, take heart, you're still loved. But a question hangs in the balance; why do we buy into temporal satisfactions, addictions and materialism, and why are we so hesitant to believe in God's promises and dive right in? I've attempted to answer those same questions in my own life experiences and have come to see there are factors beyond my self-possessed dueling with God. Besides personal guilt and failure and residual issues, fellow Christians have left a not-so-good impression that has hobbled me. But I suppose one shouldn't point the finger.

A group of people comes to mind that weighs on my heart, for I've tasted of this myself. I speak of those among us who lost what was once a vibrant experience in the Lord. I'm not addressing them as "back-sliders" or "lukewarm," but suspicious, bruised and hesitant believers, those who've been burned by embracing intimacy. Unfortunately, a growing number of people are estranged from fellowship or have quietly left on their own because they've been wounded by heavy-handed and abusive church authority, sometimes at the hands of confrontational brothers and sisters in the fellowship.

Solomon says in Proverbs that the wounds from a friend can be trusted, the inference is obvious. A true friend cares enough to speak the truth in love and is committed to staying by our side no matter how or where the wind blows. There are others that wield a knife, leaving festering scars, those who said they were friends and cared but had little empathy at how much we bled.

If you recall, I had a few run-ins with pastors and douche bags that left a sour taste in my mouth. That's putting it mildly. We've all had head-on collisions with fellow believers over church crap that offended us when it shouldn't have been an issue in the first place. For me, it's the tone of voice that I pick up on, edgy, business-like, a lot of: "in my opinion."

From my present vantage point and putting a finger on incidents that affected me in a drastic way, I wonder if some of my struggles and failing were related to "being disciplined in the Lord." The Pastor at Crossroads who challenged and corrected me on reaching out to the poor because it wasn't advantageous to the church coffers made me doubt my motives. As close a friend as Andy was when he suggested that I "sit down for a season," knocked my confidence for a loop. If I wasn't already dealing with enough insecurity to want to quit, his chastisement made me take a few giant steps backwards. Pastor Trevor's public lambasting at my object lesson during a teaching series left me feeling demoralized, ridiculously unqualified, second guessing myself if I was a minister at all or if I could do anything right. Pastor Dan of City Church basically demanded that I back off from prison ministry and sit under his teaching. Maybe he felt his agenda was more important than reaching out to the lost. I realize I can't put the blame on anyone else for my backsliding, but misguided correction rather than positive affirmation and mentoring certainly had a negative effect on my spiritual momentum. My innate conflict to measure up 100% and failing to do so was taken to another level of self-doubts, comparisons to other Christians, striving and anxiety. I think it was the lack of accreditation or reinforcement that caused my deep introspection. Honestly, it makes me wonder where I might be today if a more loving and helpful approach was taken.

I'm not comparing the notion of authoritarian leaders in Evangelical circles to a cult or inordinate practices, although it's tempting. I'm willingly laying aside my battle axe and pray for understanding. Although there are so many things done right in the church there are glaring problems that not only myself but perhaps the world at large sees as foolishness at best or erroneous and dangerous. What's perplexing to me is when a man or woman gathers a following by "anointed" preaching and it goes to their head, an ego trip fattening their pocketbook and boasting about numbers of alleged miracles and healings. Narcissism is prevalent behind the pulpit, make no mistake. It's a warped kind of Messianic complex as if God has ordained them to be the "true voice," the "guide," and insinuate or make life decisions for the congregation, especially influencing the naïve new believers. This is really scary stuff. It smacks of another charismatic minister that we all remember; Jim Jones, albeit not as blatant or with such a tragic ending. If you watched the documentaries on PBS of Jones's early days ministering to poor inner city people with a message of hope, railing against the status quo, the crowd went wild in agreement. It seemed not only relevant but compassionate and on target. But Jim Jones isn't accountable and runs off the tracks like a hell-bound train. It's frightening to see how the so-called truth of his message slipped into control and coercion as he lead a following from California to the promise land, doubly frightening to see where it went to in Guyana. How in the hell could 909 people willingly drink the Kool-Aid?

Countless church people have suffered, not a horrific Jonestown death, but died a slower death, losing identities, families divided, incomes given to support the church when the bill collectors were left in a lurch. In churches across the land, gifted and articulate leaders charm the masses while encircling themselves with those who agree with them, shoring up walls (bank accounts), with a council who feeds and strokes the hidden pride of the "Apostle." Behind glazed eyes and smiles, a council of spineless yes-men opt on going along with the program. I've seen church leadership strutting onstage as though they were King Tut and their word was God, the Amen-corner hooting in agreement. Just in case you wondered, I'm not anti-church. I'm anti-bad-church.

Here's my simple test, and please be free to draw whatever conclusion you'd like. If your pastor doesn't jostle and play with the kids in Sunday school, and we don't expect the pastor to be Santa and have chocolates in his pocket, but if he pays little to no attention other than a photo shoot it's all just window-dressing and PR. When a six year old from Sunday school tugs on his suitcoat in the hallway and pastor so-and-so shrugs it off, be wary. If you've rarely or have never seen the leadership weeping in prayer service, take note when tears are wetting your cheeks. When more of the message is about money and the senior pastor drives a brand new Tesla X and takes his wife on multiplied exotic vacations in a year, be suspicious. If there's an inner circle, the accepted circle and you're still a stranger after visiting for months trying to fit in, be on your toes. Maybe it's time to consider visiting another church. If a theme of judgement comes from the leadership Sunday after Sunday and what's posted on Twitter takes precedence over mercy with an agenda that's jack-hammered against what feels right in your gut, run! But please run to Jesus. Jesus is not like them in character, nor does the charade they play remotely come close to reflecting his Kingdom. If this test revealed anything in your mind that raises concern, it's time to reevaluate and pray like hell.

And then there are the rest of us, everyday Joe Brown's and Jane

Smith's. I hate the labels and name calling; Nominal Christians is one. Aren't you a Christian or not? The inference isn't subtle, *those denominational people*, the ones who aren't "on fire" for the Lord. I think there are more people who fit this category than any other, just normal church folks who've attended their home congregation for generations, good people who don't have John 3:16 or a fish bumper-sticker on their SUV. But why are so many church buildings half full these days?

Every city and town across the country has magnificent church buildings full of heritage and history with maybe a wall-to-wall pipe organ and beautiful stained-glass windows, but struggle to pay the utilities and an honest pastor's salary. The answer is more complex than I have wisdom to address and wonder why every time I visit an older church there's little in the collection plate. It's a shame to see so many of those landmarks being converted into retail stores or apartments, torn down like Joni Mitchell's song: *pave paradise and put in a parking lot*. Why is attendance and giving dwindling? I'll take a stab at it. I think something happened either suddenly or gradually in the lives of folks who regularly attended that caused church to become less relevant and set aside as a used item for the rummage sale. But how does that happen? Usually it involves some kind relational issue, but there are other subtle factors to consider.

We're bombarded by media hype, the new norm seems to be more conducive to keeping up appearances than having substance, and don't we all want to fit in? The catechism we learned when young is now judged as archaic and obsolete. Christianity is mocked, and who wants to be mocked? As kids we didn't know any better and sang "Jesus Loves Me" with no inhibitions. As we grew into the enlightening years of adulthood we were confronted with conflicting ideas from our peers that subtly precipitated a loss of faith, or at least made us question our religious upbringing. Going to secular college could have be one, where skepticism crept in via philosophy, or a good or not so good relationship that wore down convictions with intense sexual pressure. Maybe it was electing a career and seeking a diploma to do better than we were raised without regard to compromising integrity, like a rags-to-riches story. Misplaced priorities, insatiable greed, competition that crushed even those close to us were swept under the rug in the hopes of out of sight – out of mind. Experimenting with drugs or studying Eastern religions in an attempt to replace disillusionment about Christianity caused doubts to take root when we thought we were so wise. The world's philosophy was forced on us from many different fronts and things that once made sense no longer made sense. The message was in fine print: "God does not exist." We were lead like lemmings at the Pied Piper's tune to the edge of the precipice to join along with the crowd. I congratulate you if you have overcome and hold to your ideals. You are truly in the minority.

It's easy to succumb to other interests if we're not anchored in our faith, not necessarily bad things but things that entice us away and alter our spiritual well-being. Maybe Sunday's are made for travelling to the lake, golf or the gym routine, landscaping the property after breakfast at Denny's or watching Fixer-Upper in pj's while binging on Cinnabons instead of going to church. Whatever. We seem to make the time for our personal wants, but the tradeoff is often at the expense of spiritual priorities, gradually causing a lack of interest in God and finding interest in other things. The slope is cleverly disguised. How many of us have bagged going to church because setting a few hours aside was an interruption to our happy-go-lucky plans? "I work all freaking week; don't I deserve a day off for myself?" I get that. God's mandate to work six and take a day of rest is beneficially healthy in every compartment. I have a sneaky idea that he means for us to revitalize from our labors and responsibilities and get fresh perspective by focusing on something higher than the 9 to 5 daily grind.

I understand busyness and how easy it is to mismanage the

precious thing called "our time." The kids became active in school programs, sports or band or maybe martial arts, a hectic schedule of running two or three children in different directions was demanded and life became too eventful to carve out time for God. The excuse of: "I'm busy and need a break," is all too often a cop-out, as little by little the lamp of spiritual fervor unperceptively dimmed. How sad when sports take precedence over religion when it should be like peanut butter and jelly. There are all kinds of reasons we concoct to justify that attending church doesn't really matter; procrastination is my worst enemy.

We point the finger whether figuratively or literally at someone's face in objection. We're so easily offended. Resentments fester, family feuds erupt, politics within and without the church gets heated in debate and friends are divided, the boss is an asshole and we take work home over the weekend. We feel like a gigantic boa constrictor is squeezing our life out. And then there's a scandal in the church over money or sexual impropriety that rocks the boat. Calling Christians hypocrites, as if we aren't guilty of hypocrisy ourselves, is a travesty to hide behind and a deceptive means to write off the whole kit and caboodle with a smug self-righteous face. "I don't need this drama," drawing an X across church.

It's not a stretch to see the effects of another subtle influence that has invaded our daily lives: Social Media. Of course, it's a useful tool, but also one that steals multiplied hours of our time on Facebook or surfing the Internet while the real world goes by beyond our front door. I wonder how many people watch a fifteen minute You Tube church service instead of actually attending one. How convenient. Religion is a private matter, right? No, not really.

We're quite inventive at putting on a convincing outward image that we've got it all together, that our world revolves in peace and harmony when on the inside it doesn't. Almost without realizing it, we create a life that more resembles a house of cards, neat and pretty yet fragile. Will the foundation endure when the storm hits? They do, either like Katrina or bad Karma. I'd like to believe there's a safe place, a bomb shelter, not only to endure but to live and thrive without regret or worry; a house built upon the rock and not shifting sand.

There are havens where one can find peace and shelter from the storm. It may be in a church yet to be discovered, but for me, it was often in someone's living room with a handful of like-minded believers and a guitar player. Maybe the bottom-line answer for folks falling away from faith was losing intimacy, the give and take of love and life shared without judgement. The adage of, "Seek and ye shall find," will pay off if you keep trying.

I've bounced around many different subjects and guilty of rambling at times. My intention in sharing my story has been with the hope of clarifying my own thoughts concerning the so-called grand principles of life. Writing this account has revealed a great deal to me. Remembering and putting names and faces and locations back in place has been enlightening. The process of salvaging and reconstructing pieces from my past, however fragmented or as fresh as yesterday has for the most part been a blessing and a means to better understanding myself. From the days of playing Little League as a kid to playing volleyball in rehab, or wrestling with my brother in the backyard to wrestling with truth in my soul at a laundromat where I surrendered to Jesus forty five years ago are indelibly layered like a fossil etched in stone. Added to the layers are all the many experiences beyond my wildest dreams in the Caribbean or in prisons when I poked and hoped as a common-man for clarity of message and purpose. Memories are revelatory, even if they read like a mystery and we don't yet know the end.

I think that I've evolved from boyhood to manhood in this crazy mixed up pilgrimage. In choosing the right road for the wrong reasons and choosing the wrong road altogether, at surprising times even choosing the right road, every aspect, every choice and experience has had much to do with who and what I am. I was tempted to give up along the way but thankfully I didn't. It's fair to say that I had a lot of help on my journey or I *would* have given up a long time ago. I got high and got by with a little help from my friends.

I argued with Jackie about writing a memoir, for who am I? I'm certainly not a household name or someone famous, no George Clooney or Leonard Cohen. Who in the public domain would be interested to contemplate the musings of a no-name? My stories aren't as dramatic as other testimonials go. We're captivated by those who battled and overcame cancer, rape survivors, mountain climbers caught in an avalanche facing impossible odds; the POV of someone who struggled and was victorious are the common themes of bestsellers, the ones that give us hope and courage to keep truckin'. How in the world does my story begin to fit in?

It may be presumptuous to think that my testimony spurs an interest, but remember; most of us are everyday people seeking some improbable dream beyond ourselves and have dealt with odds that should have buried us. We're all in this together. We reach out for hope, feeling our way, groping, scratching the surface with torn fingers and sometimes catch glimmers of light at the end of the tunnel. We yearn for healing, meaning, salvation. All of us are ordinary – extraordinary people... and we all have a story to tell.

I hope that as you've read this story you've been entertained and not only got to know me better, but perhaps yourself as well. My prayer is that a dart hit the bullseye and provoked at least a question that relates to you, as we are all of us in this quagmire called life. I hope there was some random word or phrase that gave you reason to pause and ask yourself why life seems confusing, so lonely at times and broken with grave concerns of actually being repaired. When we reach the point of praying or pleading to be put back together again, like poor Humpty Dumpty, what cry comes from the depth of our soul? Is it bitterness or brokenness? My prayer is that you begin taking steps in a new direction, baby steps if necessary, even retracing steps from a familiar path that once made sense but hasn't for a long time. I pray you'll consider going back to church, or finding a place of worship to attend. If a church setting is uncomfortable, there's always someone you can contact who will meet you for coffee. Perhaps you'll discover someone who cares and listens and helps share your burden, a stranger or a friend of a friend waiting for your call. Who knows, you might even be the answer to their prayers.

It's clearly apparent that my life has been anything but perfect and it causes me to balk a bit, so please realize I'm not preaching or being holier-than-thou. I've tried to be sensitive and honest in telling my story, but perhaps at times it did become a bit preachy. I guess somewhere deep inside me there's still a preacher. At my age, I've come to the point that I no longer feel the need for exhaustive dissertation or to justify my screw-ups or boast of successes; what you see is what you get in this on-going splintered mess still under construction. Quite frankly, I can't whole-heartedly apologize for any of it or my take on how I've lived and written it. From the get-go, a flashing light never let me forget that I had to say what I mean and mean what I say. It's my story.

Being pragmatic I've always been one to seek the bottom-line. As a utopian believer I've been disappointed yet remain hopeful. Of all the crazy notions I have is that I wish we were more like the fellow with Down Syndrome that I served scrambled eggs and hash browns to at an institution in Selinsgrove forty-odd years ago. Remember my making mention of him, the young man who wore an orange hoodie and asked an innocent question so loud and so boldly that it shook my world upside-down like a snow globe. "Do you love me? Do you really – really love me?" I'll never forget his simplicity and the beaming smile on his face. I believe that in his mind, being loved was the one thing he couldn't imagine ever living without, the only thing that made sense in his world and made him secure and happy. Is our smarty-pants world so different?

It may seem out of vogue and overly simplistic, but I'm going to say it anyway. There *is* someone who loves us, and that truth is lodged in my heart and set in stone. I am convinced the answers to life's questions and pursuits are found by embracing the love of Jesus Christ. You may call it by another name, but my lover and savior is Jesus, the only trustworthy life preserver that I've found in the tumultuous sea of my life, whether I floundered and sank needing rescued or walked on water. It's so simple and easy to pass over, especially when the seas are calm, but had I not clung hard to Jesus' love I would have drowned a long time ago.

I'm now 65 years old, still very flawed, poking and hoping like some displaced adolescent questioning everything with his eyes wide open. I catch myself whistling in the dark to keep the boogeyman away, but I feel a little bit more capable to face the devils. On occasion, I find myself rummaging through moldy boxes and filing cabinets, sorting through memories still buried in the Lost and Found Department. I think I'm finding a way through the labyrinth to the light. At the least I'm becoming more at peace with myself and with God. I've learned that I can't do it on my own anymore and have gone back to church since Jackie passed. It feels right in my soul getting reconnected, yet I long for more. Maybe Jay was right; "You and me – we know too much."

There's a door with a sign on it: Lost and Found Department. It's closed but it isn't locked like a jail cell or Fort Knox. I hope you've noticed it in passing. This door is personal, accessible, welcoming, waiting for you to turn the handle and enter. You enter at your own risk, but if you have the courage or have exhausted every possible means you know to find peace and freedom, that door is open for you. There is someone who has been very patient and waiting for you on the other side, always cheering for you and has never given up. Won't you give Jesus a chance to heal your wounds? His hands and feet bare the scars that prove his love and he offers you the promise of new life if you simply ask and receive it.

An old gospel song comes to mind and may very well be my anthem. It seems apropos, and now that it crossed my mind I'll probably be singing it in my head all day. You know how that goes, when the record gets stuck and keeps repeating?

*Amazing grace how sweet the sound*
*that saved a wretch like me;*
*I once was lost but now I'm found...*
*was blind but now I see.*

# Prologue

Thank you for reading my book. This project began in the spring of 2018 and has taken three years off and on to reach completion. It's been a journey, writing something like this, as I'm a fiction writer and still have a full-time job. I feel the need to apologize for the lack of professional editing, but with some help and multiplied hours of revisions and tweaking it's as good as it gets. Sorry for typos, poor grammar and any disjointed or rambling waywardness that may have bogged you down. I pray that you've gotten the gist of my madness and give it a B+.

I also apologize for the bad language. I felt the need to interject realism for one reason; it's my way to identify with readers as salty and down to earth as I am. I pray the moments of tenderness softened the blow of being offensive and you find it in your heart to grant me grace. This could very well be one of the best books you could give to a friend in need.

If you enjoyed Lost and Found Department, I encourage you to post a review and rating on Amazon/KDP. They pay attention to comments and it will help increase my chance of success. I'm not in this for the money, but if you bought five copies maybe I'll see my picture on the cover of the Rolling Stone, (joking.)

To date, I haven't set up a website, although it's in the works. For personal contact you can find me on Facebook, Randy

Heckman, and please "like" and "share," or send me an email: yohecky@gmail.com

Made in the USA
Monee, IL
10 April 2021